The Positive Preschool

Creating Effective Learning Communities for Young Children

Muriel K. Rand

Illustrations by Catherine L. Rand

PRINCETON SQUARE PRESS

Princeton, NJ

Published by Princeton Square Press
301 N. Harrison St. No. 312
Princeton, NJ 08540

Copy Editing: Jo-Anne Mecca, Ed.D.
Cover Design: Catherine L. Rand

ISBN 978-0-9882766-2-8

To Bradstreet, Catherine, and Jason, who taught me all about young children

Contents

Introduction

Smooth running classrooms don't happen automatically. Preschool classrooms in which children are actively learning, exploring their environment, engaging socially with other children and adults, and feeling safe and cared for must be carefully crafted. Many of you have probably seen classrooms in which children are unhappy, frightened, or even humiliated. You might also have seen classrooms in which the teacher was frustrated, tired, and wishing that things would run more smoothly.

This book will examine in detail how to create the best learning environment for both young children and you. The recommendations here are based on many years of research in classroom management that gives us solid knowledge about classroom settings and human behavior (see, for example, Brophy, 2006).

There are two theoretical orientations that provide a framework for the recommendations in this book. The first is a constructivist orientation which posits that a major goal of education is for children to grow in autonomy or self-regulation (Bodrova & Leong, 2007; DeVries & Kohlberg, 1990). The second orientation is a humanistic one based on the premise that the goal of education is self-actualization or reaching one's full potential as a human being. This viewpoint is characterized by the work of Maslow (1943) and other humanistic psychologists.

This is a manual for preschool teachers who want to feel the intrinsic joy of teaching—of connecting with children—on a deep level. Throughout, I will focus on what makes children's and teachers' lives meaningful and how they can share that meaning in a learning community.

This book is based on these basic ideas that will help you create a positive, productive learning environment:

- Good classroom routines will lead to appropriate behaviors

- Classroom community is critical for preventing misbehavior

- Children must be taught social and emotional skills

- Activities that engage children effectively eliminate most behavior problems

- Culture affects teachers' behaviors and children's behaviors

- Children who use inappropriate behavior need instruction not punishment

These ideas are the foundation for good classroom management and effective teaching. They are also the basis for keeping the joy in teaching. In my experience, most teachers who get frustrated, exhausted, and burned out have not been able to develop the classroom management skills needed to have a fulfilling teaching experience. The information in this book can help you teach more effectively, ensure better student learning, and increase your enthusiasm and energy.

What Is a Healthy Classroom Community Like?

Before we can talk about the roles that the teacher needs to play in structuring a classroom community, we should be clear about our goals. What does a healthy learning community of children look like? Let's consider the characteristics we hope to find:

Respect. There is mutual respect among the teachers and children in the classroom. Young children's needs and thoughts are respected. Adult listen to children. Their ideas are valued and responded to. Children listen to each other and to adults.

Caring. Both the teacher and the children in the classroom care about what happens to all of the members of the class. The children help each other, show signs of empathy, and are comfortable expressing their emotions. Teachers willingly help and care for the children. They also encourage and model empathy and caring of others.

Engagement. The activities that are planned (or unplanned) encourage children to think, explore, experiment, and practice. All activities, even those involving transitions, care giving, or bureaucratic procedures are seen as teachable moments.

Psychological safety. Children feel comfortable in the classroom and are not afraid of punishment, humiliation, or rejection. Bullying, teasing, and shaming are not permitted. Children know they are psychologically and physically safe from harm and feel a sense of control over their life. Teachers know that they, too, are psychologically and physically safe and feel a sense of control in the classroom. Children are not afraid of taking risks in new learning experiences.

Sense of community. There is a feeling of pride in being part of the group. The members of the classroom act and feel like family.

Joy. Both the children and teachers enjoy being in the classroom. Children and teachers look forward to coming to school. People are smiling, connecting with each other, and growing as individuals. There is laughter, spontaneity, and joy.

What is an Unhealthy Classroom Like?

Unfortunately, many of us have been students, teachers, or visitors in classrooms that are not working well. In an unhealthy classroom, teachers feel they do not have control (DeVries & Zan, 1994). They raise their voice, threaten the children, and dole out punishments. Children in such classrooms are often afraid of their teacher or of the possible punishments. They respond to this fear in many ways: sometimes by rebelling against what the teacher wants, sometimes by becoming very passive. Some children in this situation will develop stress-related symptoms such as nail-biting, hair twirling, bathroom accidents, and stomach aches.

Some unhealthy classrooms have little organization and the teacher has a difficult time getting things accomplished. Much of the time is wasted in transitions that take a long time, such as getting settled on the carpet for group time or lining up to leave the classroom. The children do not know the routines and are criticized for not remembering them. Group times are dominated by the teacher trying to get the children to sit still and pay attention. The children may be restless and inattentive. Other times they may be physically hurting each other or damaging property in the room. The children have not learned a sense of self-control.

Why Do Children Use Inappropriate Behavior?

Children learn best when all their needs are met. They also use inappropriate behavior in order to get their needs met. Maslow's theory can guide us in what kind of structure is best for children by considering their human needs first. He believed that children will make good choices that help themselves grow if the environment and teachers support their needs (Maslow, 1999).

What is so helpful about Maslow's insights for teachers is his explanation of what motivates people, which helps us to see why children behave the way they do (Maslow, 1943). All humans, including young children, have a set of basic needs that motivates us. These are arranged in a hierarchy of importance. There are two sets of basic needs: *deficiency needs* and *being needs*. Let's look at the importance of deficiency needs first.

Deficiency Needs

There are two important aspects to deficiency needs: once they are fulfilled, they don't motivate us anymore. For example, when we are hungry we need to eat. Once we eat and our hunger is satisfied, we no longer need to eat and hunger is not a motivating factor for us until we are hungry again. The second important aspect is that

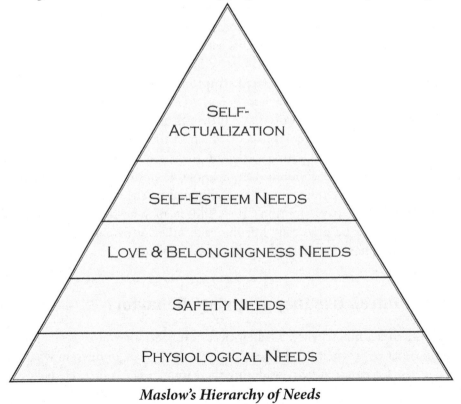

Maslow's Hierarchy of Needs

deficiency needs build on each other. Some are more important or basic than others. Once the more basic needs are satisfied, then the next level of need that is not met motivates us. These needs are usually shown in a pyramid to highlight this ordering. It is possible however, that many deficiency needs will be operating at the same time.

Physiological needs. All humans need to have food, drink, health, shelter, sleep, sex, physical activity, and various other physiological needs. These are undoubtedly the most motivating of all needs and for that reason they are shown on the bottom of the pyramid as the base of all other needs (Maslow 1943). When these physiological needs are not met, the other needs almost cease to exist. For example, when a child is very hungry, all of her energy will be put into obtaining food, and she will not be able to pay attention to anything else. Perhaps you can relate to this need by remembering a time you needed to go to the bathroom very badly and it was impossible to think of anything else but satisfying that need.

One important thing to keep in mind is that young children's bodies are still physically developing and as a result they have a physiological need to be active in a way that adults do not. For example, teachers might not realize that children who "can't sit still" are often trying to fill a physical need, and cannot therefore pay attention to what the teacher or group might be doing.

Children might also act out because they are hungry, tired, or reacting to medication. Before we try to correct a child's behavior, we need to consider what physiological need might be contributing to the problem.

Safety and security needs. The next most powerful need is for the child to be physically and psychologically safe. The child is, in essence, a "safety-seeking mechanism" and will do almost anything to maintain this safety (Maslow, 1943). This involves protection from physical harm and it also includes psychological safety, such as protection from fear, shame, and humiliation. Children's need for safety is seen in their preference for undisrupted routines and rhythms that provide a predictable, orderly world. Unfairness or inconsistency can make a child feel anxious and unsafe since the world then seems unreliable and unpredictable.

The need for safety can be a dominant force in children's home lives when they are living in chronically unhealthy situations. We can also create unhealthy situations in our classrooms if we do not carefully consider how lack of routines, unpredictable behaviors, punishment, and fear of being shamed affect the motivation of children.

Love and belongingness needs. Children hunger for relationships that provide affection and a sense of belonging to a group (Maslow, 1943). These needs include both giving and receiving love which can be seen in the characteristic behavior of young children's affection toward their teachers. Children will work with great intensity to achieve the goal of love and belongingness, and many of their challenging behaviors result from this need not being met.

Children who are seeking attention by using inappropriate behaviors are trying to get their need for belongingness and love met. Our first response is often to ignore this behavior, but the more effective response is actually to give the child more positive attention. We will examine this situation later in the book.

Esteem needs. All of us have a strong need for a stable, firmly-based high evaluation of our self that leads to self-esteem (Maslow, 1943). There are two aspects of this self-esteem. The first is a sense of real achievement, mastery, and confidence in our abilities. The second is the recognition, respect, and appreciation we get from other people. In other words, children need to feel successful in school. When children repeatedly fail and are frustrated, they will act out (often inappropriately) in ways to make themselves feel more capable.

This is why is it so important to help young children learn to do things on their own and help them see how much they've learned and grown. Children do not learn that they are capable or competent just from being told they are; they learn it from experiencing their own successes and mastery. A child who learns to put on his coat by himself does not need to be told he is capable. He knows he can do it and will develop an internal sense of esteem. We will consider this need in depth when we look at the role of praise and feedback in teaching.

Being Needs

Once the deficiency needs are met, humans are still unsatisfied in a different way; they are motivated by the need for self-actualization. This involves self-fulfillment and the need to become all that one is capable of being. Later in his work, Maslow specifically identified the need to know and understand, and the need for aesthetic experiences (such as the appreciation of beauty in art, music, mathematics, dance, literature, etc.) as conditions for self-actualization (Maslow, 1971).

Being needs have profound implications for us as teachers. In general, our society has hired us to provide for the being needs of children—specifically, the need to know and understand. However, according to Maslow, that need is not motivating to children unless all the deficiency needs are sufficiently met. Therefore, as teachers, we must provide an environment in which those other needs of children are also met.

Another important point is that being needs—unlike deficiency needs—are never fully satisfied; instead, the more these needs are met, the more they continue to motivate us. Once children begin learning new ideas, for example, they continue to be motivated to learn more. Unlike deficiency needs, they are not "turned off" because they have been met. As being needs are fulfilled, we reach the level of self-actualization, our full potential, and self-fulfillment.

Maslow's theory is a positive one for teachers. He believed that children could naturally grow and develop into healthy adults. The right environment for a child "can gratify his basic needs for safety, belongingness, love and respect, so that he can feel unthreatened, autonomous, interested and spontaneous and thus dare to choose the unknown" (Maslow, 1968, p. 59). The rest of this book will look at how to structure the classroom environment and guide children's behavior so that these needs are met and children can move towards self-actualization.

Challenges of Classroom Management

Besides your professional training as a teacher, you have also learned a great deal about teaching from your own experiences being a student in school for 12 or more years (Lortie, 2002). You also learned a great deal about managing children's behavior from your parents and family. What you learned from these early experiences might conflict with your professional training. When you are under stress, you will tend to teach the way they you were taught and to use the behavior management of your parents.

Many of us recognize that depending on the way we were taught or parented as children doesn't lead us to be an effective teacher. In some cases, the teaching or parenting we received was not effective. This can perpetuate traditions at the expense of reflective and informed change. The rest of this book will show you how to make reflective decisions about your classroom and give you a solid path to follow in developing consistency and effectiveness in creating classroom communities that best help children learn and grow.

ﾍ ﾍ ﾍ

Part I: Prevention

Chapter 1: Setting the Stage

The children in Jenna Martin's preschool class bound into her classroom first thing in the morning smiling and energetic. It is November, and they have learned the morning procedures well enough that they are now automatic routines. The children enter the room where Ms. Martin stands greeting each one and chatting with the family members who bring their children. They walk over to the cubbies, hanging up their jackets. Next they head over to the three long tables, choosing one of the manipulatives that Ms. Martin has put out. There is a low hum of voices as the children settle down to play.

After ten minutes, Ms. Martin gives a warning that morning circle will begin in two minutes. After the two minutes elapse, she rings a soft chime and the children stop what they are doing and look at Ms. Martin.

"Good morning, children! It's good to see everyone here this morning. Quietly put your toys away and come sit on the rug for morning meeting." She begins to sing a chant that they use each morning that includes each child's name. The children join in the chant as they push in their chairs and walk across the room. As they settle on the rug, each child chooses a carpet square and sits cross-legged. Ms. Martin then begins the morning circle.

A smooth running classroom depends on children knowing the procedures so well that they don't have to be told. You can see this in action in Ms. Martin's class when children arrive first thing in the morning and know exactly what is expected. Teaching these procedures took her some time and energy, especially at the beginning of the year, but she knows they are crucial for preventing behavior problems and improving the efficiency of learning (McIntosh, Herman, Sanford, McGraw, & Florence, 2004). Teaching procedures effectively is the most important step in reducing off-task behavior and wasted time during transitions.

Many behavior problems and poor learning conditions result when teachers do not specifically, thoroughly, and persistently teach the procedures that they expect children to know. Children with disabilities can have a particularly difficult time with transitions if the procedures are not directly taught because they may not pick up on what the expectations are and learn them on their own (Buck, 1999).

Imagine, for example, a 4-year old student named Francine, who has Attention Deficit Hyperactivity Disorder. After the clean-up transition at the end of center time, she is distracted by the movement, noise, and energy in her classroom. Because her teacher has not specifically taught the children how to move to small group time that is next on the schedule, Francine wanders around and needs to be reminded to join the group. She joins the group late and is unprepared for what she needs to do. She receives more directives and negative comments, and she responds with an increase in off-task, troublesome behavior. Francine is unable to settle down to concentrate on the water color painting activity during the small group time, and her teacher gets more frustrated. This becomes a vicious cycle that eventually leads to challenging behaviors and individual interventions. Fortunately we can turn this around. Much of Francine's needs can be met by providing more structure and teaching procedures.

Begin with Procedures

The first step in teaching procedures is to think through the parts of the day and how they fit together. Then make a list or description of the different procedures you want to establish. Write down what behavior you would expect from the children. For example, you would want to establish a procedure for clean up time. Write down the steps the children will follow:

1. Stop playing.
2. Look at the shelves to find a picture of your materials and put them away where they belong.
3. Look around to find something else to clean up.
4. Put those materials away, too.
5. When everything is put away, sit on your carpet square for circle time.

When developing behavioral expectations, it can be helpful to use visual imagery to ensure you are thorough. Close your eyes and picture the children engaging in the activity or transition. What do you want them to be doing? What does the classroom look like and sound like? Where are the children going to? What steps need to be taken?

Once you've determined your behavioral expectations, the next step is to teach the children this routine until they know it well enough to do it automatically. This will probably require that you teach and re-teach many times, as well as give supporting reminders while children practice this routine. The best way to teach routines is to have the children actually do them as a lesson. The Responsive Classroom (Wilson, 2012) has a wonderful strategy for teaching procedures called *Interactive Modeling*. This has four steps:

1. Students learn why the procedure is important

2. Students observe the model and create a picture in their mind of what it should look like
3. Students notice and describing what's happening
4. Students practice and get immediate feedback.

For example, at the beginning of the school year, gather the children and talk about why clean up time is important. Then have them practice how to clean up. First, pretend you are working with blocks when the clean-up song begins. Show the children how you stop playing, find the right picture to match on the shelves, and then put the blocks on the shelf. Next find another item to put away. Now ask the children to tell you what they noticed that you did. Once they've described what they saw, ask one of the children to show you how to put away the blocks. Once again, ask the children to describe what they noticed. Next have all the children practice and give them feedback on what they are doing well. The next day, practice this again in the housekeeping area and on the following days, work your way around the room. By the time you've demonstrated all the centers, they should know your expectations.

Once you've gotten through this training period, give the children positive feedback and gentle precorrection as necessary. Precorrections are short reminders of what behaviors you expect (McIntosh et al., 2004). You can use them with the whole class, such as, "Who can raise their hand and tell me what part of the story could not be true?" or with individual children, such as "Zach, remember to wash your hands before sitting down for breakfast."

Do not assume that children will do things the way you expect. Show them, allow them plenty of time to practice, and guide them in remembering. If children are not following the routines, re-teach them and provide more practice. Teachers with the smoothest running classrooms spend the first six weeks of the school year focusing primarily on teaching procedures and developing routines.

Daily Procedures

Here is a list of possible procedures to model and teach your children:

- Arrival: putting things away
- How to sit at circle
- Signal for getting the children's attention
- Going to the bathroom/washing hands/getting a drink
- Eating breakfast/lunch
- How to greet each other
- Choosing centers
- Blowing your nose/sneezing
- Working appropriately in each center
- Cleaning up after centers
- Taking turns
- Fire drills/lock down drills
- Lining up & walking in the halls
- Choosing a book in the class library
- How to turn the pages in a book gently
- Taking care of materials (putting caps on markers, etc.)
- What to do when someone is hurt
- What to do when you need to calm down
- Putting on coats
- Getting ready for naptime
- Getting read to go home

Attention Please!

I visit many classrooms in my job supervising student teachers. One of the first things that stands out is that teachers in chaotic classrooms have no consistent way to get the children's attention. Creating a quiet signal is a simple, easy to implement strategy that will give you great payoff. Simply choose a method for getting the children's attention whenever you need it. Auditory sounds are more effective than hand signals since children will not always be looking at you.

Begin teaching this procedure on the first day and practice it again and again until the children respond easily and quickly. Depending upon the age of the child and your preferences, the steps might be something like:

1. Stop talking

2. Hands at your sides

3. Eyes on the teacher

As you practice this throughout the day in the first weeks of school, try to get across the message that this signal is important, but be light-hearted in teaching the children how to respond so they begin to associate good feelings with the quiet signal. I can't emphasize enough that you will need to practice this signal and the children's response many times. If you find the children are slow to respond, or are ignoring it, go back to your practice sessions. You can make it a challenge to see how quickly the children can get quiet and create a game-like attitude when you practice. It's helpful to take a photo of how the children should look when the quiet signal is rung and post it in a prominent place.

As the school year goes on, you will still need to support children with positive reminders and perhaps play this modeling game a few more times until your signal becomes routine.

Ensuring Smooth Transitions

The most challenging times are typically transitions from one activity to another, especially if they involve the children moving within the classroom or to another location. There are some general ideas that can help in transitioning children, and there are specific strategies that work for certain kinds of transitions (McIntosh, Herman, Sanford, McGraw, & Florence, 2004). We will look at both of these. In general, all transitions go more smoothly if children know what to expect. How do you want children to clean up? What is a reasonable expectation—all the blocks or just helping to put away a few? How should the children move from circle time to centers? Think through what you want the children to ideally be doing, and then model and rehearse these procedures. Explaining to the children the reason for the procedures also helps them gain a broader understanding of why certain behaviors are necessary. For example, if you need the children to walk quietly in the hallways, you can remind them that other children are trying to work; if you want children to push in their chairs, explain to them how easily someone can trip and get hurt if the chair is in their way.

Give warnings. This may seem obvious, but sometimes you lose track of the time and try to quickly get children to change what they are doing. Resist this! Stay organized and give the children at least one warning that a transition is coming up— more might be needed for children who have trouble with transitions. You can also use timers to let children know how much time is left before a transition. This can be a personal kitchen timer for an individual child, or a timer posted on your SmartBoard or computer screen which counts down for the whole class.

Music cues. Music is a powerful way of helping children to know and be more aware of the schedule and what behaviors are expected at different times. This is why preschools have traditionally used welcome songs to begin the day, clean up songs, soft music before naptime, and good-bye songs at dismissal. Think about how playing the national anthem has become a clear signal for the beginning of sporting events, or how music in religious ceremonies lets people know when to stand, sit, or kneel.

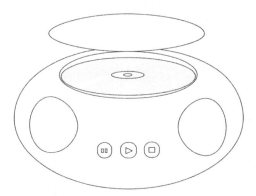

Active supervision. During transitions, things will go more smoothly if you provide active supervision in which you are scanning all areas of the room, moving to potential problem areas, making your presence known, and interacting with the children (McIntosh et al., 2004). If you are busy during transitions getting your materials ready for the next activity, talking to other adults in the room, or taking care of administrative work, the children will not get the support they need to learn how to transition smoothly. In the end, you will create more work for yourself and lose out on creating a more positive learning environment. Active supervision will require that you think through all of the day's activities and have your materials ready before the children enter the classroom. Much research over many years has shown that effective teachers have the room and the work ready before school begins (Emmer, Evertson, & Anderson, 1980; Evertson & Anderson, 1979; Evertson, Emmer, Clements, & Worsham, 2008).

Time for transitions. Behavior problems can arise if you don't leave enough time for transitions (Buck, 1999). Young children need plenty of time to figure out where they need to go or what they need to do next. Often teachers plan schedules that reflect the time they need for each activity but not the time between activities. I was recently working with a group of preschool teachers who complained that they felt constantly rushed throughout the day. When we sat down and looked at their daily schedules, we all realized that their expectations were unrealistic. For example, they had 10 minutes on their schedule for snack time; however, they needed to bring all the children to the school's lunch room each afternoon for their snack. When we paid attention to how long it actually took for snack it was closer to thirty minutes rather than ten because of the time for transition. When children are rushed, everyone's anxiety level goes up (including the teacher's) and children are less cooperative.

Another strategy in making transitions smoother is to move children gradually or in smaller groups to the next activity. For example, if you are moving children from a large group activity to getting ready to go outside, you could have half the children get their coats while you sing a song, read a book, or play a game with the rest of the children. Then the children can switch places and when everyone has their coats on they can move together to the playground. The important point in this technique is to make sure that young children do not have any time in which they have nothing to do.

Imagination and drama. A very effective strategy for gaining children's cooperation and interest during transitions is to use imagination and dramatic play. Nothing keeps children be quieter when walking down the hall than pretending to be little mice. Children will often enjoy cleaning up when they pretend to be a big dump truck or a large crane that picks the materials up. Even stubborn children will cooperate when you wave a magic wand that creates quiet voices or makes everyone tiptoe. Creating a joyful attitude during transitions reduces the tension and helps children feel comfortable. A playful, imaginative approach can create a positive climate in the classroom that will meet the safety and belongingness needs of the children.

Buck (1999) suggests a strategy of guided imagery that was successful when other approaches did not work. The teacher helped Ronald, a child who was having difficulty transitioning to group time on the carpet—falling on the floor, running, and jumping—by inviting Ronald to imagine an invisible doorway that he drew in the air, close to the story area, then pretended to open the door, walk through it, and sit down. This worked very well, showing us how important creativity and a playful attitude can be in working with young children.

Finally, try to create a positive atmosphere during clean-up time. One teacher puts on Irish dance music and the children see how many times they need to play the song before all is put away. This is not the time to raise your voice, demand that children participate, or punish children for not helping. Instead, make the cleanup routine a cheerful, social event that children will enjoy.

Special needs adaptations for transitions. Some children with disabilities will need more transitioning time than the rest of the class. You can gradually ease a child into finishing what she's been working on. Other children might need more support for knowing the daily routine. You can provide an individual set of cards with the schedule on it so the child can refer to it whenever needed. Another child can serve as a "transition buddy" to walk with or help another child transition appropriately.

Children who are highly sensitive to noise and activity may be overwhelmed by the stimuli during transitions. You might want to help the child transition before or after the other children, or to allow the child to wait in a quiet location until the next activity begins. It is also extremely important to provide positive feedback to children when they are meeting your expectations for transitions. They need to know when they are doing well!

Getting the Children into Routines

When children know the procedures so well that they do them automatically, you have developed routines. Good routines are critical for a smooth-running classroom. All of your procedures should be taught and practiced during the first few weeks of school.

Lining up and walking in the hallway. Moving the class as a whole group can be frightening for new teachers and a challenge for even experienced teachers. The trick lies in teaching the procedures for lining up or walking in the hallway clearly. This should be started on the first day of school, and repeated as needed afterwards. If children are not behaving properly in the hallways, it is important to stop right away and bring the children back to the room. Keep a positive attitude without making any nasty comments or complaints, and have the children simply practice how to walk in the hallway again. The second important trick is to give positive feedback to the children who are behaving appropriately. Do not spend time trying to correct children. Instead point out who is walking properly or behaving as they should.

Clean-up time procedures. In many early childhood classrooms, clean-up time is the most challenging part of the day for keeping children on-task and reducing inappropriate behaviors. This is not surprising considering the amount of stimulation—noise, movement, materials, and the intensity of the work. I have visited some classrooms in which I myself felt overwhelmed at clean up time by the immense amount of work it would take to put everything away. There are a few strategies that can ease the difficulty. First, keep in mind what your learning goals are for clean-up time. These might be to develop a sense of responsibility, to show helping behavior, to learn how to sort and classify by putting things away where they belong, and to develop motor skills.

How important is it, really, that everything is put away perfectly within the time period allotted? Be sure your goals are not unreasonable. Throughout the work time/center time period, help children put things away as much as possible so the job at clean-up time is not so difficult. As children finish playing with the dress-up clothes, help them put them back. When the block area is overloaded with blocks, you can start to replace some on the shelves. It is often unreasonable to expect that young children can put everything away themselves. It's too big a job.

It can help to assign very specific and relatively small jobs to children. Asking a child to clean up the block area may be too much, but asking her to put the triangle blocks back on the shelf makes it more doable and more like a game. Similarly, a child can be assigned a puzzle to put away, or to put a few books back on the shelf. This might also help prevent the children from finding other things to begin to play with.

Some children will quickly retreat to a quiet area of the classroom—often their cubbies. In many cases, these children are overwhelmed by the stimulation and truly can't emotionally handle the commotion. Instead of fighting with them over cleaning up, offer them a job in a quiet area of the classroom, away from the major noise (typically the blocks and housekeeping area). Perhaps this child can clean the paint brushes in the sink, straighten your books, or even hang up some pictures on a wall in a quiet spot. The important thing is that the child has a job and feels like he is contributing to the clean-up effort. The actual amount of work is not the important part.

Taking care of classroom materials. Like the other procedures we want children to do, taking care of classroom materials needs to be taught. Here are some tips:

- *Be organized.* Have a specific place to put things away—markers, books, papers, blocks, etc. Label the area, adding pictures to make it really clear for young children. The more organized you are, the more organized the children will be. This is the critical first step in teaching children to care for classroom materials.

- *Introduce materials.* Don't let children use materials until you've introduced the procedures to use them appropriately. Model how you want children to care for the materials, whether it is how to make sure the tops of the markers click when you put them on correctly, or how to turn the pages of the class books so they don't rip. Nothing is too simple to model. In fact, teachers typically don't get specific enough. Next have the children practice what you've modeled. Then give them opportunities to try using the materials independently.

- *Offer reminders.* Children will need many reminders to learn the proper care of materials. Be supportive by repeating the modeling as needed, or just reiterating things to remember, for example, "As you work on your drawings, remember to put the caps back on the markers and push until they click," or "When you are reading silently, remember how we learned to turn the pages in the books gently."

- *Give positive feedback.* Acknowledge when children *do* take care of their things. "Bryan, I noticed you remembered how to turn the pages carefully when you were reading." This way they will begin to pay attention to their own success and know when they are on track. Do this every day!

- *Use logical consequences.* If you've followed these steps, and children repeatedly fail to follow your guidelines, it is important to set boundaries by using logical consequences. If a child does not put the caps back on the markers, then she can't use them. If a child doesn't turn the pages of the books gently, he won't be allowed to use them independently. When using logical consequences, your tone of voice must be calm, and the child should always get another chance to use more appropriate behavior soon.

If many children are not following the guidelines, then you should go back and have another group lesson on caring for the materials.

Children will make mistakes and will need time to learn to control their impulses and take control of their bodies. With plenty of modeling, practice, and positive feedback, you should be able to develop a learning environment in which children care for the materials and use them properly.

Creating Classroom Rules

All communities need guidelines for acceptable behavior so that people's needs in the community are met (Ashford, LeCroy, & Lortie, 2006). Let's consider the difference between rules and procedures (Evertson et al., 2008; Wong & Wong, 2004). Procedures are simply the steps for getting something done in a particular time and place. Rules are general guidelines for behaviors that are expected all the time. For example, "raising your hand" is a procedure because it is only used in certain contexts. When you are talking one-on-one with a child, hand-raising is not necessary. It is only in a specific context—usually a large group activity—that hand raising is needed to regulate who is talking. On the other hand, "be kind to others" is a rule because it is expected at all times.

In a constructivist classroom, rules should reflect our desire to get children to understand that other people can have different feelings and that we all have a responsibility for keeping people and things in our classroom safe (DeVries & Zan, 1994). For that reason, I recommend only a few rules which all focus on how we treat others, how we take care of our things, and how we take care of ourselves. Here's one suggestion:

> *We are kind to others*
> *We stay safe and take care of ourselves*
> *We take care of our materials and classroom*

All other general rules are versions of these three ideas. For example, "Respect others" is a form of "We are kind to others." Avoid including behaviors that are specific to certain settings or situations such as "Raise your hand" or "Walk." These should be taught instead as specific procedures. Rules should refer to behaviors that are always expected, such as being kind.

Children's involvement in rule-making. The process of developing and deciding on rules can be shared with the children through class meetings. Begin this process by focusing on typical classroom problems: "I noticed that some children were upset today because someone was calling them names. What do you think we can do about this problem?" By focusing on specific problems in the classroom, you can help children understand the reason for rules. It is very important for children's moral development that they understand these reasons rather than follow the rules because of a fear of getting in trouble. You can repeatedly emphasize how rules help keep us all safe and keep the classroom in good shape.

You may find that you will need to break down each rule into simpler, more specific behaviors. For example, children may want to create a rule, "We don't call each other names." Remember, however, to keep your discussion of rules focused on behaviors that are true all the time—otherwise you may be describing procedures, which are much simpler to just teach children through modeling and repeated practice. In essence, rules are about living as a community and maintaining good relationships with each other. Procedures are about how to get specific things done. The difference is important in how we help children develop moral reasoning and an understanding of living in a classroom community (DeVries & Zan, 1994).

Checklist for Getting Ready for the Start of School

☐ Make a list of all the procedures you want to establish

☐ Develop and teach your Quiet Signal

☐ Plan and teach procedures for major transitions

☐ Teach other procedures gradually over the first month

☐ Develop rules with the class

☐ Refer to rules often during the first month

☐ Use positive feedback frequently to help children learn appropriate behaviors

ℰℐ ℰℐ ℰℐ

Chapter 2: Building a Classroom Community

Julie rang the chime that signaled her four-year old preschool children to come together on the colorful rug they used for group activities. The children moved over to the rug from the tables where they had been working, wiggled around a bit and settled themselves into a circle around the edge of the rug. It was the end of the first week of school, so the children were getting used to the transition and being together as a group. Julie began by saying, "Okay children, today we have some special work to do. We are going to decide on a class song. This will be our own special song for our class—to help us remember that we are a community and that we care about each other." She smiled with enthusiasm. "I've picked out three songs that we have sung this week and you will all be able to vote on which one you think makes the best class song."

Julie led the children in singing and moving to the three songs. Then she brought out a laminated chart with three columns and she explained how they would vote. "I will give each of you a sticky paper and you will take turns putting your piece of paper in the column that shows which song you like best." She helped them read the name of each song along the bottom of the chart and then called each child up one by one. The excitement grew as the numbers of papers filled up the columns. Finally they were done, and Julie asked the children to count the numbers in each column and write them on the chart, giving support as needed. The song Hand-in-Hand was the winner so she led the children in singing it one more time.

The next day at group meeting, Julie showed the children the large chart she made with the words to their class song on it. As the weeks went by, the children learned how to track the words to the song with the pointer as they all gathered together each morning, celebrating their togetherness as a class. Charlene was pleased when she thought about how well her class had started to bond as a group.

Have you ever wondered why some children act as bullies, even at a very young age? Why some children cling to your legs and give hugs that knock you over? Why some children sit quietly in their cubby just watching the classroom activities? Many of these behaviors stem from children's need to feel love and belongingness (Devereux Early Childhood Initiative, 2004; Maslow, 1943). This is a powerful need for all humans and as a result, children come up with unique and persistent ways of getting their needs met, including attention-seeking behaviors that can be disruptive in the classroom.

Building Positive Relationships

Classrooms with positive social climates have strong interpersonal relationships between the teacher and the children and between the children themselves. You might think of building these relationships as making deposits in a social piggy bank (Joseph & Strain, 2006). You will need to make many deposits to build those strong relationships so that children begin to trust you, and so that your relationship stays strong even when you need to set limits for children. Having a strong positive relationship with children goes beyond just making the child feel good; it is so important that research shows it even affects the future peer relationships of children (Hughes & Kwok, 2006). In one study, classrooms in which teachers developed high quality relationships with their students had fewer behavior problems throughout the year than classrooms where the teachers did not (Marzano, Marzano & Pickering, 2003).

Relationships flourish not because there is not conflict but because we are able to manage conflict and repair breaks. You might also think about this process as growing a garden in which you need to provide plenty of sunshine, fertilizer, and water in order to withstand bugs, drought, or severe weather and bring forth a harvest. Children who are relationship "starved" will not be able to learn how to socialize or emotionally regulate themselves. The paradox here is that the children who present challenging behaviors are often difficult to build relationships with. These are the children who often trigger our "hot button" issues and we can find it hard to promote a strong bond with them. This is the point where you will want to fight your initial reactions and instinct to withdraw or get angry. Instead, push yourself to get closer to the children that are easily rejected or rejecting. Ask about their interests outside of school, talk about their family members, and join in their activities.

Be friends with the children? Many new teachers are warned not to be "friends" with the children. This advice might stem from a fear of losing control or not having enough authority. It is possible and desirable, however, to have a personal relationship with each child that might look like friendship from the outside, but actually represents a caring bond with unconditional positive regard. This must go along with also setting limits for children and helping them develop their self-regulation. You can, and should, do both—have a personal relationship with each child, while retaining your authority in order to maintain safety, direct learning and set limits on behavior.

How can you build a positive personal relationship with children? Here are some suggestions:

- Greet each child warmly every day

- Ask children about their life outside of school—what they do at home, etc.

- Get to know something personal about each child that you can talk about

- Watch children's TV shows and be able to talk to children about the shows

- Let children talk to you about their feelings without being judgmental

- Get to know the children's families

- Spend a few minutes as often as you can individually talking to a child

- If you are angry with a child, wash the slate clean at the end of the day and let him or her know you are starting over again fresh the next day

- Let children know they are missed when they are absent

- Put up photos of the children's families

- Provide positive feedback as often as possible throughout the day, aiming for more positive comments than negative ones

Helping Children Feel They Belong

One of the reasons that teaching is such a hard job is because we are simultaneously planning for the learning of a whole community of learners. Working with each child individually would undoubtedly be easier and less complicated, but it would also miss the potential benefits of being in a group. These benefits, however, don't just happen because you put 15 or 25 children together in a room for a year. In some classrooms, the children do not feel part of a community. Instead they may be competitive, highly individualistic, and subgroups may exclude each other, forming cliques, or rejecting certain children from social activities. For example, if your classroom has many instances of tattling, teasing, and bickering, you have a problem with group cohesion.

Other classrooms have a deep sense of group cohesion. The children help each other, look out for each other, collaborate and feel a sense of pride in being part of their classroom. What I've found in my own observations of classrooms is that this group connection—this sense of a community of learners—happens when the teacher values it and works hard to make it a priority. This chapter provides various strategies to help you develop a stong sense of community in your classroom.

Using Getting-to-Know-You Activities

Starting the first day of school, plan activities that help the children get to know one another. Here are a few examples:

Classroom family book. Children each draw a self portrait and dictate something about themselves. The pages are laminated or covered in page protectors and put in a binder and become part of the classroom library. Read the book frequently during the beginning of the school year.

Picture name cards. Take a digital picture of each child and laminate it on a small index card. Punch a hole through the cards and put them on a binder ring. Choose one child to start in the middle of the circle. That child looks at one of the cards, finds that child, says "good morning" and then takes that child's place in the circle. The next child then turns over the next card and starts the process again.

Duck, Duck, Goose name chase. Play by the standard rules for Duck, Duck, Goose, but instead, the child who is "It" says the name of each child (instead of "Duck) as he or she goes around the circle.

Who am I? The children will dictate or write something about themselves privately during the day. Then at group time, you can read each description without telling the name. The children will play a guessing game to figure out who you are describing.

Teaching Children to Say Kind Words

If we want to create a postive environment in which the children are loving and kind towards each other, we need to teach them the skills to do this. It is an unfortunate truth that some children do not hear many kind words directed towards them and they need those models desperately. All young children can benefit from direct instruction in how to use kind words. Young children are still learning about what the boundaries are for their behavior, and they need us to be clear about what is okay to say in school and what is not. At group time, you can begin by using puppets, dolls, or pictures of children and put on a little skit in which you act out a child saying mean words. Ask the children how they would feel if they heard those words. Next ask them what we can say to each other to make each other feel good, instead of sad or angry. Make a list of the words on chart paper and post it in a place the children can see.

For the next few days, at the start of group time, re-read the chart of kind words. Tell the children you will be listening during the day to hear how many of the words they use. And really listen! Children need lots of practice to develop new habits, and they need feedback to know how they are doing. When you hear children using kind words, draw attention to it. At the end of the day, gather the children together and share the kind words you heard that day. Add any new ones to your list. You should see a great decrease in teasing as you focus children on kindness instead.

Even after the first week of this practice, you will still need periodic reminders. Choose one day each week to

Kind Words:

I like your picture!
Can I help you?
Great job!
Thank you
Please
Want to play?
Thanks for your help
You look nice
I'm sorry
Excuse me
Do you want some, too?
Are you okay?
Good answer!

go over the Kind Words list and continue to provide positive attention and feedback when you hear children using them.

After the children have gotten good at this, you can use the same method to teach them how to do kind things for each other. Start by having the children brainstorm a list of kind things they can do. Put these on a large poster and hang it where you and the children can refer to it frequently. Then have the children act out scenes in which they do kind acts as practice. Finally, be sure to point out whenever you see children being kind.

Stopping Negative Behavior in its Tracks

Children will naturally test the limits on what they are allowed to say and do. This includes bullying, saying disparaging things to other children, and rejecting classmates. In order to create a healthy classroom community, it is critical to stop these behaviors immediately. If you let even the smallest negative comment go unchallenged, you will give the message to the children that being nasty to others is acceptable. It's not.

For example, you might overhear children saying things like:

"You can't come to my birthday."

"She smells bad."

"Look at what she's wearing!"

"Oooh, that's for girls!"

"You can't play with us."

"You're stupid."

"I don't like you."

When you hear children say these types of things, you have a teaching opportunity. I recommend having a quiet, private talk with the child and saying something like, "Jenna, I heard you tell Kayla that she's stupid. We don't use mean words in our classroom. I'd like to see you say something kind to make up for that." Later in the day, when you have the children at a group meeting, tell the children, "I've heard some unkind words today so I think we need to review how we talk to each other in our classroom." Then you can review your poster with kind words, and talk about how it feels when others say mean things to us.

After a few instances of this type of discussion, the children will come to an amazing realization: they are psychologically safe in your classroom! This will help stop the type of behavior that leads to bullying, because children will not have to constantly worry about other people being unkind. In other words, if you can jump-start the kindness, it will take off and "go viral." The critical step is to intervene immediately and consistently when children are unkind.

Creating a Positive Classroom Culture

Each classroom is similar to a unique country or cultural group, having certain behaviors, rules, values, and traditions. You can let this classroom culture develop on its own, or you can help to guide children (and other adults) into a classroom culture that supports the children's learning in positive ways. When I visit different classrooms, I am continually impressed with the different feel of each room. This is in part from the many cultural-group behaviors that children bring to the classroom, but in part each classroom is truly unique.

You have a big influence in creating a positive classroom culture. Imagine for a moment what you would want your ideal classroom to feel like. What behaviors would you want to see? What would you want children to believe about learning, their relationships to their classmates, their abilities, their differences? Once you have created this image, it is easier to guide this into reality.

There are no right or wrong classroom cultures, but there are clearly cultures that support children's learning in better ways than others. My experience leads me to believe the most important elements for success are that a teacher believes that she can create a positive environment and that she has a clear image of what that environment would be.

Giving Positive Attention

The most important tool you can have in helping children learn appropriate behaviors is your own positive attention. It is very easy to fall into the trap of correcting all the misbehaviors you notice. Even though we know that children respond well to positive feedback in the form of praise or social approval, studies consistently show that teachers do not use positive feedback as often as they should and, in fact, often reinforce inappropriate behaviors with their attention. (Alber & Heward, 1997; Landrum & Kauffman, 2006).

Instead, push yourself to notice the children who are behaving appropriately and systematically give these children positive feedback. This is called narrating the positive (Lemov, 2010). Chris Young gives a perfect description on his blog of the success he's had with this strategy compared to his previous habit of telling the children what they were doing wrong (Young, 2010):

> I'll give you a real-life example from my class this year: "I can't believe this is the third week of school and we still don't know how to walk through the halls." I traded this in for: "We're whispering as we walk, facing forward, one behind the other." I'll give you one guess as to which statement motivates the students to do it right. And they have been doing it right! Finally!

I have found that using positive feedback frequently is one of the things that separates the effective teachers from those who are struggling. Some teachers find this hard to do, so I encourage you to practice again and again until you get comfortable. Aim for giving a positive comment every couple of minutes. These can be public so everyone can hear, but not use a specific name so that you don't embarrass a child. You might say, "I see children who are cleaning up and putting lots of toys away." or "I notice that some of you are sharing your paint with your friends. That's a nice thing to do." You can also provide this positive feedback privately, directly to a child: "Morgan, you sat through all of circle time today and kept your body still!"

Effective Positive Feedback

Although positive attention can be extremely important, not all teacher attention and praise is as effective as it could be. Recent research, for example, shows that praising children by telling them they are smart can actually lead to children not trying as hard on tasks (Dweck, 2007). This is because children do not internalize the message that it is through persistence and hard work that learning occurs, rather than just being smart. Praising children in order to manipulate their behavior (*I like the way Billy is sitting….*) is also not very effective at gaining children's compliance. Children quickly learn that the teacher is using them to get others to behave. Although many teachers use praise as a way of motivating children, research shows that in many instances praise can decrease a child's desire to do something (Kohn, 1993). Similarly children notice that when the teacher says "good job" or "I like your picture" to all the children the praise becomes meaningless.

Instead of such empty praise, use positive feedback or encouragement to help children develop positive behaviors and reflect on their learning. The Center on the Social and Emotional Foundations for Early Learning recommends four principles for using positive feedback and encouragement. (Hemmeter, Ostrosky, Santos, et al., 2006):

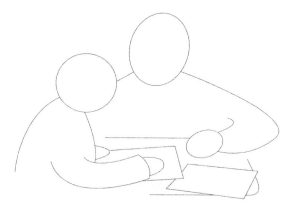

1. ***Provide positive feedback for appropriate behavior.*** Notice when children are following procedures, demonstrating newly learned behaviors, or showing kindness. This is like the old adage of "catch them when they're good." In a positive, healthy classroom, children should receive many more times as many positive comments as negative ones.

2. ***Use descriptive feedback.*** Children need to know exactly what they've done that has been positive. If we simply say "good job" or "well done" the children will not learn much from our feedback and will not value it as much. You can think of this type of praise as junk food—empty calories that do nothing for the child's nutrition. Instead, give specific feedback such as "You put away four blocks today. That's more than you've done before" or "You got right on your cot for naptime and read quietly." These types of statements provide solid nutrition and help children learn. However, for most of us, this type of feedback does not come naturally or easily. It takes more thinking and more work, which is why it's more valuable to children. But with practice over time and a commitment to helping children grow, it can be learned and become natural for you.

3. ***Convey positive feedback with enthusiasm.*** Our tone of voice and attitude convey much more to children than just our words. We want children to know we are paying attention to them, that their behavior matters and that we will celebrate their accomplishments.

4. ***Provide positive feedback for effort.***   Be sure to point out the process, strategies, and effort that children use rather than just the accomplishment: "You worked a long time on that picture. It looked like you were thinking hard." Sometimes children have also worked hard and have only a little to show for it. Noticing their effort can help them see what they have accomplished. For example, Nichole might be struggling with self-help skills in putting on her own coat. She can't yet pull up the zipper, but it will help her to point out that she is working hard and is now able to get the bottom pieces of the jacket together.

Some starters for giving positive feedback

- "You have worked really hard to _____."

- "You've been so busy today. Tell me how you _____."

- "I noticed you were working cooperatively with _____.

- "You got right to work today. That helped you get more done."

- "You participated in the story today. Is that a special story for you?"

- "You got your work done today all by yourself. You must have been focusing very well."

- "I see so many colors in your painting. Tell me about them."

- "I noticed you were working so well with _____ today."

- "I noticed that you helped _____ today. That was very kind and I bet she was happy you did that.

Positive Teacher Responses

In addition to increasing the amount of positive comments you use, it's important to monitor other types of language that are more harmful. The following list describes the types of comments typically used in classrooms, moving in order from appropriate to inappropriate. As the graphic shows, be sure you are staying in the healthy zone with all of your comments and you will find your classroom culture becomes more and more positive and conducive to learning.

1. ***Positive feedback.*** "I see three children have their coats on and are ready to go outside." "Marcia and Judy, you shared your materials well today." "You mixed red and blue in your painting. How did you make these lines?" This is encouraging talk that describes the positive things your children are doing, whether it is good behaviors or academics. It shows that you are interested in their work and efforts. It is non-judgmental and non-manipulative. This language is effective because it provides clear feedback to the children about what they are doing right. The children who overhear your feedback are also learning from what you are saying.

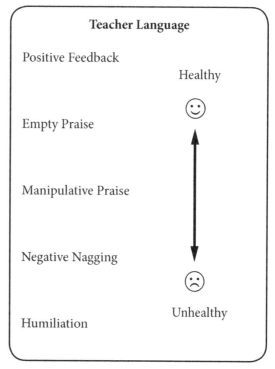

Teacher Language

Positive Feedback

Healthy

Empty Praise

Manipulative Praise

Negative Nagging

Unhealthy

Humiliation

2. ***Empty praise.*** Short comments like "good job" and "nice work" feel good and help create a positive environment, however children don't learn much from them about why they did a good job, or what aspect of their work is good. These comments are like junk food. They taste good, but are not very nutritious.

3. *Manipulative praise.* "I like the way Kody is cleaning up." Children quickly learn that these statements are coercive and are not sincere. They pit one child against the others and can lead to resentment. Instead, try describing what children are doing that is appropriate in an anonymous way: "Some children are ready, sitting quietly on the rug with legs crossed." This will probably take some practice to get used to but it's worth the effort.

4. *Negative nagging.* "Jared, stop that." "No calling out." "You were all very noisy in the hall." "Shhh!" "We don't hit!" These statements draw attention to the behaviors you don't want to occur. Why would you want to draw attention to inappropriate behavior? Even worse, they don't let the children know what they *should* be doing. Instead, use positive feedback to focus the children's attention on what your expectations are. If a child needs correction, it should be done privately.

5. *Humiliation.* "You'll never make it to kindergarten if you keep that up." "Who do you think you are?" "What's wrong with you?" "How many times do I have to tell you to stop?" These statements are never appropriate and come from extreme frustration—a sign that a teacher needs extra support to turn things around and plenty of work on her own emotional regulation. Needless to say, these comments encourage children to become defensive and act out, or humiliated and shut down. They also teach the children that it's acceptable to use humiliating language and to bully each other.

When I observe new teachers, the most common mistake I see is a focus on negative nagging. The teachers too often point out every little inappropriate behavior, slowing down the transitions and lessons, and creating a negative climate. It's a joy to see a teacher use plenty of positive feedback instead. Invariably, the classrooms using positive feedback are calmer, with more learning taking place.

Try tape recording or videotaping yourself for a little while. Keep track of the types of comments you make and notice the children's responses. Try practicing using more positive language throughout the day and especially when things get chaotic. The higher on this scale of teacher talk you can stay, the better the learning environment will be!It can be an interesting observational exercise to actually monitor the instances of positive and negative attention in your classroom for a few hours as a method of self-reflection using the following form (Hemmeter, Ostrosky, Santos, et al., 2006):

☺ Positive Attention	☹ Negative Attention

Class Meetings

Modeling democratic decision-making can be an important role teachers play in early childhood classrooms. Children are more likely to understand and adhere to rules, procedures and decisions that they have had a part in creating. Whole–group meetings are the ideal time to engage the children in group decision–making about classroom community issues (DeVries & Zan, 1994). You can involve children in developmentally appropriate discussions around proposing, planning, and choosing group activities, caring for the classroom, and dealing with class problems.

For example, you might elicit from the children ideas for a class party, or what books or songs they'd like to use. Perhaps you've been noticing that clean-up time is taking longer than usual. You could ask the children for suggestions on how to solve the problem. This can easily be integrated into your language arts goals by recording the children's ideas on chart paper and modeling language analysis strategies.

The advantage to class meetings lies in the opportunity to have children participate in a modified form of democracy, learning to listen to others, and to think about meeting the needs of the whole group rather than just individuals (DeVries & Zan, 1994). Class meetings model the process of everyone's voice being heard. This gives children more of a sense of power over their lives and develops a healthy sense of community. Children are more likely to behave appropriately when their belongingness and self-esteem needs are met in this way.

Group problem-solving strategies. When conflicts or behavior problems arise, class meetings can help the entire class use problem-solving steps, focusing especially on stating the problem, asking for solutions, and providing follow-up support.

A few words of caution are in order. For this problem-solving process to work, you must be able to set aside blame for the problem and focus on positive changes to prevent future issues (Gartrell, 2006). This process can easily turn into a mean-spirited, negative, and humiliating experience if you spend time on accusations or resort to group punishments ("No playground time today because clean-up took too long"). Move quickly past who-did-what statements and focus instead on what changes can be made. You might also need to be firm about not allowing children to accuse each other, to hurl insults, or make disparaging comments of any kind. Set up these guidelines before any discussion begins and remind children as necessary to follow them. If children are still negative and upset, it might be better to stop the process and use the problem solving process alone with the individuals involved. Some topics may be too intense for the group to handle.

Decision-making and voting. Besides problem solving, there are many other topics and issues that children can decide upon as a group. Being able to make good choices is an important skill for young children to learn and practicing this in a group provides excellent learning support.

Children can be allowed to make choices about class activities, such as:

- Materials to purchase

- Books to read

- Songs to sing

- Topics to use for writing workshop

- Science experiments to try

- Where to go on a walk around the neighborhood

- What food to serve at a family night event

- How to remember to be quiet in the hallways

- How to decorate the room for spring

- What play themes to use in the housekeeping area

In general, there are two ways to do group decision-making. You can use consensus-building in which you try to get everyone to agree to a particular choice. This typically means you might have to compromise until you get something that everyone can live with. It doesn't mean everyone gets their first choice but rather that no one can't live with the choice. The advantage to reaching consensus is that no one is usually upset by the choice.

The other process is through voting, which holds a strong place in the American culture. Voting gives everyone a chance to express their choice formally, and leads to a sense of having control since everyone has an equal weight (each vote counts the same). The downside is that the minority—the people whose choice did not get the most votes—can often be unhappy with the outcome and feel left out. Many teachers feel that even with this possibility, voting is still an ideal way to teach children about American civics while also supporting group identity, responsibility and empowerment.

DeVries and Zan (1994) offer the following guidelines for voting with young children to ensure that the process is effective for developing group processes and in helping children learn mathematical concepts:

1. ***Choose appropriate issues.*** Children should vote on things that are interesting to them and that affect the entire group. Do not focus on issues that affect only one or a few children. Do not vote on issues that are related to disagreements about facts. Instead, model for the children how to get the information needed.

2. ***Encourage discussion and define the alternatives.*** Help the children to describe what the alternatives are that they want to vote on. These should be in the children's words as much as possible, and you can write them on large paper so it is clear what is being voted on. Encourage the children to provide their reasons for and against the choices available: "Why do you want to vote for that choice?" "Can someone else tell us why he or she wants to vote for the other choice?"

3. ***Choose an appropriate counting procedure.*** Asking children to raise their hands to vote can lead to chaos and incorrect votes. Because impulse control is difficult, children will raise their hands immediately, or repeatedly for each choice.

    »   ***Polling.*** You can poll the children by calling out each name and recording the child's name on the large chart paper underneath their choice. After the polling, you'll want to have the children help count the votes. This is a good time to use tally marks to help the counting process. You can also use children's name cards that you might have already, and simply call out the child's name, then put their card into one pile or another depending on their vote.

    »   ***Body Vote.*** Children can physically move to different sections of the room depending upon their vote. You will want to put a sign up that designates the particular choice for that particular area. For example, if the children are voting on what books to read for the next thematic unit, you could place each book in a different area of the classroom and have children move to the book they choose.

4. ***Foster acceptance of majority rule and respect for minority views.*** Voting provides an opportunity for you to focus on empathy and remind those whose choice got the most votes how the others may be feeling. You can emphasize that the decision is fair since more people wanted that choice, rather than emphasizing winning or losing. You may also decide that the choice which did not get the majority vote may be done at a later time if possible.

Checklist for Building a Community of Learners

- ☐ Develop a positive relationship with each child in your class

- ☐ Plan activities to help the children get to know each other

- ☐ Teach children to say kind words and do kind things

- ☐ Intervene when children say or do hurtful things

- ☐ Re-teach and practice kind words and behaviors

- ☐ Hold class meetings to settle on class rules and decisions

- ☐ Use group problem-solving to address classroom problems

- ☐ Encourage children to vote in order to make choices in the classroom

❧ ❧ ❧

Chapter 3: Teaching Classroom Success Skills

When Martin first entered preschool, he was a whirling bundle of energy and movement. He couldn't sit still during circle time, had trouble writing his name, pushed his way into line, and regularly tripped over children on his way to the carpet.

His teacher, Miss Washington, recognized that Martin needed to learn some new skills to help him be successful. She started by brainstorming a list of skills, and then picked out the top three that she thought could help him immediately. These included: controlling his body, using words instead of pushing or shoving, and calming down.

She began with whole-group lessons on these skills, since she thought all the children would benefit from a review. Next she conducted mini-lessons with Martin each morning during center time. She used puppets, made photo cards, and had him practice for a few minutes each day.

By the end of two weeks, Miss Washington noticed Martin saying to one of the other children, "Excuse me" as he squeezed past her. She called attention to this, saying, "Martin, I noticed you using excellent manners to ask to get by. You've really learned how to work well in our classroom!" Martin smiled and skipped over to the table.

Being successful in school requires much more than being smart. It demands a whole set of skills for surviving and flourishing in a classroom with many other children and one or more teachers. In order to succeed in this environment, children also need to be able to:

- Listen to the teacher and do what she asks

- Control their impulses (stop doing what they want to do, or when they want to do it)

- Tolerate frustration (when they don't get what you want, or have to stop)

- Focus on one task and ignore distractions

- Ask appropriately for what they want or need

- Get attention in appropriate ways

- Initiate friendships

- Make amends when they do something wrong

- Say "no" or "stop" in appropriate ways

There are many more skills we could add to this list, of course. Children who do not yet know how to do these things often end up using inappropriate behavior like grabbing, ignoring requests, distracting others, fighting, or daydreaming. Teaching these skills on a regular basis can prevent challenging behaviors and create a positive, harmonious classroom.

Self-Regulation and the Brain

Psychologists refer to the brain functioning of self-regulation as *executive functioning* (Kaufman, 2010). The prefrontal cortex of the brain that controls executive functioning affects the following:

Inhibition. The ability to stop oneself from exhibiting a behavior at the appropriate time. It is the opposite of being impulsive and also involves delayed gratification and the ability to wait.

Emotional control. Being able to calm down, and also to logically realize what type and what level of emotional response is appropriate.

Initiation. Starting new tasks and independently generating ideas and strategies.

Working memory. Being able to keep information in one's mind long enough to act on it. A child with poor working memory often has trouble remembering what she was just asked to do, or what the directions were that you just told the class.

Organization. Keeping materials and belongings in their places in an ordered way.

Planning. Being able to systematically think through the steps needed to complete a task and keep track of time.

Self-monitoring. Being able to compare one's behavior and performance to some standard and being able to tell whether one is meeting expectations.

Hopefully, by now you are thinking, "Wow! These are all the behaviors of the children who make us want to pull our hair out." Yes—it is problems with executive functioning that lead children to being impulsive, emotional, disorganized, and forgetful. Here's a typical scenario that shows a child with problems in executive functioning:

Group Time is about to start on the rug. Kevin, a young five year old shoves his coat in his cubby and it falls onto the floor, along with some papers and small toys. He ignores these and bounces over to the carpet, knocking down a chair and bumping into Jennifer. He finally sits down and settles himself. During the lesson, Kevin blurts out answers and after about 5 minutes he gets up from the carpet and goes over to the art area. The teacher assistant quickly redirects him back to the carpet. After Group Time, he makes a plan to work in the block area. As soon as he gets up, however, he is distracted and sits down at one of the computers. The children who chose computers as their plan complain and ask him to leave. Kevin gets angry and starts pushing the children away from him. Ms. Grayson hurries over before he can hurt anyone. She wonders how she can help Kevin adapt better to being at school.

Recent research is helping us to understand that self-regulation plays a critical role in school success. In a series of classic studies, Mischel and his colleagues found that 4-year-old children who could delay gratification longer in certain laboratory situations showed more cognitive and social competence in adolescence, achieved higher scholastic performance and coped better with frustration and stress (Eigsti et al., 2006; Mischel, Shoda, & Rodriguez, 1989). In one recent study, students' self-discipline and control was a stronger predictor of academic success than other measures of intelligence (Duckworth & Seligman, 2005). Other researchers found that kindergarteners who had higher levels of behavioral regulation in the fall, including focusing their attention and controlling their inhibitions, reached higher levels in mathematics, literacy and vocabulary skills in the spring (Ponitz, McClelland, Matthews, & Morrison, 2009).

Many early childhood teachers are overwhelmed by the growing number of children with difficulties in self-regulation. Because many teachers burn out, or begin to feel helpless in the face of this lack of self-control and behavior problems, children are being expelled from early childhood classrooms at an alarming rate (Gilliam, 2005; Hastings, 2003).

The good news is that research shows self-regulation can be taught (Bodrova & Leong, 2007). Some of the following techniques and activities are appropriate for the entire class to improve all children's performance, and some are intended as one-on-one support for children who need extra help learning to regulate their behaviors and emotions.

Teaching Children to Regulate their Behavior

Because children learn self-regulation better when it is embedded throughout the day, rather than as separate teaching activities, you can integrate the following self-regulation strategies into your classroom management plans (Bodrova & Leong, 2007):

Planning activities. Provide children with choices and planning time to help them develop the ability to think through their actions and be purposeful. If you are the one who always decides what will be done, children will not learn how to make good choices and follow their own plans. Children can draw a picture of what they are planning, choose from a written list of ideas or photos of centers, dramatize what they want to do, or describe verbally their plans.

Freeze games. Children often learn things first through their body and then transfer that learning into more abstract cognitive skills such as using manipulatives or sitting still for group time. Therefore, you can focus on movement activities to develop self-control. Include games in which children must listen and regulate their bodies' actions within a fun framework. You can, for example, ask a question, put on music, and when the music stops, ask the children to freeze, then respond. *Hopscotch, Mother May I* and *Simon Says* are other games that help children regulate their physical behavior.

Stillness time. Build into your schedule a meditation or relaxation time in which all the children sit quietly for a couple of minutes. Teach them to sit comfortably with their eyes closed. Ring a bell or make another sound to get started, then guide the children in listening to the sounds in the room, or paying attention to how their body is sitting. Start with just a minute at first, then gradually build up to three or four. This will be challenging for some children in the beginning, but if you practice it every day, you'll be amazed at how quickly children can learn to control their bodies. This relaxation also has health benefits and teaches emotional regulation as well.

Picture and symbols. Use pictures and symbols (called concrete mediators by psychologists) of what behavior children should be exihibiting to help them learn self-discipline until they can do it independently. For example, when children are sharing with each other in pairs, one child can hold a stick with a picture of an ear on it (for the listener) and the other child can hold a stick with a picture of a mouth on it (for the speaker). A photo of how a child should be sitting can be laminated and held in the child's hand during group time. Other mediators include picture cards to help children remember rules and directions, graphics of the daily schedule for children to refer to, and squares on the carpet to designate personal space.

Teaching Children to Control Emotions

In addition to regulating their bodies and actions, children also need to learn to regulate their emotions. Research shows that emotional regulation, along with other aspects of emotional competence, affects children's long-term social competence (Denham et al., 2003). In social situations, the experience of emotions may be too little or too much to fit the demands of the social world. Emotional regulation consists of monitoring, evaluating, and changing one's emotional reactions in order to accomplish one's goals (Thompson, 1994). Young children usually need support from you and other adults in order to develop these regulation skills, as seen in frequent outbursts, temper tantrums, distress and withdrawal that get in the way of social interactions. In particular, children need to learn to calm down when they are upset and to tolerate frustration when things don't go their way. In order to use these skills, children need to be aware of and identify their own emotions. This is more complicated than it seems.

Identifying and labeling feelings. Emotional awareness means that children understand that feelings are different from thoughts, they can identify and name their feelings and realize that others may have similar or different feelings (Epstein, 2009). When children understand emotions better, they are more likely to be responsive to their peers, and rated as more sociable by teachers and more likeable by peers (Denham et al., 2003). Emotionally knowledgeable children can identify the expression on a peer's face and are more likely to know how to react appropriately to peers' displays of emotions. Often children exhibit challenging behaviors because they are unable to understand or cope with their own feelings or understand others' feelings. The first step for us as teachers is to help children recognize how emotions are expressed. This can be done directly through picture cards that you might hold up and have the children discuss, or by reading children's literature related to emotional expression, such as:

- *Glad Monster, Sad Monster: A Book About Emotions* (Emberley & Miranda, 1997) is a charming book for preschoolers with masks children can try on. Feelings are represented as different colors.

- *The Rainbow Fish* (Pfister, 1992) provides a situation for discussing how it feels to be rejected by peers and the importance of friendship. Appropriate for preschool through primary grades, the book is beautifully illustrated and appealing to children.

- *Today I Feel Silly: And Other Moods That Make My Day* (Curtis, 1998) reviews various different moods that will help preschoolers reflect on their own changes in mood.

- *Let's Talk About Feeling Sad* (Berry, 1996) is one of a series of books appropriate for preschoolers about specific feelings. Other books in this series include feeling afraid, embarrassed, angry, disappointed, and jealous.

There are also a variety of children's books available for bibliotherapy which help children cope with behavioral and emotional challenges by relating to the stories in the books, or helping them to discuss difficult subjects such as divorce, death, adoption, bullying, self-esteem, worrying, and many other emotional and social topics (Abdullah, 2002; Sridhar & Vaughn, 2000). These can be found through an Internet search or by asking your school or local librarian for recommendations.

Throughout the normal events of the day, and when conflicts occur, it is helpful to label children's emotions for them so that they begin to distinguish between different emotions and know what specific emotions feel like. For example, when A'isha comes into the classroom and slams her backpack down on the desk and scowls, you might say, "Hi A'isha. It looks like you are very angry this morning. Can you tell me about it?" Or imagine that Mariah has just bumped into Robert as she tries to sit down for group reading time on the carpet. Robert blows up and tries to push her away. You could intervene and use this as an opportunity to label emotions while still helping children learn more appropriate responses: "Robert, it looks like you are angry that Mariah bumped into you. I can understand that, but I can't let you hurt Mariah. Does anyone have some suggestions for what we can do when we are angry at someone that won't hurt them?" You can then elicit suggestions that might include telling the other person how you feel, for example.

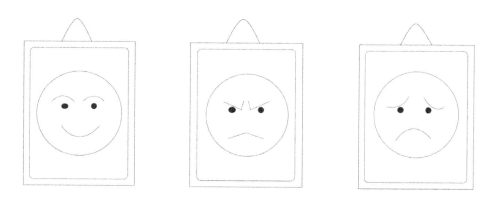

You might consider taking photographs of the children to hang on the wall with the emotions labeled. You can refer to these when children are expressing emotions and scaffold the children's use of these pictures and labels in their writing, discussions and interactions. Create a thermometer that has a moveable "mercury" center. As children relax they can use the thermometer as a concrete way of showing their emotional intensity. This can also be helpful in getting children to express their emotions.

Acknowledging and accepting feelings. Children, like adults, exhibit a very wide range of feelings and it is important to acknowledge and accept these. Feelings and actions are separate and you can help children to see the difference. For example, we might feel angry (justified or not) but it is our choice of how to express our anger that is most important in social settings. We should never criticize or demean children for their feelings, or else they will learn that their feelings don't matter or that they are not really feeling what they think they are feeling. Instead, say something like, "Martin, I can see you are very sad. Let's think of ways for you to feel better while you're at school today." Or "Shelly, you seem very frustrated, but I can't let you hurt anyone. Let's go to the Quiet Corner for a little while."

Teaching Children to Calm Down

One of the most important skill–sets a child (or adult) can have is the ability to regulate emotional reactions and moods. The following section provides practical ways of teaching children to calm themselves down. The only way these exercises work, however, is if they are regularly practiced when the children are calm. These skills must be learned before they are needed. Pick a few of these that you like and try to fit them into your daily routine so that it is easy to remember to practice them.

Breathing exercises

Controlling your breath is the easiest and most effective way to calm down. These activities can be taught to the entire class and then brief reminders should be used to give individual support when needed.

- *Flower and candle.* The children hold up their fists and pretend they are flowers. They deeply smell the pretend flower. With the other hand, they pretend their fists are candles. After smelling the flower, they slowly blow out the candles. Be sure to remind them to blow out the candle gently so that they slow down their respiration.

- *Balloons.* Get the children in a relaxed position, then have them close their eyes and breathe in deeply. Then tell them to pretend to *slowly* blow up a balloon. "Breathe into the balloon a little bit, a little bit more, a little bit more, now let out the rest of your breath." This works best if you model this first a few times and have them do it with you before starting to close their eyes.

- *Blowing bubbles.* You will need bubble mix for each child, so this might work best as a small group activity. Have each child practice gently blowing through the wand to create bubbles. Encourage children to make different size bubbles and to slow down. For very young children, this will take some practice. Once the bubble is created, encourage the children to watch it drift away until it pops before blowing the next bubble.

- *Snow globe.* Shake up a snow globe (or a clear bottle filled with water, glitter and glycerin) and ask the child to watch the glitter slowly settle, breathing along with the movement.

Body grounding

Grounding exercises focus on using the child's body to help him or her stay in the present moment and not get caught up in worries about the past or future (Najavits, 2002). They are particularly helpful when the child is over-stimulated or needs to come down from an agitated state and with children who are chronically anxious, have experienced trauma, or have unstable lives.

- *Tighten and release.* While the children are sitting down, have them tighten their fists and count to three slowly and then completely relax their fists, and count to three slowly. This can be repeated three or four times and is helpful at the beginning of activities to get children to calm their bodies and get ready for more focused work. Children can also be taught to use this technique when they are angry, before taking any action.

- *Growing roots*. This works best when children are in chairs. Have them place their feet flat on the floor and really feel the solid weight of their feet connecting to the floor. Then have them imagine that they are a plant with roots which are growing deep into the ground to keep them safe and solid, so they won't be blown around by worries.

- *Cool down*. When faced with a child who needs to calm down, encourage him to get a damp paper towel to hold on his forehead that will take away the worries/anger/frustration/sadness. Encourage the child to sit in a quiet spot for a few moments and feel the coolness. Let him decide when he is ready to rejoin the activities.

- *Special calming objects.* Children can choose a small object, such as a stone, piece of cloth, or something with an interesting texture since the sensory effects are helpful. When children are upset, they can reach into their pocket, cubby or desk and spend a couple of minutes feeling these objects. This can be linked to calming thoughts which are described in the next section. It is fun to have a special ceremony in which their objects will become the Special Calming Object as you wave a magic wand over them.

- *Peaceful colors.* Gather the children together in a comfortable spot and have them close their eyes and pick a color that makes them feel quiet and calm and peaceful. Then have them imagine that with each breath they take the peaceful color spreads all over their body, calming each place it goes—for example, down their neck to their chest, then their stomach, arms, legs, and so on until they are filled with beautiful color and peaceful feelings. This is helpful to do after an over-stimulating activity such as outdoor play, gym, recess, or lunch.

- **Soothing music.** Make or purchase a CD or audio file of soothing music that children can listen to in your Quiet Corner when they need some peace and quiet. Classical music works well, as does meditation music or those recordings made especially for relaxation, such as ocean sounds, sounds of the forest, etc. Be sure to include headphones which help a child block out the stimulation around him and keep the rest of the class undisturbed. You can make these available during free times during the day, center time, or you can suggest that children might want to use them when they are showing signs of agitation.

Yoga Poses

Yoga is a way of moving one's body that is synchronized with breathing. Yoga can help children gain body awareness and self-control of their bodies, which is an important step in self-regulation. The following are some possible poses to use with young children. Have the children pay attention to their breathing while in their poses. Once you know three or four poses, you can move from one to the other in sequence.

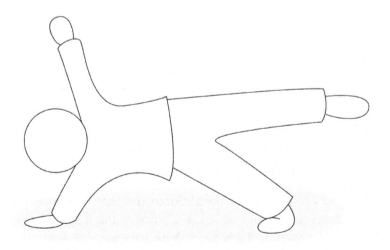

This can be done by taking a breath and then breathing out as you move to the next pose. Hold it for two breaths, then take a breath and move to the next pose and then exhale. Have fun with these and encourage children to create their own poses, too!

- *Mountain.* This is a good pose to start with. Show the children a picture of a mountain and have them imagine how straight and tall and steady they can be while standing still. Shoulders should be slightly back and feet flat on the floor.

- *Cat/Dog.* Get down on hands and knees. Arms should be right under the shoulders with your back flat. Gently arch your back up high like a cat as you breath out. Then as you breath in, let your back sag down like a dog. Gently alternate between the two for a few more breaths.

- *Tree.* Stand on one leg with the opposite foot resting against your ankle or calf. After you've gained your balance, gently raise your arms like a tree as you exhale. Keep your "branches" up in the air for a few more breaths.

- *Happy baby.* Lay on your back and grab the soles of your feet in the air. Gently rocking back and forth provides a back massage and loosens tight muscles.

- *Cobra.* Lay on your stomach and gently push up with your arms, arching your back.

Calming Thoughts

In addition to using the body to calm down, children can also learn to use thoughts to calm themselves down or to feel better when they are frightened, sad, or angry. Teach these strategies to children when they are calm as a fun way to learn how to care for themselves. Practice frequently.

- *Describe the room.* In this exercise, the children look around the room and begin to describe it out loud. "I see a table with books on it. It is shiny. There is a pencil next to the books. Under the table, the floor is grey with lines in it." You can model this a few times and have children take turns practicing it. When needed, remind children they can play the "room game" to calm down.

- *ABC's.* Teach the children to use the alphabet as a calming routine. They can quietly whisper the letters to themselves. Have them go through the alphabet once, then repeat it a second time, stretching out the sound of each letter. Once again, remind children to use this strategy as needed.

- *Kind thoughts.* Help the children make a list of kind things they could say to themselves such as "I am a good person," "I am loved," or "I can do this." Help the children practice saying these phrases to themselves, perhaps in a whisper. Older children may be able to hear these thoughts internally, but younger children will do better with moving their lips. Remind them to use their kind thoughts when they need them.

- *Favorites.* The children can practice thinking about their favorite things. It might be helpful to offer categories such as favorite foods, people, toys, pets, places to go, friends, etc. Once again, remind children to mentally list their favorite things when they need to calm down.

- *Friendly photos.* Ask families to send in photos of people who are important to their child. Laminate these and attach them with a small-ring binder or twist-tie. When children are feeling sad/angry/lonely they can pull out their photos for a moment or two and let the photos sooth them.

- *Visual imagery.* Have the children close their eyes and imagine themselves in a calm, happy place where they feel warm and safe. Tell them that they can go back to this place and feel good by closing their eyes and bringing this image into their mind. As children get tired or cranky throughout the day, you can remind them to close their eyes for a moment and go back to their happy place. This can also be done to quiet the entire class before beginning a new activity.

- *Self-talk.* Help children to mediate their emotional responses by having them repeat words quietly out loud (or in their head if they can). These words might be, "I am calm," "Stop and think," "I can wait, I can wait," or counting to five before doing anything. This can be learned as a game when it is first introduced. You can put on lively music and have the children dance vigorously, then stop the music and have them say in a quiet voice the phrase you are teaching, such as "I am calm." In the next round, have the children only mouth the words, then the next time have them say it in their heads only. Practice this game often and provide reminders throughout the day to prompt their use of self-talk. For example, this can be done before nap time in preschool, or while waiting for lunch to be served. When children show signs of agitation, they can be reminded to use self-talk by you modeling it.

Turtle Technique

This strategy involves teaching children to have self-control by pretending to be a turtle when they are upset or angry (Center on the Social and Emotional Foundations of Learning, n.d.; Webster-Stratton, 1991). They go into their "shell," count to three, and then think of a better solution. Here are the steps:

1. Model remaining calm

2. Teach the child the steps of how to control feelings and calm down ("Think like a turtle")

    Step 1: Recognize your feeling(s)

    Step 2: Think "Stop"

    Step 3: Tuck inside your "shell" and take three deep breaths

    Step 4: Come out when calm and think of a "solution"

3. Practice these steps frequently

4. Prepare for and help the child handle possible disappointment or change and "to think of a solution"

    ### Possible solutions:

    a. Get a teacher

    b. Ask nicely

    c. Say, "Please"

    d. Ignore

    e. Share

    f. Say, "Please stop"

g. Trade a toy/item

h. Wait and take turns

5. Give positive feedback and attention when the child stays calm

6. Teach families the "Turtle Technique" to use at home

Classroom Quiet Spot

Design a place in your classroom where children can go to calm themselves down. This can be a large appliance box, a corner with a rug, pillows, and stuffed animals, or some other place that is calm, quiet, and apart from the rest of the action in the room. The rule for this place should be "one child at a time" to allow children to retreat to cope with over–stimulation or frustration (Moore, 1996). Allowing children to go to the Quiet Spot whenever they need to will help them learn when they are overwhelmed and give them a sense of peace and control. In the beginning you might need to firmly suggest to the children that they should go to the Quiet Spot to relax for a few moments, however, try to let each child make the choice about when he or she is calm enough to leave the space; otherwise it becomes a punishment and defeats the purpose of teaching self-control.

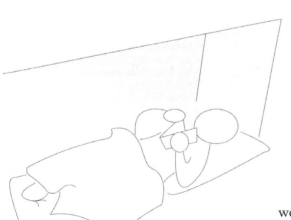

When children show stress throughout the day, you can help to coach them by reminding them to use emotional regulation skills. Most children will not be able to use these on their own yet, and will need scaffolding to work through them and learn when to use them independently. For example, when Vanessa begins to argue with others and shows signs of distress, you could gently approach her and say, "Vanessa, it looks like you are frustrated (labeling her emotion), let's take a calming breath (teaching her skills to self-regulate), and say to yourself 'I am calm' (using self-talk)." You will probably need to model and practice this with her many times until she can do this on her own. Children can also help to support and remind each other to use these tools.

Teaching Classroom Skills

Some children use inappropriate behavior because they have not learned how to behave in school. You might have a tendency to think children are just "acting out," but they may need support in learning how to behave in school. These skills include:

- Doing what the teacher asks for instead of what you want to do

- Looking at the teacher while she is talking or leading an activity

- Waiting for a turn with materials

- Waiting for snack, outside play, lunch, and so on

- Raising one's hand and waiting to respond

- Organizing one's coat and personal belongings

- Nodding to show understanding

- Getting attention in appropriate ways

These skills are often overlooked because many children learn them without extra help. But other children need direct instruction. I've found that teachers are often angry and frustrated with children who lack these skills—and often make the assumption that the children just choose not to use them. The older the children get, the more difficult it becomes for them because these classroom skills are building blocks for later learning. Children with disabilities are particularly likely to need support in these behaviors.

Try out a simple skills training program. Pick one or two skills from the list above. Designate some time during the school day to model and support the child in practicing the new skill. Use puppets, photos, role play and books. Give positive feedback when the child is successful. Practice this over the course of a few weeks, at least, because it takes time for children to develop new skills to the point where they can use them on their own.

Teaching Children How to Share

Most preschool children find sharing very difficult. This is partly because of their immature brain and partly the previous experiences that children have had. It is easy to think that children who can't share are spoiled or selfish but in most cases, children really don't know *how* to share.

The first step is to give children examples of what sharing looks like. There are actually many ways to share. Children can take turns with an item (such as a computer), or both children can use matierlas at the same time (such as markers or books). At circle time or group time you can introduce this idea by bringing over some markers and having the children show what it looks like to share. Be very specific and have them notice what the children are doing. Next show them how to share by taking turns. Bring out a chart and show the children how they can put their name on the chart when they want a turn. Demonstrate how to move the names and how to count how many children will get turns ahead of you. Also show the children how to use the timer.

Puppets can help demonstrate problems with sharing. Pretend the puppets both want to use the same dress up clothes and then show how they can problem solve to take turns. Or one of the puppets can grab a block from another one, giving you the oportunity to show how to work together in the block area. On a regular basis, you can role play any problems that you have seen occur in the classroom and ask the children for solutions.

Teaching Children How to Wait

Let's face it - we all find waiting very difficult! For young children, waiting for something they want can be extremely difficult because the part of the brain which helps them control impulses is not well developed yet. Two- and three-year olds cannot be expected to wait for more than a minute or two, while older preschoolers can stretch that a little bit with enough practice and good strategies.

We can teach children ways to make waiting easier. Model for the children ways to distract themselves - perhaps by counting, or singing to one's self, or looking around the room to find things that are interesting. Take opportunities throughout the day to remind children how to distract themselves. You can also teach them to say to themselves, "I can wait. I can wait. I can do it!" Some children may need extra help with this. During center time, you can work one-on-one with them, modeling again how to wait, and having them practice by pretending to be in different situations.

Teaching Children to Get Positive Attention

What's the difference between the children who are a joy to have in class and the children who push our buttons and challenge our last bit of patience? One important difference is that some children have learned how to get adults' attention in positive ways and others haven't. Consider the subtle ways that children interact positively with you:

- Saying, "Good morning, Ms. Jones!"

- Bringing you pictures they've drawn

- Giving you a hug

- Saying, "You're the best teacher in the world!"

- Making eye contact and smiling

- Asking you about your personal life: "What's your dog's name?"

These interactions represent a way of building personal relationships that we as adults also use in everyday life. You can think of these interactions as the grease for the wheels of relationship-building. And without that grease, the wheels turn slowly, squeak, grind, and wear down.

So it may seem strange at first, but what you can do is teach children how to get attention in positive ways. Tell the child that you are going to help her get attention in a good way. Model positive things she can say to you and other adults, and have her practice. Suggest to the child that she can shake your hand or get a hug when she comes into the classroom, or ask how you are feeling. Perhaps she can draw a picture for you, or just ask for some "talking time" with you. Some children may need pictures of what they can do as reminders. When the child begins to use any of these strategies, give plenty of positive attention and feedback.

Also consider the ways that children are currently getting attention with inappropriate behavior - perhaps by tugging on your clothes, whining, stomping, or demanding what they want. Try to ignore this behavior as much as possible and when it occurs, remind children of how to get your attention in a good way. If you've made pictures of good behavior, you can just point to the picture.

As children begin to get more attention in positive ways, they will have less of a need to get this attention by using more challenging behavior. Helping children learn these new strategies takes a while, so be patient.

Teaching Peer Relationship Skills

Social skills are also critical for children's success in school. Many times children use inappropriate behavior like poking, hitting, or biting because they have not learned how to get other children's attention or manage social demands. In addition, children who are rejected or lack friends experience school as an uncomfortable place. This social anxiety prevents them from using the part of their brains they need for learning. Here's a list of the most basic peer relationship skills (California Services for Technical Assistance and Training, 2012):

- Says "Hi" or "Hello"

- Introduces self by name

- Asks questions about other students (name, likes, etc.)

- Identifies common interests and discusses them

- Shares something about self

- Provides compliments

- Asks for permission

- Shares objects with others

- Assists others who desire assistance

- Invites others to participate

- Smiles

Supporting the development of friendships. At the base of social relationships are friendships. Some children will easily develop positive relationships with other children. Some will not and will need more direct instruction, modeling, and support from you and the environment.

You will want to help aggressive or withdrawn children to join their peers. We might be tempted to conclude that some children are aggressive or shy and we need to live with it. Not so. Children need help in learning social strategies and will benefit from your careful observations and modeling. For example, if you were working with a boy who has difficulty getting the group in the block area to accept him in their play, I might join the play with him, modeling strategies: "Look kids, Kenny has some flat blocks that would be great for ramps. Where do you think he should put them?" Encourage Kenny to be persistent in his attempts.

To help with shyness, be sure to set up a variety of activities that can be done in pairs. For children who have not yet mastered social skills, having to coordinate a relationship with more than one other person can be overwhelming. Encourage parents to make play dates with another child by suggesting children who might be good playmates.

Some children will be left out frequently, either because of withdrawal or excessive aggressiveness. What might happen is that such children begin to be seen by  the other children in a role—for example, the kid who's always in trouble, or the class clown, or the quiet kid. Help children get un-stuck from such roles by allowing the child (and the other children) to see themselves in a different light. For example, imagine that Kendra has little impulse control and is often bossy. She occasionally hits the other children and they have learned to avoid her. In addition to using some of the interventions described later in the book, you can point out whenever you catch Kendra doing anything kind. For example one of the children might have dropped a book that Kendra picks up. You can say, "Kendra, thanks for picking up that book for Michael. *You're such a good friend.*" When Kendra and the other children hear this enough, it will start to become a self-fulfilling prophesy.

Outside recreational time is also an important setting for social skills development. Children act differently when they don't have the structure of the indoor classroom and friendships often bloom in this setting. Children can bond with each other through activities that are not as language dependent—building together in the sandbox, climbing the slide again and again or running fast to chase bad guys.

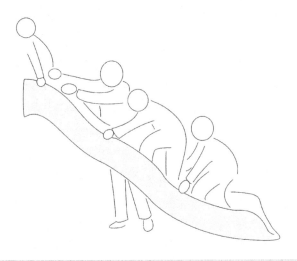

Checklist for Teaching Classroom Success Skills

Behavioral Regulation throughout the Day
- ☐ Planning activities
- ☐ Freeze games
- ☐ Stillness time
- ☐ Pictures and symbols

Emotional Regulation
- ☐ Identifying and labeling feelings
- ☐ Acknowledging and accepting feelings
- ☐ Teaching children to calm down
- ☐ Breathing exercises

- ☐ Flower and candle

- ☐ Balloons

- ☐ Blowing bubbles

- ☐ Snow globe

Body Grounding

- ☐ Tighten and release

- ☐ Growing roots

- ☐ Cool down

- ☐ Special calming objects

- ☐ Peaceful colors

- ☐ Soothing music

Yoga poses

- ☐ Mountain

- ☐ Cat/Dog

- ☐ Tree

- ☐ Happy baby

- ☐ Cobra

Calming Thoughts

- ☐ Describe the room

- ☐ ABC's

- ☐ Kind thoughts

- ☐ Favorites

- ☐ Friendly photos

- ☐ Visual imagery

- ☐ Self-talk

- ☐ Turtle technique

- ☐ Quiet spot

Classroom Skills

- ☐ How to share

- ☐ How to wait

- ☐ How to get positive attention

Peer Relationship Skills

- ☐ Friendships

- ☐ Helping children to join activities

- ☐ Get children get unstuck from roles

- ☐ Support peer interactions on the playground

ೞ   ೞ   ೞ

Chapter 4: Engaging Children in Learning

Miss Harrison was frustrated with the way her morning circle was going. Her mixed class of three- and four-year old children seemed to have more and more behavior problems every day. The circle time started out well with all the children singing the morning greeting song, but when they moved onto their calendar routine, many of the children started wiggling, talking to each other, and occasionally turning around and grabbing some blocks to play with. After calendar, the children were not at all interested in sitting through storytime, or practicing the letter of the week. After about 20 minutes, she lost her patience and started reprimanding the children. She knew her approach was not working, but what should she do instead?

At the heart of classroom management is the ability to keep the children engaged in learning. Many behavior problems result when children are not actively participating in the learning activities. This is often because the work is not in their zone of proximal development (Vygotsky, 1978) or not age appropriate. In this chapter, I will offer some suggestions for keeping the children's attention and helping them to stay involved and on task.

Kounin (1970), a famous educational psychologist, was the first theorist to emphasize that classroom discipline and instruction are deeply connected, rather than separate elements of teaching. After observing classrooms for many years, he found that planning and organization are keys to good management. In addition, he identified the following characteristics of teachers with good classroom management.

Withitness. The teacher is aware of what's going on in the classroom all the time. This refers to the proverbial "eyes in the back of the head" that good teachers seem to magically develop. This teacher will notice Bryan starting to get agitated and decide to call on him to choose the next song. She will notice when Marissa is focusing on the story better than usual and gives her positive feedback for her effort.

Multitasking. The teacher is able to carry out multiple tasks at the same time such as singing a song while watching all the children's behavior and signaling the paraprofessional to set up the tables for lunch.

Smoothness. The teacher has all the materials ready ahead of time so that there are not interruptions during the activity and the children are not ever left waiting for the teacher.

Momentum. The teacher keeps the pace of the lesson brisk so that children do not lose their engagement. This includes redirecting children towards appropriate behavior quickly with the least possible intervention and maintaining the focus of the group on the lesson. These teachers also moved the children from one activity to the next without having children wait for each other. For young children, momentum is especially important since children who lose interest in your lesson can quickly find something else to interest them in a way that you might not want, such as playing with materials on a nearby shelf, talking to a neighbor, or roaming around the room.

Keeping children engaged in learning also requires good judgement about what format is best for a particular activity. There are four basic structures you can use to engage children in activities:

1. Whole group activities, in which all the children participate at the same time with you leading the activties.

2. Small group activities, in which you lead 3-7 children in the same activities in a designated area of the classroom such as a group table or sectioned-off carpeted area.

3. Centers, in which the children choose what area they want to work in and what activity they want to do in that area. You are facilitating the children's learning but the children are leading the activity.

4. One-on-one, in which you lead one child in an activity during center time. This is typically used to give a child more attention, support, and guidance in learning new skills.

An important teaching decision is whether you should use whole-group, small group, one-on-one interaction, or a play center for any given activitiy. The following list gives my recommendations for how to structure common activities in order to be most successful:

Singing, music, and movement: whole group

Art activities: small group or centers

Science activities: small group or centers

Cooking activities: small group or centers

Storybook reading: small group or one-on-one

Social skills activities: whole group, small group or one-on-one

Lunch or snack; whole group or centers

Writing activities: centers or one-on-one

Engaging Children in Whole-Group Activities

Whole-group activities are effective only when all the children are able to participate. When children have to wait for a turn to participate, or listen at length to other children talk, they will quickly lose interest and may become disruptive. Whole-group settings are not appropriate when many sets of materials are needed. For example, it is relatively simple and effective to use clay or watercolor paints with a small group; it is difficult to do the same activity with all the children at once. Therefore, virtually all art activities work better in small groups or centers. The same holds true for science activities. Conducting an experiment and having children watch you rather than use the materials themselves is not effective.

Once you've decided that a whole–group setting is indeed the best format for your activity, it's time to think through the management needed for children to experience success. There are other simple techniques for keeping children engaged during your whole group activities:

- *Keep it active.* Get the children moving their bodies in purposeful ways. Hand motions, full body actions, or even finger plays help children to focus.

- *Give choices.* Have the children choose what song is sung, what poem comes next, or what story will be read. Try to build choices into all your activities.

- *Use variety.* Plan for many different types of activities which are all short. This keeps children interested and prevents them from getting bored or distracted. Keep a close eye on the children's body language. When you see some fidgeting and wiggling, it's time to move to a different activity.

Using Alternatives to Hand Raising

Many classrooms use a hand-raising ritual. A teacher asks a question and waits for the hands to go up. Many do, some waving wildly: "Me, me!" Some children sit staring into space or playing with the rug. Some children seem to still call out, no matter how many times they are told to raise their hands. When the teacher eventually calls on a child, often he doesn't know the answer and stumbles for a minute or so before the teacher moves onto to someone else. Sometimes the child rambles on about a different topic while the rest of the children zone out or anxiously wait for their own turn. The teacher is often exhausted from trying to keep the children on task.

Sound familiar? Besides the management challenges of controlling children's behavior, the part of this ritual that concerns me the most is that during these exchanges only one child at a time is fully engaged in the learning interaction. Young children don't learn well from sitting and listening to others, even if they can get themselves to be able to focus on the interaction. This is an ineffective learning pattern, yet teachers repeat it because it's so familiar and comfortable.

In general, I don't recommend having children raise their hands to answer questions. You will quickly lose the engagement of the children. Here are some better alternatives to the hand raising routine:

Turn and Talk. After the question is asked, pairs of children turn to each other. One listens while the other answers. This way half of the class is engaged in talking, and it is easier for children to pay attention to the speaker in a paired situation. Be sure that children know ahead of time who their partner is and that they practice how to pair up. This should move quickly, so keep the pace brisk to support children staying on task.

Think-Pair-Share. This technique is similar to Turn and Talk, except that children are first given time to solve a problem or answer a question individually, then they turn to their partner, quickly share responses with each other and come up with the best or most interesting answer (Lyman, 1981). Next the teacher calls on a few

pairs to share with the class. Being able to listen to a partner is a challenge for young children, but the practice they get will help them develop more self-regulation. They also benefit from being able to share their thinking.

Choral responses. To increase student engagement and reinforce simple concepts, allow the children to respond all together. This works best for questions with one answer, and as a quick review of previously covered material.

Individual whiteboards. Each child has a whiteboard and marker and they write down their answer to the question. Children hold up their boards so the teacher can judge how well the children are understanding the concepts. If your class doesn't have these boards, you can also use plastic plates that the children write on with dry erase markers.

Cold call. Keep a list of children's names, put their names on cards, or sticks, and randomly pick children's names to answer. This helps to improve the pace of the lesson, and keeps children engaged since they don't know when they will be called on. However, it should still be used sparingly since it suffers from the problem of only one student at a time interacting with the question.

Giving Directions

Young children typically have difficulty in following teachers' directions. This is most likely a result of both the child's immaturity in being able to cognitively process the information given, but it is also likely to stem from ineffective ways of giving directions. If you are giving directions to the whole class, use your quiet signal first and be sure that you have the children's attention.

Only give one or two directions at a time. Often we overwhelm children by giving them too much information. Only give directions that are necessary in that moment, and give them in a way that tells the child specifically what to do. Be clear and concrete; telling a child to "settle down" or to "get ready" does not state what the behaviors the child should follow. Instead, say, "Sit with your legs crossed and use your whisper voice," or "Go to your cubby and put on your coat." This lets the children know exactly what they should do. Give the children time to respond to your request before making another one. Monitor the children to be sure they follow your directions.

Some children, especially those with disabilities, may need personalized directions. For example, some children will respond better when you give them a physical prompt (pointing, guiding, demonstrating). It is helpful to also have picture prompts for directions that are given often, such as washing hands, hanging up coats, getting books out for lessons, or pushing in chairs. For children with verbal processing problems, pictures can help them manage the complex verbal environment of the classroom.

Sharing Time or Show and Tell

Another common form of group activity is "Show and Tell" or "Sharing Time" in which each child takes the floor and provides a narrative about something he experienced outside of school, often with a concrete object to go along with the talk. Similarly, many teachers build in these types of group discussions after reading a book to the class and have the children take turns describing their personal responses.

These types of discussions are difficult to manage in any classroom, and there are added challenges when working with young children (Carter & Doyle, 2006; Parker, 2001). In order to participate in discussions, children must learn to take turns speaking, and you will need to decide how those turns will be managed. Will you call on children who raise their hands? Call on children in order so everyone gets a turn? Go around the circle? Next, children will need to speak relevantly on the topic. This is very difficult for younger children who tend to be egocentric in their speaking and easily flow from one idea to the other without regard for their listener. It takes practice and skill for you to redirect children or ensure that the rest of the group doesn't become restless and lose interest in the speaker. Another important issue is that children's ability to gain access to speaking is connected to their social class and ethnicity (Cazden, 2001; Weinstein, 1991).

Given the complexity and difficulty in leading discussions with young children, there are some adaptations that will help things go more smoothly:

- Keep discussions short and use them sparingly. Don't have all the children take turns sharing at one meeting. Break it up over a few days with a few children at a time.

- Use visual aids to help children keep their attention and focus. If you are discussing the best part of a book, show that picture. If children are sharing what they did, encourage them to create a picture or dramatize what happened with the help of friends.

- Teach the children to keep their eyes on the speaker. This will help them focus better.

- Redirect children as needed. It may feel rude to interrupt children, but you are also serving as a guide to help them realize when they are not holding the interest of the group. This can be done gently: "Marisa, what a wonderful story. We need to move on to the next child, though, so I hope you will tell me the rest of your adventures later during center time."

- Try to engage all the children as much as possible. Encourage the group to ask questions or to comment on what the speaker is saying in order to help them stay focused and interested.

- Remember the children's developmental levels. What might seem like misbehavior will often be immaturity and inability to sustain focus in discussion settings. Watch the children's body language carefully. When they are fidgety and restless, try to speed up the pace, or cut the discussion short and move onto a different activity.

Engaging Children in Small Group Activities

Small group activities are often easier to manage because there are fewer children to engage and you can meet children's individual needs better. This structure is an excellent way to build language competence and vocabulary since children can talk to each other and to you while engaging in the activity. Therefore the best small group lessons include open ended activities in which children can explore materials such as art activities, science experiments and group games. Reading children storybooks is also more effective in small groups than in whole group settings since it is easier for children to comment on the book and discuss what is happening (Morrow & Smith, 1990).

To keep children engaged during small group activities, following these guidelines:

- *Group size.* Keep your groups small. Three to four children works best, although many centers and schools will plan on seven or eight children in small groups.

- *Materials.* Each child should have a set of materials so that all children are working simulatansously. Don't make children wait for a turn because that is lost learning time. Young children learn better by doing than watching.

- *Freedom.* Allow children to work in their own way as much as possible. Except for group games which include simple rules, children should be able to be creative and go in their own direction.

- *Boundaries.* Even though you are allowing children freedom to work with the materials, be sure that they know what limits they have. For example, insisting that children work at the group table, or stay on the group rug is appropriate. Designate a particular location such as a table or carpet area for your small group time so that children know where they must stay during this time.

- ***Plan for when children are done.*** Some children may want to spend more time on your planned activity than others. It is unlikely that all children will be done and ready to move onto the next activity at the same time. Have a plan for when children are done or when they lose interest. You might want them to leave the group to go to play centers or begin to work on another activity at the group table or carpet.

Keeping Children Engaged in Centers

The major portion of the day for learning in a preschool should occur in child-directed, child-initiated play activities. Some programs call this Center Time, Play Centers, Play Time, or Work Time.

Format. Center time in preschools can be formatted in a variety of ways. This might be determined by the curriculum model that your school or center uses, or you might have some choice in how to implement center time. Some programs, such as High Scope, allow children complete freedom to go to any play area, to work with any materials, and to stay in that center as long as they want. Other programs, such as Tools of the Mind, have the children remain in the play center they've chosen for the entire center time, or those such as Creative Curriculum might limit the number of children in a center but allow choices if there are open spots in other centers. In all effective programs children will have choices for what activities they do and what centers they play in.

Planning. There are many benefits in having children plan what activity they are going to do. Planning helps them develop the ability to control their actions in a thoughtful way which is critical for success in school. In High Scope programs, children plan in small groups in playful ways such as talking to puppets, using pretend microphones or pointing to a planning chart with photos. In Tools of the Mind classrooms, planning time is done in small groups at tables. The children plan and draw a picture of what role they will play. With scaffolding from the teacher, they either dictate or write a sentence with their plan. By the end of the year, many children can do this independently. In other classrooms, teachers have developed laminated planning boards with sections for each center. The children put their name tags in the center they are planning to play in. Some teachers have the children's names of clothespins and they clip their name onto a chart in the center area. When the chart is full, the child needs to choose a different center.

Popular Centers. You may find that some centers are so popular that you need to regulate turns. This can happen with the computer center, easel, tricyles or other activities that are limited in how many children can participate.

Conflict. Young children are still learning how to control their impulses and how to use language to manage social relationships. This means conflict is inevitable. Consider these incidents as teachable moments. Children do not need to be punished, but rather taught how to behave in centers. For exmple, children need to be taught how to take turns with the dolls or dress up clothes and how to work collaboratively on building with blocks. You might need to teach children how to walk around someone's block creation so they don't knock it over. You can set up certain rules such as "Don't knock down someone's structure unless he gives you permission." Don't assume that children *should* know how to behave in centers. Instead think about the social skills you can teach while children are playing.

Preparing the Physical Environment to Engage Children

"He knocked my building down!" cried Jake.
"These are my blocks! Get out of my way." Kyle screamed back at him.
Janine rushed over to calm the situation down. This year she seemed to have more problems in the block corner than anywhere else. The kids always seemed to be fighting, buildings were getting knocked over, and the noise level was uncomfortably high. As the school year progressed, more and more children were choosing the block are during center time in her preschool classroom. She was getting tired and frustrated of having to spend so much energy keeping the area problem-free.
As she discussed the problem with her teacher assistant, Marcy, they brainstormed various solutions. Perhaps they could station one of the teachers in that area during center time. That would limit their flexibility in working with different children however. Perhaps they could limit the area to fewer children? That solution seemed to discourage the increasing interest in block play that Janine wanted to encourage. Perhaps they could make the area itself bigger? Janine and Marcy spent some time at the end of the day figuring out what they could try. The block cabinet consisted of two long shelves attached with a hinge in the middle. It was currently in an "L" shape with one side against the wall. They decided to open

the cabinet fully and place it flat against the wall. This would increase the area and make it easier for the children to get the blocks without stepping over each other.

The next week was amazing. Janine could not believe the difference this simple change made. There were as many children in the block area, but the fighting all but stopped and the noise level decreased. The best part was that the children started building more sophisticated structures since they weren't knocked over as much, and since they could see the choice of blocks better. Janine and Marcy were so pleased, they decided to look carefully at the rest of the room to see what else could be improved.

The physical environment is an important, and often overlooked, teaching and learning tool. It is often thought of as a "third teacher" along with parents and teachers (Gandini, 1998). Because young children need concrete materials, movement, and plenty of interactions, the physical environment of the classroom is critical in the learning process. In a recent study, for example, Lorraine Maxwell (2007) found that for children between the age of 3 and 4, the physical environment was related to children's cognitive and social competency. Certain aspects of the physical environment were particularly important. In classrooms that scored high on having (a) compatible or complimentary activity  areas, (b) support spaces, (c) children's access to large motor development areas (indoors and/or outdoors), and (d) children's access to personal care (e.g., toilets), both 3- and 4-year old children perceived themselves to be more competent in the classrooms than their peers who rated as inadequate on these items.

Many classroom spaces designated for early childhood programs are less than ideal. It takes a great deal of creativity and thoughtfulness to create spaces that supports a positive community of learners. Many teachers often overlook the great impact that the physical environment can have on children's behavior. For example, most of us feel a sense of place, or an emotional attachment to places that are important in our lives. Children, too, need to feel a sense of place in their center or school which will provide them with emotional stability, a chance to learn through their senses, and evoke home-like characteristics (Read, 2007).

Planning the Classroom Space

In her classic book about preschool and primary classroom environments, Vergeront (1987) outlines the following important ways to plan your classroom space:

A Sense of Arrival. Children develop emotional attachment to meaningful places like their classroom, which can provide a sense of belonging and stability (Read, 2007). Children, families, and visitors will enjoy a sense of welcoming when your classroom is planned out to provide a sense of arrival. This can include a sign in sheet that is easily accessible, bulletin boards that highlight children's work and create connections to families, important announcements, and a view of exciting activities in the classroom that entice children to enter. Plan to have enough space to greet family members who may be pushing strollers or arriving with other children in tow. This space is where you will also want to post information for families about the daily schedule or upcoming events.

Personal Space. When living in a community such as a classroom, children also need their own personal space such as a cubby that can hold their coat, extra clothes, and naptime things. For very young children who may have difficulty separating from their family members, photos of their family can decorate their personal space.

Storage . You will need three kinds of storage: 1) Materials that children have access to now in the classroom, 2) Materials you want the children to use later in the year, 3) Your own teaching materials that the children will not use.

Early childhood classrooms typically have many more materials than those of older children, because of the need for concrete, sensory-based experiences and activities. One way to organize your materials is to think about each area of your classroom and consider what activities will take place there. This may include your learning centers or activity areas, space for whole group activities, and areas for small group activities. The following questions can guide you (Scheuermann & Hall, 2008, p. 208)

- What materials need to be stored in this area?
- How will those materials be stored and labeled?
- What materials will children be able to use on their own?
- What materials will be used only with adult supervision and need to close by, but out of the reach of children?
- What type of cleanup will be required at the end of the activity?

Labeling shelves, cabinets, and walls with both words and pictures can help children gain independence and benefit from the cognitive tasks of classifying and

seriating objects as they search for items and put
them away.

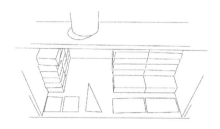

With some luck, you will also have shelves
or closet space that is not within the reach of the
children. You'll want to store materials to bring
out at various times throughout the year. This is
important for keeping children's interest high.
Do not store materials where children can easily
get them unless you want them to access them! Don't waste your time and attention on
preventing children from using materials that are visible and easy to get to.

You will also want to plan space for your own teaching materials that are not
available to the children. This might be your own computer, your observation materials, children's files, teachers' guides, planning materials, and your personal items.

Pathways. Think through carefully how the children will get from one area
to another. Pathways that cut through working spaces can lead to children accident-
ly disturbing the work of others. And when you have children who have low tolerance for stress this can cause a fight to erupt or other behavioral challenges. Be sure
there are clear pathways around areas, and not too much open space or children will
wander aimlessly or run through the areas. If the pathways are too congested, there
will be a bottle neck and hard to reach areas will be less frequently used. If you have
a child using a walker or wheelchair, or other assistive movement devices, plan carefully
for pathways that are wide enough with plenty of space for turns. Also plan for your
own movement.

Activity spaces with defined boundaries. Children can be overwhelmed by
large spaces that are common in the adult world. Breaking down the classroom into
smaller spaces provides children with a sense of security and competence. This can
be done by arranging low cabinets to close off spaces such as a dramatic play area or
science center. The arrangement of tables can also set off different areas of the room.
Rugs work well for creating visual boundaries that let children know certain areas are
designed for certain behaviors such as sitting in a circle for group activities, or quietly
reading books.

Programs for young children include many concrete learning materials.
Children will use these materials most effectively, and learn the most, when they are
grouped together in logical ways. Having designated activity areas such as a dramatic
play center, art area, book corner, or science center will help children make choices
and reduce wandering. When activity areas are grouped together, such as placing the

block area adjacent to the dramatic play center children show greater creativity and more equitable gender-based play. Grouping activities can also keep noisier areas and quiet areas closer together to help children concentrate. This will also give children cues about expectations for noise levels.

All activities do not take up the same amount of space and controlling the size can promote certain behaviors. For example, a dramatic play center that is too large might encourage too many children in that area and lead to disorganized play. On the other hand, a block area that is too small may create conflict when children bump into each other or inadvertently knock over the other's work. If you notice that certain areas of the classroom are generating many behavior problems, consider that the size of the space may be too big or too little. You will also want to avoid having a center with a high level of activity (such as dramatic play) close to quieter activities (such as the library corner).

Noise control. A busy classroom of young children can be a very noisy place and the physical environment can make this better or worse. Carpeting effectively cuts down on all noise, and is especially helpful in the block area where the sound from wooden blocks hitting the floor is bothersome. Unfortunately, rooms with high ceilings, such as those in old school buildings and church halls allow the noise to reverberate more. Curtains and other "soft" materials such as partitions, plants, and even stuffed animals cut down on the noise level, as well as adding a home-like feel to the room.

Types of play materials. Keep in mind that some activities can be done easily by only one or two children, such as a puzzle, tricycle, painting at the easel, computer game, or journal writing. Other activities are more complex, such as a water table with various pouring materials that can accommodate a few children. Areas such as the dramatic play center are very complex and can often accommodate small groups of children. In planning the classroom environment, a balance of simple activities and complex activities is most effective (Kritchevsky, Prescott, & Walling, 1969).

There are many views about how many materials should be available in each activity area. Vergeront (1987) suggests that enough activities overall in the classroom should be one and a half times the number of children in the class. That would mean that for a class of 15 preschool children, you would plan at least 22 different activity slots. This might mean 5 in the block area, 4 in dramatic play, 4 at the water table, etc.

Wolfgang (2004) provides a helpful classification of play materials into three categories depending on their use. The first group includes fluid materials such as water, sand, easel paints, and play-doh. These materials are designed to encourage sensori-motor stimulation and creativity. They also require the child to control or master the materials by deliberately structuring them so they contribute to a child's self-regulation. Children first start out in random movements, then gradually learn to control and elaborate on the material.

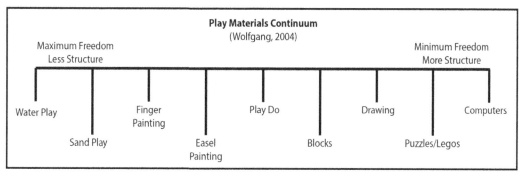

The second group comprises structured materials such as unit blocks, Legos, puzzles, and other building blocks. These materials are solid and have a specific structure and form. They can range from being more open-ended like unit blocks, to more structured in how they are used, such as pegboards or puzzles. Similar to their use of fluid materials, children's play will begin as random exploration before they learn to use the materials to create their own symbolic products.

The third group includes symbolic materials which encourage make-believe and fantasy play. These can be small materials that children manipulate such a miniature cars, housekeeping props, zoo animals or small people. They can also be large materials which children can use for role play, such as a refrigerator, stove, dress-up clothes, or toy telephones.

The categorization of materials can be visualized on a continuum which ranges from the most structured to the least structured. This can be helpful to consider when working with children who are aggressive or passive. Aggressive children may have difficulty with very fluid, unstructured activities because they do not offer enough control. As a result, the child may get overly stimulated, frustrated and lose a sense of self-control. Through gradually exposure and learning, the child can eventually learn to use such materials in a productive way. On the other hand, children who are very withdrawn will often avoid symbolic materials because they pose a social challenge and require the child to be more exposed and interactive. Similarly, the child will need gradual exposure, modeling, and support to be successful with those materials.

Quiet Corner. Children need privacy and it's important to have a place they can recover composure so they can learn how to regroup and regain self-control. Think of this as a pleasant cool down spot such as the library corner or a place with a rug, pillows, and secluded from the rest of the room so a child can go and spend time to calm down. This should not be thought of a time-out area in which children are sent as punishment. Instead, the focus should be on helping children to gain self-control as they need to.

Some children are easily overwhelmed by the stimulation in a classroom. The movement, the amount of children, the noise, lights, and even the walls that are covered in stimulating materials can cause children to act out behaviorally. They might over-react in anger, whine, tantrum, or become withdrawn. Your quiet place should also provide some respite from the stimulation of the classroom. An area in which there is lower lighting, less visual material, and less movement is ideal. This might need to be created – such as a large appliance box, or a space created from the backs of cabinets. This is a chance to use the children's creativity as well as your own in helping to design the "quiet place". This area can be used in many ways, especially in helping children learn emotional skills and self-calming behaviors.

Whole group meeting area. If the children will be sitting on a rug, be sure there is enough personal space for each child. I have seen many group activities turn into chaos because the children were squeezed together in too little space. Many children with stress in their lives, such as those living in poverty, dealing with difficult family situations, or those with certain disabilities can have a very low threshold for any kind of negative stimulation and require more personal space than you might expect. A simple push can set off challenging behavior. Simply providing enough personal space can prevent many behavior problems and encourage appropriate behavior.

If you find that children are not focused during your whole group activities – perhaps annoying each other, or complaining – first try to enlarge the space you are using for the group, as well as designating boundaries for personal space by using mats or a rug printed with lines or shapes. Also check to make sure all children can easily see you. Teach the children to recognize when they are too close to others and how to stay in their designated space. You can have them imagine a bubble around themselves that will pop if they are too close to others. I recommend having enough room so that you can sit children in a circle. When children are in rows on a rug, there is more tendency to bump into each other and it's harder for children to see each other.

Music and movement activities work well in large group settings, however, you'll need plenty of room for movement. Think through the limits you might want to set on movement such as children needing to stay within their square on the rug. It is also helpful to plan and teach children how they can move in a circle for songs and activities with jumping, walking, skipping, etc. This might be around the edge of the rug, or you could place a tape on the floor that children can follow.

Think through what materials you will use on a regular basis during whole group lessons, such as:

- Portable white board for morning message,

- Chart paper for language experience stories,

- CD or audio player for music activities,

- Markers

- Puppets to help demonstrate procedures

- Chair you are comfortable on

- Smart Board, Promethean Board or other technology equipment

You'll want to find a way to store these next to your rug or meeting area. You can designate a cabinet, shelf, or other area that is the "teacher's area" and teach children that these materials are only for the teacher's use. Also consider positioning yourself during whole group activities so that you can see the door to your classroom and keep an eye on anyone coming in who might need your attention.

Outdoor Learning Areas

Recess has been under attack in recent years as schools give up time for outdoor play in order to squeeze in more academics. Educational researchers have helped us see that recess and outdoor play have implications for educational and developmental growth (Pellegrini & Smith, 1998). For example, a study of four-year-old girls and boys showed that attention to classroom tasks was greater following sustained outdoor play periods (Holmes, 2006). Even the United Nations Convention on Children's Rights states that, "Parties recognize the right of the child to rest and leisure, to engage in play and recreational activities appropriate to the age of the child" (Office of the United Nations High Commissioner for Human Rights, November 1989). Some centers in urban areas substitute an indoor play space with climbing apparatus instead of an outside playground. While this is certainly better than providing no space for gross-motor activities, it is not an adequate substitute for being outside.

While you might not have control over the outdoor space for your children, it can still be helpful for you to understand criteria that make such space better for children. The National Association for the Education of Young Children uses the following general criteria for accreditation of a preschool or kindergarten program (NAEYC, 2005) :

- Play areas are protected by fences or natural barriers

- Play areas are arranged so staff can hear and see all children easily

- There is at least 75 square feet of outside play space per child

- The play area protects children from injury from falls (with resilient surfacing), sharp points, entrapment, tripping, excessive wind and direct sunlight

- The play equipment is safe and well maintained

- The play area accommodates abilities, needs, and interests of the age group it serves.

- Motor experiences such as running, climbing, balancing, riding, jumping, crawling, scooting, or swinging

- Activities such as dramatic play, block building, manipulative play, group games or art activities

- Exploration of the natural environment, including a variety of natural and manufactured surfaces, and areas with natural materials such as non-poisonous plants, shrubs and trees.

- The outdoor space meets the ADA accessibility requirements so that children with disabilities can fully participate in the outdoor curriculum and activities

You might be fortunate to have a well-designed play area accessible for your children. Even if you do not, however, there are materials you can acquire to bring with you to improve the outdoor environment and create appropriate outdoor experiences for children.

Gardens. Whether you are in a beautiful rural area where space is abundant, or perhaps in an urban school with a small balcony or roof area, you and your children can create an outside garden that supports their learning (Pecaski McLennan, 2009). Gardens can be created in a corner of your play area, on a lot adjacent to your center, or in moveable planting containers on any outside area that gets enough sun during the day. The planned location will also need to be somewhat close to a source of water. Big plastic tubs can serve as planters by drilling drainage holes through the bottoms, or families can be enlisted to create more substantial planters or to break up the soil for planting. Planning and creating a garden is also a good opportunity to use community resources such as a local gardening center or hardware store to come to your class and do a presentation. The garden can then be used for children to learn about science concepts, taking responsibility, and enjoying the beauty of nature.

Technology in the Early Childhood Classroom

Some experts in the field believe that we are well past the point of asking if technology should be included in learning environments for young children; instead we need to focus on what kind of technology we can be using and for what purposes (Parette, Quesenberry, & Blum, 2010). Much has been written about the use of technology in early childhood classrooms (see for example the November 2003 issue of Young Children published by NAEYC). There are two considerations: the first is the use of technology as a teaching and learning tool. The second is the use of technology for adaptations to the needs of children with disabilities. We can use the framework of universal design for early childhood education (Darragh, 2007), in which we create environments that provide access and equity to all children in an inclusive way. Technology provides an excellent opportunity to create this inclusive learning environment as well as providing access to poor children who might not have the opportunity to learn about technology outside of school.

You may be fortunate enough to have a classroom equipped with a variety of technology resources. However, if you don't currently have such resources, knowing about what is helpful and available can assist you in advocating for the materials you'd like to have. Let's first consider larger technology pieces such as a SmartBoard or Promethean Board, which are interactive white boards combined with a computer.

These can project your computer screen while allowing interaction through the large touch screen and various teaching applications. These are wonderful for children who benefit from viewing a large screen and from the opportunity to use the touch screen rather than a mouse. These boards come in versions which are permanently mounted on a wall like a chalkboard, or that are on a moveable stand which can be rolled around to different locations. Even though some boards can be moved, they still need to be hooked up to a computer so it's important to plan where you'd typically be using the board, making sure that an electrical outlet and computer hook up are close by. You will need to plan out where you will have your own personal computer in the classroom (and to advocate for one if you don't currently have one!)

A simpler LCD projector for a computer can be mounted permanently on the ceiling or just brought out when it will be used. These machines get hot and will need

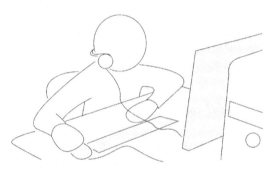

to be placed so that very young children won't inadvertently touch them. You'll want to designate wall area to use for a screen. You may find that you are in a classroom that still has an overhead projector. The use of the overhead also requires planning for a screen and area to situate the cart it sits on. If you regularly use these types of projectors you may find that a Smart Board will do the job better with much less classroom space.

Another environmental challenge is finding space for computers that the children will use independently. They will need to be located in an area where there are electrical outlets and connections to the Internet if the school does not use wireless connections. Also consider situating them where you can easily monitor the children's work and behavior. In order to encourage children to get the benefits of socializing and cooperative work, leave room for two chairs at each computer if possible. You'll want to plan on space for a printer and space to keep the associated paper and ink supplies. Also be sure to plan for assistive technology devises such as switches or digital voice synthesizers, or amplifiers.

In addition to these larger items, consider how you will store and use other technology such as digital cameras, video cameras, voice recorders, and audio players. Many teachers have moved away from tapes and CDs and are using digital music players such as iPods or smart phones to keep play lists of favorite songs. The digital players allow you to easily customize what audio tracks you want to use and to switch easily from one track to another without finding the right CD or cueing up the tape at the right place. Free software is available online to assist children in creating their own music, video, and voice recordings as well (see for example (Skouge, Rao, & Boisvert, 2007). Plan on where you will have speakers for the devices, or whether you want to also have headphones available for children to use during center times.

Because technology devices require special wiring, electrical outlets and other spatial requirements, it is best to start laying these out first, then consider working in the other areas of your classroom which can be more flexible.

Assistive Technology Toolkit. Teachers working in inclusion classrooms can help all children with access to the learning materials and activities by having assistive technology available and making adaptations in the physical environment for children (Doctoroff, 2001). These items would be available to all children, rather than just assigned to specific children with disabilities. In that way, they can support many children and avoid stigma in their usage. The following list includes items that are most often recommended by special education teachers (Judge, Floyd, & Jeffs, 2008). The great thing is that most of the items of this list provide low tech solutions.

- *Visual schedule:* Pictures or symbols representing a desired activity or task are inserted into a schedule or calendar or list

- *Picture boards:* Sets of pictures that children can point to in order to communicate

- *Talking switches:* Child activates a switch to communicate simple phrases or words

- *Weighted vests:* These heavy vests give children sensory input that helps calm them while increasing attention and concentration

- *Positioning devices:* Equipment that is designed to help children stay stable and comfortable in standing or sitting positions.

- *Adaptive seating:* Chairs with firm backs that are adjustable in height and depth. Can be used with adjustable tables.

- *Adaptive scissors:* Easy-grip scissors with loop handles or a second set of handles for adult assistance.

- *Pencil grips:* Soft plastic triangle that fits over pencil to help position fingers correctly.

- **Switches.** An adaptive item is connected to a switch which can be touched anywhere to operate it.

- **Slant board:** Desk-sized easel that helps child with posture and stability. Can promote better writing facility.

- **Computer touch screen.** Allows children to use computer by touching the screen and without the need for a mouse.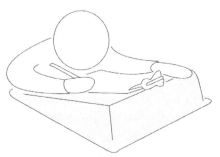

- **Adaptive keyboards:** Computer keyboards with well-spaced keys in high contrast colors to help children locate letters and numbers.

The Physical Environment and Challenging Behavior

The reality is that is it often easier to change the physical environment than it is to change children's behavior. Your classroom environment can be used as prevention tool so that challenging behaviors don't occur. This requires an attitude of experimentation to see what might work, and a willingness to adapt your room to meet a child's needs. Some people react strongly to the idea that it's unfair to change a classroom for one child, or even that we should invest more time and energy in one child, but that's exactly what is needed. When a child's challenging behavior disrupts the other children and drains your energy, you will realize that all the children, in the end, benefit from the accommodations. So if one child needs to be able to sit alone during story time, or right next to you, or one child needs more time for transitions, or to have additional room to work, it is beneficial to all. This is an opportunity to build empathy in the children and help them see that all children's needs will be met – including their own. Your classroom becomes a metaphor and model of the idea that all children need different things and that fairness comes from meeting those needs, not from giving everyone exactly the same thing.

Checklist for Engaging Children in Learning

- ☐ Plan whole group activities which keep children active, give choices, and use variety

- ☐ Use alternatives to hand-raising such as turn-and-talk

- ☐ Give directions clearly

- ☐ Keep "Show & Tell" time short and use visuals

- ☐ Plan small group activities that allow all children to participate freely with materials, while knowing their boundaries

- ☐ Decide on a format for center time

Plan your classroom space carefully:

- ☐ A sense of arrival

- ☐ Personal space

- ☐ Storage

- ☐ Pathways

- ☐ Activity spaces with defined boundaries

- ☐ Noise control

- ☐ Variety of play materials

- ☐ Quiet corner

- ☐ Whole group meeting area

- ☐ Plan your outdoor space carefully following NAEYC guidelines

- ☐ Integrate technology to allow children independence, collaboration, and include assistive technology as appropriate

৩ ৩ ৩

Chapter 5: Developing Cultural Competence

Marta has been attending Ms. Harkins' class for three months now. She speaks Spanish in her home, and only knows a few words and phrases in English. Most of the time in class she has trouble understanding what the teacher is saying. She doesn't want to ask for help or draw attention to her lack of knowledge though, so she smiles and nods her head. The teacher assumes she understands and moves on with the lesson.

Antoine is a strong, curious, and active preschooler. He loves to explore the materials in his classroom and rarely comes when called for circle time. His teacher, Mrs. Harrison, thinks he has attention problems; however, Antoine is encouraged to be active at home. His parents are delighted to have a boy that is so smart and engaged in the world. They value his activity level and strong will.

Miss Maggie has noticed that the girls all run to the housekeeping area as soon as center time begins. The boys prefer to huddle together in the block area. This morning, Michael ventured over to the dress up clothes and put on a straw hat. Another boy teased, "Oo, that's for girls!" Michael immediately dropped it on the floor and walked over to the computer instead. Miss Maggie can't undertsand how the children have already learned so many gender stereotypes at such an early age. She wonders how she can teach the children to be more accepting and less rigid.

We all have different expectations of children's behavior based, in part, on our own cultural and family background. In order to be more effective as a teacher, you'll need a level of cultural competence that will enable you to understand children's expectations, interpret their behavior, and communicate better with families. Many behavioral strategies will backfire if you don't have some prior understanding of children's culture, gender, ethnicity, social class, or language—as seen in the anecdotes above.

In addition to cultural differences in behavioral expectations, there is also the issue of bias. In order to create a learning environment in which all children are respected, valued, and treated fairly, you will need to consider how your own classroom management might encourage respect for diversity or instead reinforce stereotypes.

In our professional journeys as teachers, we develop our cultural competence in a slow progression forward. Cultural competence is a set of behaviors, attitudes, and policies that enables us to work effectively in cross–cultural situations (Cross, Bazron,

Dennis, & Isaacs, 1989; Isaacs & Benjamin, 1991). We are all at different places in this process, and it's helpful to think about your own progress. In the 1970's, Noel Burch of the Gordon Training International outlined four stages that we pass through in achieving competence:

1. *Unconscious cultural incompetence.* Teachers who have very little understanding of other cultures or bias issues, and do not realize that they are lacking this competence. They often claim they are color-blind and treat all children the same because they ignore difference rather than respecting and embracing it.

2. *Conscious cultural incompetence.* Teachers who have very little knowledge or understanding of different cultures and bias issues but who know that this is important. They are actively trying to gain more knowledge and are working on developing the skills for anti-bias education.

3. *Conscious cultural competence.* Teachers in this stage have obtained a great deal of knowledge and skills in cultural competence and anti-bias education, however, they have to carefully think about how to integrate this into their teaching. They work hard to be culturally competent and it doesn't yet come easily.

4. *Unconscious cultural competence.* Teachers in this stage have achieved a level of understanding and experience that allows them to easily meet the needs of diverse children and provide a learning environment that affirms the value of all cultures.

This chapter provides an introduction to some of the cultural and social values that will impact your classroom management. It will provide a foundation for understanding the types of issues that impact you as a teacher, and a framework to help you continue to gain more cultural knowledge in the future.

High-Context and Low-Context Cultures

Children will respond and benefit from classroom activities in different ways based on their cultural backgrounds. It's important to consider the ways in which cultural values and beliefs affect children's thinking about themselves and their identity. For many white, middle-class children in the United States, their sense of self is one of independence. This leads to valuing independent work, individual successes and failures, and personal responsibility for one's actions. Cultures with an emphasis on individuality have been called *low-context* and are typically western European and North American (Hall, 1977). Our schools are predominantly aligned to the low-context cultural perspective as seen in our emphasis on doing one's own work, giving out individual grades, and valuing independence.

Such a perspective, however, is not held by most non-white ethnic and racial groups (Greenfield, 1994; Greenfield, Keller, Fuligni, & Maynard, 2003). Instead, cultural beliefs emphasize an interdependent self in which a child's identity is defined by relationships to others. These cultures are considered *high-context* and they value being closely connected and a member of a group (Hall, 1977). Therefore, standing out in a crowd, bringing attention to one's personal success, or becoming independent in daily living activities are not as important as getting along with others, bringing honor or status to your social/family group, or allowing others to help you. This may show up in your classroom when children share their work with each other or help a friend to complete a problem, even though you have been calling for independent work. You may think that children are cheating, and feel frustration with their behavior. However for some children, it may seem strange and even inappropriate to not help each other. They have been taught to value this at home.

These cultural differences can also show up in the discussions you have with family members about their values and desires for their children. For example, studies show that in countries with high-context cultures such as Japan, China, Russia and Brazil, group values and social identity are heavily emphasized (Han & Thomas, 2010). In contrast, individual identity and personal interests are more valued in low-context countries such as the United States, Canada, Italy and Australia. It's easy to believe that parents don't care about their children's education when they are really caring about different aspects of that education than what you might personally value. The following figure shows other characteristics which vary culturally (Han & Thomas, 2010, p. 471; Kaiser & Rasminsky, 2007).

Continuum of High-Context and Low-Context Cultures

$\longleftarrow \hspace{6cm} \longrightarrow$

Low-Context Cultures	High-Context Cultures
• Western European and North American	• Asian, South Asian, Southern European, Latino, African American, Native American
• Individual identity, independence, and personal interest valued	• Social identity, interdependence, and group interest is valued
• Encouraged to use more verbal expression in direct, precise logical ways	• Compliance, harmony, and respectfulness emphasized
• Assertiveness, initiative and leadership emphasized	• Encouraged to use more subtle communication cues such as facial expression, movement, and shared traditions and experiences
• Withdrawn behaviors more negatively associated with peer rejection	• Withdrawn behaviors are more appreciated than aggressive behaviors

---

These differences can cause miscommunication problems, as well as misunderstandings about why children might use certain behaviors. Many European American teachers have a hard time realizing that they have a culture. Instead, they think of their own values, beliefs, habits, and preferences as "normal" because most of the people around them share these, including those they see on television, movies, in government leadership positions, and so on. People who differ from this norm are considered as having a culture, and are often seen as exotic or unusual. This is, of course, a clear sign of the cultural dominance that white European groups have had in the United States for centuries. This makes it all the more important for teachers to take the time and effort to examine their own beliefs and values and to understand that many of the behaviors that seem odd, rude, inappropriate or confusing, might be very understandable to people of other cultures.

Although cultural differences should not be used to stereotype children or predict their behavior, they can be used to better understand children's thoughts, perceptions, and motivations. Some children will prefer to not answer questions in whole group. This requires them to stand out publicly in front of the whole class which can be stressful if the child values being part of the group but not standing out from the group. Similarly, some children may resist competitive activities you plan—such as seeing how many books a child can read in the 100 Book Challenge and then comparing the children to each other. Even a simple request to see who can finish cleaning up fastest may seem threatening or confusing to children whose culture does not value competition. Becoming a more culturally responsive teacher requires deep knowledge about the children in your care, a commitment to valuing diversity, and the skills to create an environment in which children with a variety of backgrounds and individual personalities can learn equally well.

Cultural Interaction Styles

If children's behavior is aligned with our cultural expectations, we are satisfied; however, if children's behavior is different from what we expect, we might jump to the conclusion that the child is deficient in some way, rather than think about the culture in which the child is living. Cultural interaction styles vary across cultures on a number of dimensions and you may be able to reduce or prevent behavior problems by keeping these in mind (The IRIS Center for Training Enhancements, n.d.-d)

Degree of directness. People in some cultures get right to the point in what they want to say. In other cultures, it is considered more appropriate to be indirect and hint at what you are trying to convey. For example, in Anglo families, it might be fine for a child to say, "I want a doll for my birthday" whereas in Korean culture, it is more likely a child would be taught to say, "I really like dolls a lot, do you like dolls, too?" as a way of indirectly getting the message across. Some children will not understand a request such as, "Would you like to close the door, please?" as the demand it is intended to be. Instead he or she might honestly reply, "No, I wouldn't." It might be a cultural misunderstanding to think this child is being fresh or uncooperative if he is used to a more direct style: "Please close the door." In a similar way, some children may find the direct request a bit confrontational, even rude. This requires patience, understanding, and a basic assumption that children are trying to behave in an appropriate way, in order to adapt to each other's communication styles.

Level of emotionality. In some cultures, communication is done in a more dramatic emotional style with intensity of voice, gestures, and facial expressions. Other cultures value being restrained in one's outward emotions. This can be confusing in cross-cultural interactions when you misinterpret a child's expression as showing the child doesn't care, or is deliberately being unfeeling. The child might be feeling his emotions deeply, but is not displaying them in the way you are used to. Similarly, you might feel that some children are over-reacting when they are very dramatic. This might also be an issue of the cultural style the child is used to.

Degree of vocalizations. In some cultures, it is expected that listeners will chime in, repeating phrases and talking at the same time. This is a way of offering support and showing that the listener is involved with what the speaker is saying. In other cultures, speaking at the same time would be considered rude and speakers might be offended. This is often true for gender differences. Deborah Tannen describes women's talk as "rapport talk" in which we join in talking with the speaker, and men's talk as "report talk" in which each person takes a turn and does not interrupt (Tannen, 2001). As you can imagine, this frequently leads to misinterpretations: men may feel that women interrupt too much, and women may feel that men aren't really listening. In reality, we are perceiving cultural differences in how we were learned to communicate from our family and those who spend a lot of time with us.

Speaking and listening. In the United States, we tend to be speaker-focused, assuming it is the speaker's job to make sure that communication is understood. Children are encouraged to share their ideas openly, often doing so whether someone is listening or not. In other cultures, especially Asian groups, children are encouraged to listen as a way to learn, and that too much speaking is inappropriate (Kume Tokui, Hasegawa, & Kodama, 2000). In a classroom setting, some children may be uncomfortable with the expectation that all children freely express their ideas. In addition, some children are taught that small talk that is used to affirm ties between people is intrusive and one should only speak when there is something truly important to say (Minami, 2002). While teachers may 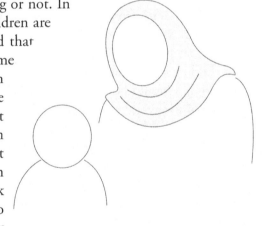 find such behavior helpful in not interrupting instructional activities, it may make the child seem unfriendly to others.

Personal space. As you may have noticed in your own interactions with other people, some cultures prefer to have more space between people who are speaking than other cultures (Beaulieu, 2004). This can lead to discomfort for children if we remain too close to them while talking, and lead us to assume that children are not interested, or being distant when they back away from us. This can also be troublesome in rooms where children are asked to squeeze in close to each other for story times, or to stand close while waiting in lines. Children may misinterpret others' actions as too intimate or even aggressive.

Attitudes towards sharing. In some cultures, property is communal and people are more comfortable with the idea of sharing. In contrast, some children are raised in cultures which value individual rights to a greater degree. Tensions can arise when people have different views on what is an appropriate amount of sharing, or what specific things are appropriate to share.

Responses to authority figures. How we respond to people in authority also varies by culture. Some of us are taught that we should make eye contact when an adult is speaking; others are taught that such behavior is rude and we should lower our eyes to show deference (Torres-Guzman, 1998). Some children are also taught not to speak back to those in authority, while others are encouraged to share their ideas as a way of showing their critical thinking skills and motivation. If your own culture taught you to expect quiet obedience, you may misinterpret children's questions or complaints as rudeness when they have simply not yet learned your interaction style or expectations.

English Language Learners

Children who are English language learners can be at a great disadvantage during some activities such as center time since they do not yet have the language skills to negotiate and plan with other children. When developing activities, it is helpful therefore to have available at least some materials in which a child does not have to negotiate interactions with other children such as LEGOS, math manipulatives, or science activities (Okagaki & Diamond, 2003). This can offer the child a welcome break from having to work so hard to understand and communicate.

In preschool, it is helpful for a child to have opportunities to watch others play from the sidelines as a way of improving their comprehension skills. Most children who are learning English will go through a non-verbal period in which they are watching, listening intently, and rehearsing by talking to themselves (Tabors, 2004). On the other hand, be careful that children who are English language learners do not become socially isolated. English language learners can be caught in a double-bind in that they need social interaction to learn the new language however they might not have enough skill to participate in social activities. This can lead to the child being treated like a baby or being invisible.

Provide the child with an opportunity to observe, and to follow what other children are doing. Social experiences such as working on buddy projects or small group activities are important support strategies for language learners. Tabor (2004) offers other suggestions for helping second language learners to be successful in classroom activities:

1. Use plenty of non-verbal communication

2. Keep your messages simple

3. Talk about the here and now

4. Emphasize the important words in the sentence

5. Combine gestures and talk

6. Repeat certain key words in the message

There are two major aspects of classroom management which can help children who are English language learners feel more secure in your classroom (Tabors, 2004). The first is to have a consistent routine so that children can participate easily in the daily schedule without needing linguistic clues. Because they will catch on more quickly, they will look and feel more like members of the group, helping them social integrate.

The second is to have places in the room where children can spend time away from the demands of communication and focus on developing other skills. This could be a quiet reading area, an area for math manipulatives, computer games, or art activities. This will allow the child to take a break from trying to communicate, observe others and join in when he or she feels comfortable. Build in time that you can talk individually to children. In one research study of a dual language kindergarten, adding interesting materials to learning centers did not necessarily generate much language use, however, when children had to negotiate or were engaged in meaningful conversation with the teacher, more complex language emerged (Hayes, 2005).

Cultural Bias

A very important consideration in guiding children's behavior is our own cultural bias. Research by sociologists presents us with some disturbing findings: African-American children are rated by teachers as having poorer classroom behavior and less academic engagement (Ainsworth-Darnell & Downey, 1998; U.S. Department of Education National Center for Education Statistics, 2001). The question this raises is whether such teachers' evaluations of African-American children's behavior is a result of racial bias or whether the behavior is actually more problematic.

Some sociologists view the problem as one of cultural mismatch. Many types of behaviors that are valued and accepted in African-American cultural settings are not those that are typically valued by teachers in classrooms (Boykin, 1978). Others have pointed out that cultural differences themselves are not the issue since the behavior of Asian American students, while culturally different from most white teachers, is typically evaluated as positive. These scholars have proposed that it is not the difference in culture alone that is the issue, but the difference in status combined with cultural differences (Alexander, Entwisle, & Herman, 1999). In other words, teachers who have adopted mainstream white cultural values may perceive African-American children's behavior as more problematic because of the cultural differences and low social status that African-Americans have traditionally been given.

Another consideration is racial matching. Perhaps African American children behave differently with a white teacher than when matched with a black teacher. For example, Ogbu's research proposes that African American students resist schooling because of their historically subjugated relationship with whites in American society. They adopt an oppositional cultural identity and are sanctioned socially for "acting white" in school (Ogbu, 1991, 2008). Based on this perspective, African-American students might show more resistance with white teachers than with African-American teachers. One study showed that African American first-graders were more likely to be rated as immature when they were "mismatched" with white teachers or teachers with high socioeconomic status (Alexander, Entwisle, & Thompson, 1987). The authors explained these results as stemming from the teachers' discomfort with unfamiliar behaviors of students with low-status characteristics.

In order to tease out the different possibilities about African American children's behaviors, Downey and Pribesh (2004) examined data from a national database of about 13,000 black and white kindergarten children. They looked specifically at children who were matched with a teacher of the opposite race (70% of the black children had a white teacher, while only 2% of the white children had a black teacher because of the predominance of white teachers). Their analysis showed that black children had more behaviors such as arguing, fighting, getting angry and acting impulsively when rated by white teachers but fewer when rated by black teachers. In fact, there was evidence that when black and white students were placed with same-race teachers, black students' classroom behavior is rated more favorably than is white students.

So, what can we conclude from this research? Perhaps the clearest message is for us to be more self-reflective when responding to children's behavior. We can ask ourselves about what our expectations for children's behaviors are, and more importantly—where did our expectations come from? How did we learn to have these expectations? Are there other interpretations of the child's behavior? Would I react the same way if this child had a different racial, ethnic, or socioeconomic background? These are difficult and uncomfortable questions to consider, but the alternative is for us to keep perpetuating a social system that is unfair to some children.

Warm Demanders

Often, novice teachers struggle to set limits for children or push for higher achievement, because they perceive their own actions as "mean" or "uncaring". Other teachers have mistakenly interpreted developmentally appropriate practice to be an approach in which the teacher passively supports children. In contrast, research shows that many children living in poverty, especially those whose cultural background is not the same as the teacher's or the school in general, have difficulty engaging in academic tasks (Bondy & Ross, 2008). They may end up frustrated, angry, and use challenging behaviors in the classroom context. They may also learn very little, and get caught in a cycle of failure that persists throughout elementary school.

A growing body of research has identified an effective style of African American teachers as "warm demanders" (Beauboeuf-Lafontant, 2002; Ware, 2002, 2006). This effectiveness, especially in high-poverty schools, stems from a teacher's actions "that communicate both warmth and a non-negotiable demand for student effort and mutual respect" (Bondy & Ross, 2008, p. 54). Research reveals that successful African-American teachers of African American students have the following characteristics (Irvine, 2002, p. 142):

1. Focusing on caring in all aspects of a child's life rather than in narrow interpersonal ways

2. Caring for students by providing honest and truthful feedback to students about their performance

3. Caring for students but never relinquishing their authority or attempting to be friends of their students

4. Demonstrating that their caring is representative of a history of African-American, culturally-specific teaching behaviors

These efffective teachers who are "warm demanders" do not accept behaviors which get in the way of the students' achievement. They build relationships deliberately with the children in a way that convinces the children they are cared about, while holding them to high expectations for academic achievement. Warm demanders ensure that children know the teacher believes in them. Because of this deep belief, the children interpret the teacher's demands—even those which sound harsh—as being caring. Excuses such as living in poverty, difficult family lives, and lack of school readiness are not tolerated. Instead, effective teachers have high expectations, try more creative ways to teach, and are more persistent in helping children who are struggling. In essence, they insist on good behavior, respect, and hard work.

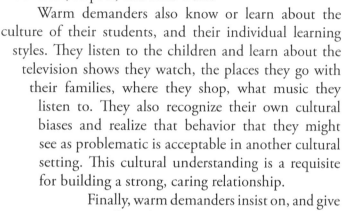

Warm demanders also know or learn about the culture of their students, and their individual learning styles. They listen to the children and learn about the television shows they watch, the places they go with their families, where they shop, what music they listen to. They also recognize their own cultural biases and realize that behavior that they might see as problematic is acceptable in another cultural setting. This cultural understanding is a requisite for building a strong, caring relationship.

Finally, warm demanders insist on, and give respect to all students. When behavior problems arise, they might be frustrated, but they approach the child with a belief in the student's ability to improve. They use problem-solving strategies, thoughtful reflection, observations and dialogue with the child to approach the problems rather than blaming the child or family. This is not easy to do, especially when there are cultural differences between the teacher and children. For example, white teachers are less willing to exercise authority than African American teachers are while teaching (Irvine, 2002), yet African American children are often expecting such use of authority and may react poorly when it is not there. It may be advantageous for all teachers working with African-American students to adopt the characteristics of warm demanders.

Gender Bias

There is plenty of evidence that boys and girls are treated differently in our classrooms—in ways that can be damaging to both genders (Chapman, 1995-2012). Recently, researchers have noticed that in general, girls outperform boys in elementary school. At the same time, boys are more frequently in trouble for inappropriate behavior.

According to Mulrine (2001), boys earn 70 percent of the D's and F's that teachers give out while also making up two thirds of the students labeled learning disabled. Boys account for 80 percent of high school dropouts and attention deficit disorder diagnoses.

So what's going on here? In part, we can attribute this to the socialization of girls to be neat, quiet and helpful, as compared to the socialization of boys that focuses on being active, verbal, and assertive. Boys are at a disadvantage because early childhood and elementary classrooms are so predominantly based on female interaction patterns and expectations. Research shows that boys' and girls' brains have different "rest states" (Gurian & Stevens, 2010). When a boy is bored or not engaged, some parts of his brain stop functioning which interferes with his ability to listen and learn. Girls' brains, on the other hand, stay active when they are bored or unengaged. Using physical activity and movement in classroom activities can help boys' brains to remain alert and active. You can see how boys' brains can get them into trouble in a classroom that expects all students to be quiet and still.

Girls are also shortchanged in many classrooms. Research over the past 20 years has shown that girls are praised less often, and teachers give boys greater opportunity to expand ideas and be animated than they do girls (Marshall, 1997; Sadker & Sadker, 1994). I've been in many classrooms in which boys were taunting each other for acting like girls. In almost all these cases, the teacher allowed this to go unchallenged, even though "acting like a girl" was considered an insult (a clear indication that acting like a boy is more valued). How do girls feel after hearing that they are less valued than boys over and

over again? And how do boys feel when they have such a limited range of acceptable behaviors?

I'm always surprised to see teachers make a conscious decision to separate boys and girls in activities in school, such as lining up, taking turns, or creating teams. This is problematic. It contributes to gender bias and discrimination and is damaging to *both* boys and girls. Imagine for a moment that you heard a teacher tell the children, "Okay, let's have the Black children line up on this side, and the White children on the other side." Most of us would think this is completely inappropriate. Yet we often do the same thing with gender. The only time this might be acceptable is going to the bathroom, but children shouldn't line up for the bathroom, so even that instance is not one I would advocate.

I've seen teachers use a pattern of calling on a boy, girl, boy, girl to answer questions during lessons. Why differentiate children by gender during lessons? You might be thinking that this allows for more fairness. But would you be comfortable using a White child, Black child pattern? Probably not, and that raises the question of why we are comfortable separating by gender. What may result from years and years of hearing these phrases and being separated by gender?

- Children may learn that boys and girls are different intellectually

- Children may learn that they should be considered as different kinds of people because of their gender

- Both boys and girls get locked into gender stereotypes at an early age

Are boys and girls different? Of course! But the physical differences should not lead to unfairness. We've made great progress in gender equity but there is still a long way to go, by any measure. It's interesting to note that girls and women have made great strides in entering college in numbers greater than men, yet they are still underrepresented in many fields, especially science and math. At the same time, boys, especially Black and Latino, are rapidly dropping in number in college enrollment. They are also psychologically discouraged from entering many "helping" careers such as teaching, nursing, and social work which have been traditionally female jobs. I wonder why these differences still persist so strongly at a time in which we are so aware of the value of diversity. Perhaps it is because we are still reinforcing those gender differences throughout a child's early years.

The good news is that teachers who are made aware of their gender-biased teaching behaviors and provided with strategies and resources to combat bias are better able to promote gender equity in their classrooms (Jones, Evans, Byrd, & Campbell, 2000).

Religious Diversity

One of the most tricky aspects of working in a diverse setting is balancing the values, traditions, and customs of different religious groups. Holidays can be especially challenging, especially for children and families who are not from mainstream religious groups in your area. Sometimes religious views are not compatible with each other and you can't please everyone. It takes great sensitivity, tact, and knowledge about religious differences to be culturally competent.

Here are some general strategies that can be helpful:

1. Learn about religious practices and values. Survey your families to learn about their religious affiliations. Invite them to share family customs or books with the class.

2. Allow for children to have the choice of participating in any kind of religious activity such as coloring Easter eggs, dressing up for Halloween, or creating Christmas decorations. Confer with family members as to their preference for their child's participation.

3. Consider teaching *awareness* of holiday traditions, rather than *acceptance*. Refrain from celebrating holidays if you have children who are not comfortable participating. Reading books about holidays, or listening to guest speakers are often more acceptable than creating the holiday celebration. Check your school policy on holiday celebrations.

4. Be aware of religious practices that may affect children in school such as Muslims' fasting during Ramadan, or food restrictions of Jews or Hindus.

5. Be sure that you are not privileging some religions over others just because you are more comfortable and knowledgeable about them. For example, spending a week on Easter activities and then doing only one short activity for Passover gives the message that Christian holidays are more important.

6. Remember that not all children have a religious background. Some families choose not to be involved in any religious tradition.

What Would You Do?

Below are some very thought-provoking scenarios from Kirmani and Laster (1999, p. 62) which show the complexity of religious diversity and need for sensitivity:

Scenario 1: Parent: "It's almost the end of October. All of my child's friends are getting prepared for Halloween. Their talk is filled with discussion of their costumes, the candy, the decorations. My child said to me, 'I know what I want to be. I want to be an ugly wicked witch! When are we getting my costume, Mama?' I am an evangelical Christian; my religion doesn't condone the Halloween celebrations. We believe that Halloween has historically celebrated the dark side of spirituality."

How would you advise the parent to respond?

Scenario 2: Teacher: "We are having a class play, and I want all the children to participate. I made a mistake, I guess, when I assigned Jovinder to be an angel. His mother, a Sikh, was very polite and apologetic, but seemed nervous when she explained that he couldn't be an angel in the play."

How could the teacher have handled this differently?

Scenario 3: Parent: "I am a parent in the Buddhist tradition. My child is asked to take a gift to school to exchange. We want our child to develop a sense of giving but we also want him to learn not to focus on material things. We feel pushed into what the majority of people expect of us."

How could this parent support the class project and also voice his or her concerns?

Creating a Culturally Relevant Classroom Environment

An important aspect of the children's environment should be the ability to support the social identity development of children, including those who are biracial, multiracial, and multiethnic. Young children need support for developing their own social-group identity and for understanding and feeling comfortable with children from diverse backgrounds, yet a large study of 1,000 kindergarten teachers in Florida showed that less than 25% of the classrooms had books in other languages in their classroom, provided opportunities for students to experience poetry from other cultures or invited non-native speakers of English to speak or read to their students (Gayle-Evans, 2004). Less than 23% used materials and objects depicting ethnic groups, and although most of the classrooms had dramatic play centers, only 50% indicated having a variety of racial/ethnic and special needs dolls in the dramatic play area. Only 50% included a variety of skin-tone paints in their art activities.

An effective way to start exposing children to diversity and opening conversations is with books which offer multicultural themes, pictures of diverse ethnic and racial groups, a variety of different languages, different family structures, and non-stereotyped portrayals of elderly, disabled, or poor people. This can also be done by ensuring that posters, curriculum content, manipulatives such as puzzles and games, and artwork represent diverse families and children and various age groups and genders (Wardle, 2004). The Early Childhood Equity Initiative of Teaching for Change has developed a classroom checklist to help teachers ensure that all children can see themselves reflected in the classroom environment and are treated in a fair way (Early Childhood Equity Initiative, n.d.) Below are some of the sections of the checklist to help you evaluate your own classroom:

Physical/Visual/Aesthetic environment

☐ Are images of children and adults from all major racial/ethnic groups in the U.S. present?

☐ Are there images of different family make-ups such as single parent, extended family, gay or lesbian-headed family, multi-racial family in addition to the traditional nuclear family?

☐ Are there images of differently-abled people of various backgrounds shown doing work and with their families?

☐ Is there a fair balance of men and women doing jobs inside and outside the home, in blue, pink and white collar jobs, as well?

☐ Do the images present in the classroom depict people from different cultures in everyday activities and dress or are they only in traditional costumes and in ceremonies?

Children's Books

☐ Do books reflect diversity of racial, cultural, class and religious backgrounds?

☐ Do books reflect different gender roles?

☐ Do books show a wide-range of occupations (blue, pink and white collar)?

☐ Do books show variety in family make-up?

☐ Do books show children and adults with special needs and abilities?

☐ Are books written in different languages, particularly the home languages of children in the classroom?

☐ Do books depict interactions between children of different racial backgrounds, including conflicts and their resolutions?

☐ Are there books addressing issues of skin color within and between different racial and cultural groups?

Children's Toys and Materials

☐ Is tempera paint the color/shades of children's skin provided on a regular basis?

☐ Do the dolls represent a fair balance of ethnic and racial groups in the U.S.?

☐ Is there a balance of male and female dolls?

☐ Do dress-up clothes and dramatic play objects and artifacts reflect a diversity of cultural norms, especially those of the families served in the program?

☐ Are musical instruments from different cultures a part of the everyday music area and experiences the children are exposed to?

Classroom Rules and Processes

☐ Are boys *and* girls encouraged to play in all areas of the classroom and yard (including large motor toys, climbing equipment, housekeeping and art areas etc.)?

☐ Are both boys and girls offered help when they need it?

☐ Are stereotyping behavior and language challenged by classroom teachers and staff?

☐ Do teachers and other staff members give matter-of-fact feedback about racial/ethnic physical characteristic and questions about the same?

☐ Are all children encouraged to express feelings, as appropriate?

In their early years, children begin to construct a personal identity which includes that child's individual characteristics such as age, personality, sibling positions, height, interests and so forth. At the same time, children will also develop and become aware of a social identity that is assigned to them by society (Derman-Sparks & Edwards, 2010). This might include gender, ethnicity, race, religion, and social class. Many teachers mistakenly believe that young children live in a color-blind world in which they do not recognize social differences or pay attention to issues of race or ethnicity, but research shows us that very young children recognize such differences as skin color (Katz, 2003). In the early grades, children can and do discriminate and show prejudice for others' social identities and if we do not actively challenge this, then we inadvertently contribute to it (Derman-Sparks & Edwards, 2010).

The physical environment can provide cultural and language models. It can also impede children's cultural competence. Children learn the messages they receive that are both direct and indirect. They might learn, for example, that race is not something adults are comfortable talking about and shouldn't be brought up (Bronson & Merriman, 2009). Other messages might be more overt. I have often heard young boys chastise each other for playing with "girl" materials or acting like a girl. Teachers might also hear children call each other racial slurs as insults or tease a boy about acting "gay." On the other hand, I recently visited a classroom in which the teacher comfortably talked about racial differences with her children when they noticed that a visitor had the same skin color as one of the children's grandmother. This led to a spontaneous discussion about skin color differences and families. In this way, young children are learning about who is and isn't important in their world. A child might think, "If there are no pictures of people that look like me, or no one talks about my kind of family, then I don't matter" (Derman-Sparks & Edwards, 2010).

It is appropriate to provide direct instruction to children in understanding cultural differences, and using children's literature is one of the best strategies. Many children's picture books provide cultural settings and stories that help children learn about other racial and ethnic groups. For example, *The Color of Us*, by Karen Katz

(2007) provides a rich variety of skin color descriptions which children can use to build a positive social identity.

Children's cultural competence. In addition to being culturally competent as teachers, we can also help children achieve cultural competence in a way that will improve the climate of our classroom community, help children develop positive relationships with children who are culturally different from themselves, and begin to have a positive sense of self-identity that includes their own cultural, racial, or ethnic group (Derman-Sparks & Edwards, 2010; Harriott & Martin, 2004).

Checklist for Developing Cultural Competence

- ☐ Determine if you have children from low-context or high-context cultures

- ☐ Consider cultural interaction styles when communicating with children and families in your class

- ☐ Plan ways to support English language learners by allowing observation time, planning social interactions, and providing time without communication demands

- ☐ Examine your own possible cultural biases

- ☐ Determine if using a warm demander style of teaching would be appropriate in your classroom

- ☐ Study your classroom procedures to ensure gender equity

- ☐ Gather information on the religious background and preferences of your families

- ☐ Evaluate the physical environment of your classroom to determine if it supports diversity and is culturally relevant

ℰ ℰ ℰ

Part II: Positive Behavior Interventions

Chapter 6: Guiding Children's Behavior

Ms. Patel had just helped her children transition to centers for work time. There was a low, production hum of children's voices in the room. She scanned the room carefully to see whether the children were settling in and starting their activities. In the table toys center Mark and Wayne had picked out a partner game to play. They began arguing over who would go first. Ms. Patel decided to just watch them and see if they could resolve the problem without her intervention. After a few minutes, the boys decided that Kyle would go first for this game and Wayne could go first the next game. Ms. Patel was impressed with their problem solving ability. She thought to herself that if she had stepped in and given them her solutoin, they wouldn't have had the experience of figuring it out themselves. She said to the boys, "You both figured out who would go first in such a clever way. You worked hard to figure out that problem!" They smiled up at her as they continued their game.

As she continued to scan the room, she noticed that Chloe had just grabbed a hold of Julissa's hair in the block area and was pulling her to the ground. She quickly intervened by gently and firmly removing Chloe's hand and saying, "Chloe, you're hurting Julissa and you need to stop. Julissa, are you okay?"

Julissa pouted and said, "Yeah, I'm okay, but I hate her!"

Ms. Patel took a calming breath and said, "I can tell you are very angry, Chloe, and I bet that Chloe, you are pretty mad, too. Let's all take a few deep breaths to calm down. Julissa, can you tell me what happened?"

"She took my bridge piece!" Julissa said with force.

"I was using it first and then she grabbed it!" yelled Chloe.

"Okay," said Ms. Patel, "It sounds like the problem is that both of you want to use the bridge piece and we only have one of those. What could you two do about this? Do you have any ideas?"

Julissa answered right away, "She can leave me alone. I was playing with it."

"No, I had it first. She should play with something else." added Chloe.

Ms. Patel said, "Well those are two ideas. Can you come up with a few more ideas before we decide what to do?"

The two girls sat quietly, Chloe with her arms folded and Julissa looking down at the rug. Ms. Patel waited. Chloe finally spoke, "She could use it first, and then I can have it." Ms. Patel was surprised that Chloe offered to let Julissa have it first and she wondered if she was feeling badly about pulling her hair.

"Would that work for you, Julissa?" She silently nodded. "How long do you think a fair turn would be?"

"Ten minutes?" asked Chloe.

"What do you think Julissa? Is ten minutes fair?"

"Yeah, okay."

"Then let's go with that idea." Now that the children were calmer and able to think more clearly, Ms. Patel decided to address the hair pulling. "Before we do that, though, I need to be sure that you will be safe here in school. We never hurt each other, and Jennifer, when you pulled Julissa's hair it hurt her. What could you do instead when you are angry?"

"Get the teacher?"

"Yes, you could come get me. Or use your words to tell Julissa why you are angry. You may not pull hair and if you do it again, you will not be able to play with the blocks until you learn other ways to show your anger. You know, when you hurt someone, you should really try to make her feel better. What could you do to make Julissa feel better now?"

Chloe sat quietly, not moving. Julissa's eyes were bright and she looked eager to see how this would turn out. "I'm sorry, Julissa."

"Does that help you to feel better, Julissa?" asked Ms. Patel.

"Yeah. I'm okay." said Julissa, turning and picking up the blocks.

"Okay, then. Let's see if your idea will work. Julissa, we'll set the timer for ten minutes, then it will be Chloe's turn." Both girls returned to their building.

Later Ms. Patel checked in with the girls to make sure that their solution was working. She also decided to add a few more lessons this week on the classroom rules, recognizing when we're angry, and having the children review positive ways to demonstrate their anger.

This chapter offers a variety of strategies that can help you maintain positive interactions with children. As always, the goal is to establish positive behaviors so that intervention is not needed. It is a proactive approach to working with young children.

In early childhood education, we have a long history of using a guidance approach to behavior management. This means that we view children's behavior through a developmental lens, seeing "misbehavior" as "mistaken behavior" or behavior that serves a purpose for the child in order to get his or her needs met (Gartrell, 2010). Early childhood strategies for guiding children focus on ways to teach children the behavioral skills they need rather than punishing them for what they do that is inappropriate.

Positive interactions between teachers and young children don't always happen naturally. Because young children are developmentally different from adults, they can often seem illogical and frustrate us since they don't often respond to our reasoning attempts. Most adults are at least two or three developmental stages beyond young children and our evolutionary amnesia makes it difficult and perhaps impossible for us to really empathize with how young children feel and think.

The Perils of Punishment

I am often able to convince new and experienced teachers that punishment is very limited in its usefulness in the classroom and can be damaging to children's sense of self and autonomy. However, I realize that it is difficult to let go of this model without something else to take its place. This chapter will provide concrete suggestions for how to use a humanistic and constructivist model of guiding children's behavior instead of punishment. Because these ideas may be new to many readers, and may seem unusual at first (because you have not experienced them as a child yourself), I encourage you to try these out and practice them often. These strategies will often not come as easily as many of the reward and punishment strategies that you might have grown up with and are more familiar with.

Guilt and Shame

Although punishment is prevalent in our schools, there is little evidence that it is effective, and much evidence that it is damaging to children. To understand why this is true, we need to look at the emotions of guilt and shame (Tangney & Dearing, 2002).

Feeling guilty. Because we live in social groups, we need to have social rules and expectations that keep us all safe and help us get our needs met. When our behavior violates those expectations, we need to feel badly so that we are motivated to change. The emotion of guilt functions in exactly this way. When we violate our own standards for what is right and wrong, we feel guilty. It is difficult to tell the difference between guilt and shame, but one of the important characteristics of guilt is that we can usually make amends and the guilt subsides. For example, if you got angry at a friend and said something that hurt her, you could try to make amends by apologizing, being especially kind, or trying to make it up to her. In this way, you can get rid of your guilt and get back into an emotional balance.

Another example can be seen in a child who damages another child's book, gets caught, and feels guilty. You can help this child learn how to get rid of guilt in a positive way by scaffolding her in replacing or repairing the book. The big difference between children and adults lies in where the standards for behavior come from. Adults have internalized a set of behavioral standards and they feel guilty when they violate their own standards. Children are still learning to internalize those standards and our classroom rules help them in that process.

The important characteristic of guilt for us to remember is that we can get rid of the feeling of guilt by making things "right"—that is, by fixing the problem that our behavior created. Therefore, when children misbehave, a constructivist approach is to help children figure out how they can make things right, rather than punish them. Taking responsibility for fixing the problem they created helps them to construct and understand the reasons behind rules for good behavior. Punishing them does not teach them why they were wrong, or what strategies they could have used instead.

Feeling Shame. Unfortunately, adults often use shame instead of guilt to get children to conform to behavioral expectations. Shame is a different emotion from guilt, even though many of us confuse the two. When we feel that we are inadequate as a person, we are feeling shame. This is the emotion of feeling "not good enough" or simply bad as a person. The emotion of shame is directed at our deep identity. Guilt, on the other hand, is directed at our behavior. Shame is not helpful in getting us to change our behavior because it feels like an inadequacy of our personality. We are overwhelmed by trying to change who we are as opposed to changing what we do.

Shame is very damaging to children and adults. You can think of it as a poison or toxin that is introduced into our sense of self. That toxin slowly eats away at our identity and soul, and if it is not stopped, it can disable us. The worst part of shame is that is it very difficult to get rid of it. Because it is directed at our identity rather than our behavior, it does not go away by trying to fix the problem. This can be seen best in a classroom example. Let's imagine a teacher who is frustrated with a child who is not following the classroom procedures and causes disruptions in the class work. She yells at him, "Daniel, what is the matter with you? I just don't know what to do with you!" In these short statements, she has communicated the message that there is something wrong with Daniel as a person. Daniel may now be thinking, "There is something the matter with me," and feeling ashamed. This shame will stay with Daniel, poisoning his sense of self. Because there is no focus on specific mistaken behaviors that Daniel did, there is no chance for him to make changes.

You might be wondering why teachers would shame children. I believe it is because they were shamed as children (and adults). It is a method we are all familiar with. Shame is also such a horrible feeling that we want it to go away. Because there's no easy way to get rid of it, we try to feel better by making others seem to be worse. In a way, we try to dump our shame onto others to relieve our own discomfort. This doesn't work, however, because we feel guilt or more shame as a result of shaming others. It is a difficult, vicious cycle to break.

One way to work on recognizing when we are shaming children is to think about whether we are correcting a child's *behavior* rather than criticizing their *character*. This table provides some examples of both.

Teacher talk that shames children	Teacher talk that helps children see the effect of their actions
"What's wrong with you?"	"When you swing your arms like that, you could hurt someone."
"You should be ashamed of yourself."	"If you want a turn with that truck, you need to use your words to ask, not hitting."
"Why don't you listen? How many times do I have to tell you this?"	"It looks like you've forgotten how to line up, let's practice it now."
"I don't know what to do with you."	"When you come to reading group, you need to have your book. You can quietly get it now."
"You drive me crazy."	"Remember to use your whisper voice now."
"How could you do that?"	"When you took Ariel's snack, she got very upset. Look, she is crying. What can you do to make her feel better? How can you fix this problem?"

"I'll have to tell your mother you were bad today."	"You had some problems remembering our rules today. Let's go over them again and I bet tomorrow you will remember them better."
"You'll never make it in kindergarten"	"What are you having trouble with? Let me teach you how to write your name."
"Why aren't you more like your brother?"	"You are a very funny person. That helps our whole classroom have fun and laugh. Let's go over what you need to do during center time, though, so you can remember what you need to be working on."
"What I am supposed to do with you?"	"It seems like you are angry today. Would you like to talk about it?

Punishment is not as effective as other strategies for changing behavior. Punishment does not help children develop respect for others, or to learn to construct moral and social rules (DeVries & Zan, 1994). Instead it demands that children respond passively to adult coercion. Many strategies we have become used to are forms of punishments. These include:

- Using a color card system in which a child's card is moved to yellow and red when he misbehaves

- Sending a child to the office because of inappropriate behavior

- Giving a child a zero or lower grade for not completing homework

- Making the whole class miss outside recess because a few children were misbehaving

- Threatening to call a parent when the child misbehaves

We know that punishment leads to lower self esteem in children. In addition, many children quickly learn to be sneaky about behaviors that they know will result in punishment rather than adopting different behaviors. Many children who lie and cover up the actions that they think are unacceptable have experienced punishment as a consistent form of interaction with adults. It is easy to see how punishing children can destroy trust and lead to children feeling unsafe emotionally. Consider the following questions from the Center on the Social and Emotional Foundations of Early Learning (Hemmeter, Ostrosky, Santos, et al., 2006, p. 5):

> If a child doesn't know how to read, we teach.
>
> If a child doesn't know how to swim, we teach.
>
> If a child doesn't know how to multiply, we teach.
>
> If a child doesn't know how to drive, we teach.
>
> If a child doesn't know how to behave, we... teach?... punish?
>
> Why can't we finish that last sentence as easily as we can finish the others?

Time–Out as Punishment

One of the strategies that was often advocated in years past was the use of "time-out" and especially a "time-out chair." When children used inappropriate behavior, they were sent to a chair or other location that was separate from the group and quiet. Children are often admonished to "think about what you did" while in time-out, and teachers typically control the amount of time spent isolated. When time-out was advocated as a humane strategy, it was intended to help parents and teachers find an alternative to corporal punishment—hitting, and spanking, for example. While I would certainly agree that time-out is a more humane strategy than corporal punishment, it is not appropriate for helping children develop more positive behaviors.

Isolating children is almost always a painful psychological experience. Children who are often sent to time-out develop a reputation for being a trouble-maker or bad kid. They often internalize these judgments about themselves and become anxious and depressed. As children begin to see themselves as a bad kid or as a trouble-maker, they act in ways that fit that inner view of themselves. The label becomes a self-fulfilling prophecy.

Time-out is not successful because it does not teach children what positive behavior or skills they need to learn. One can easily see that time-out is not particularly effective by observing which children are sent to time-out in October and then observing which children are still seen in the time-out location in March. It is often the same children, which shows us they have not learned anything from this technique, other than that they are a "bad" kid.

It is also possible that time-out is serving a positive function for the child. If his inappropriate behavior is used in order to get him out of something (like clean-up time, or seatwork in math) then the child might actually prefer time-out. Even if this is not on a conscious level for the child, it is possible that the teacher's actions in sending the child to time-out will increase his or her inappropriate behavior.

Another consequence of time-out is that the teacher ends up controlling the child's behavior. In a constructivist, humanistic classroom, we want children to learn self-control so they eventually will not need an adult to help them distinguish between appropriate and inappropriate behaviors. We also want them to learn to control their own impulses and they won't learn that if the teacher is doing the control work for them. This is a clear example of heteronomy, or being governed by someone else, when our goal in education is autonomy or self governing (DeVries & Zan, 1994).

So why do teachers use time-out so frequently? My guess is that they often need a break from behaviors that are destructive, disruptive, or bothersome to them. Having a child separated and quiet for even a few minutes can give a teacher a needed break to gain her own self control, protect other children, and maintain the flow of the classroom. The other unfortunate reason is that many teachers don't have alternative strategies to use instead of time-out. In the following section, we will consider some alternatives that are effective in helping children develop positive, appropriate behaviors.

Alternatives to Punishment

Some behavior that teachers see as misbehavior and in need of elimination can be interpreted, instead, as the child's lack of social and emotional skills, and needs that are not met. Behavior can be understood as a form of communication. Instead of jumping to the conclusion that the child is wrong, it is helpful first to look at the social, physical, academic and emotional environment in the classroom. Have the children been sitting too long? Is the space too crowded? Are the activities too challenging? Not challenging enough? Is the child hungry, tired, or not feeling well? A great deal of inappropriate behavior occurs because of the classroom context, not because there is something deficient in the child. To put it more simply, sometimes our efforts as teachers cause inappropriate behavior from the children. That's why the strategies in the first several chapters of this book are so important in creating a positive, effective classroom environment. Too often teachers jump right into trying to correct student behavior without a thorough review of their own classroom practices.

The next issue to consider when children use inappropriate behavior is child developmental patterns. There are some inappropriate behaviors that we expect young children to use because they have not yet developed the social, emotional, and cognitive skills to handle the demands of classroom communities. For example, when children grab things from each other, we can ask, "What has the child not learned yet that can help her behave more appropriately?" We will explore this more in the next chapter when looking at interventions for challenging behavior, but it's always important to consider positive behaviors the children need to learn. Consider a child who has trouble working independently and constantly talks, interrupting the other children. What skills does the child need? What learning strategies can help the child develop more appropriate behaviors? Teachers sometimes assume that the child is "stubborn," "fresh," "rude," "aggressive," or "lazy," without realizing that many children *cannot* use the skills they need rather than choosing not to use them.

Responding to Children's Inappropriate Behavior

Your response to a child's behavior can range along a continuum from the least amount of intervention to the most amount. If at all possible, it is best to intervene as little as possible to try to allow children to develop their own ability to problem solve. The Teacher Behavior Continuum, shown in the following figure, contains a range of different possible teacher responses to inappropriate behavior (Wolfgang & Glickman, 1986).

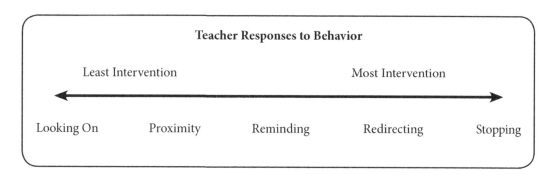

Teacher Responses to Behavior

Least Intervention   Most Intervention

⟵————————————————————————————————⟶

Looking On   Proximity   Reminding   Redirecting   Stopping

Looking on. Before you intervene, you can observe closely and see whether or not you are needed. By watching carefully, you will also be ready to step in if it becomes necessary. In other words, learn what to let go.

For example, Barbara was watching her 4-year old preschoolers playing in the housekeeping area during work time. She noticed Benjamin and Steven standing next to each other, pretending to prepare a meal. Benjamin wanted a spatula that Steven had and began grabbing it as Steven resisted. Barbara moved closer but said nothing and watched. The two boys struggled for a few moments, each pulling on an end of the spatula. Finally Benjamin relented and said, "Okay, you can have it. I'm gonna make soup." He walked away to get some other materials, then joined Steven again at the counter. The two boys continued playing and talking as if nothing happened. Barbara made a mental note to work one-on-one later with Benjamin to model how to ask for a turn, rather than grabbing.

   Proximity. Because adults represent the moral conscience of young children, just moving closer to a child engaging in inappropriate behavior may help the child to make a different choice or be more mindful of her actions. Proximity, or physically moving closer to children can scaffold the behavior you'd like them to learn. For example, if a child is not paying attention, or disturbing another child next to her, you can simply stand closer to her. Likewise, if children are arguing with each other, you could walk over close to them and just quietly watch. Your presence will encourage children to think differently about their actions.

   Redirecting. Much misbehavior is the result of children not having the skills or knowledge to get their needs met in a socially safe and acceptable way. That is why we work so hard to get preschoolers to "use words" instead of actions when they are unhappy or when they want something. Redirecting a child's behavior can be seen as subtly teaching them a more appropriate behavior that gets the same result. Redirecting works best when you have determined that the child doesn't know what behavior is appropriate or when she needs a reminder of what she could do instead. Imagine Tanya is playing with Latisha and she grabs one of the blocks that Latisha has layed out next to her. You calmly say, "Tanya, if you want a block, get one from the shelf. Those are the blocks that Latisha is using and she won't like it if you take them."

   Stopping. There are times when children's behavior is dangerous to themselves or others and they must be stopped immediately. Stopping children's behavior must be done without anger or humiliation. Keeping calm yourself is the best guarantee that you will be effective with the child. Once the behavior has stopped, your next step is to use other guidance techniques to ensure that the child will calm down and be able to learn more appropriate behavior.

   For example, Justin is on the playground and is forcibly wrestling with Hannah to get the tricycle she is using. He puts his hands around her neck and you quickly and calmly pull Justin away from Hannah without talking to him (so that you don't reinforce the behavior with your attention). You check with Hannah to make sure she is not hurt and reassure her that you will keep her safe. You tell Justin to go play somewhere else because he is not being safe with the tricycles. When you see that he is calm, you remind him of how to use his words to ask for a turn and let him know that you will not allow him to hurt any one in school. You make a note to work with him again tomorrow on how to ask for a turn and you help him practice this during outside play time. You give hime plenty of positive feedback for using his words.

Positive Time-Out

Although I don't advocate using time-out as a punishment when children misbehave, I do believe it can play a role when used as a strategy to help children calm down and gain self-control.

The first step in this method is to create a new name for this procedure. Children have learned to associate "time-out" with punishment, so a name that helps convey the idea of self-control is better. For example, you might consider, "Quiet Time," "Alone Time," "Break Time," or something that the children choose. Choose a place in the room such as a comfortable chair, carpet square, pillows, or other spot that is removed from the action, but not really isolated.

Model for the children how the Quiet Time will work and explain that this is a time to calm down. Pretend that your friend just made you angry and you feeling like hitting him. But instead you go over to the Quiet Center, hug a pillow and show them how you are taking three deep breaths. Then get up and pretend to go back to playing. You can also role play with your assistant teacher being upset and you tell her to go to Quiet Time to calm down, and then she can also model how she calms down, perhaps by reading a book.

The most critical aspect of using time-out as a positive process is your attitude and tone of voice. Children can tell when you are annoyed and frustrated and then this will turn into an ineffective punishment. Use your time-out process for minor behaviors. It is essential to redirect inappropriate behavior before it gets out of hand. For example, you might send a child to the Quiet Corner if she is poking another child at circle time, pushing others during transitions, or using materials inappropriately.

The second important aspect in making the process effective is to welcome the child back to the class activities in a positive way. Show the child that she is cared for and an important part of the group and get the child involved in work right away. Some children might need a discussion with you later about why they needed a break and how they might behavior more appropriately in the future. The focus should always be on what better choice the child can make. Instead of "think about what you did" the child should be encouraged to learn how to calm down so he can make better choices.

Acknowledging Feelings When a Child is Upset

What do you do when a child is upset? Young children are often confused and overwhelmed by their own feelings. Some children can become emotionally flooded so that their heart rate increases, their muscles tense, breathing feels more difficult, thinking becomes confused and toxic feelings wash over them. Obviously, this is not the time to reason with a child, even if he is only mildly upset. The physical effects of this emotional flooding can take 30 minutes or so to wear off, and that's if they haven't been triggered again. In some children who are under great stress in their lives, the hormonal responses do not often subside and they live with chronic emotional flooding.

Too often we are also uncomfortable with the child's strong emotions and we want them to go away. We might say things like, "Oh, relax, there's nothing to be afraid of." But to the child who is feeling afraid, this is another way of saying, "There is something wrong with you." or "I don't have time for your problems." Sometimes we might tell a child who is upset, "You know, if you just didn't push him, he wouldn't say mean things to you." Once again, this presents the child with the notion that her feelings don't matter and she won't even hear your logic. Perhaps a child is moving slowly, looking sad for most of the day. I've heard teachers say things like, "You're not going to get your work done if you keep moping around like that." Unfortunately, these methods—denying feelings, reasoning, and criticizing—don't help the child.

Instead, a powerful technique is to acknowledge the child's feelings (Faber & Mazlish, 1995). You can do this by labeling his emotions, as we learned earlier in this book, or simply saying "oh," or "uh huh" or "mmm" which lets the child know you are listening. Often, the child will open up and tell you more about what is bothering him or her.

For example, one day Jeremy was pouting in the corner of the classroom and his teacher approached him and said, "What's up, Jeremy?" He replied, "I hate school." Although his teacher was disturbed by this and was tempted to contradict him, she kept him calm and just said, "Oh." After a moment, Jeremy added, "My sister gets to stay home all day, but I have to come here. I hate it." Jeremy's mom had had a baby a few months earlier and she was taking a family leave to stay home for the next few months. This was the first time the teacher noticed that it was affecting Jeremy. She said, "You must miss your mom a lot when you come to school." Notice how she acknowledges the child's feelings rather than fixing the problem. Later, when Jeremy is calmer, she will talk to him more about how to cope with his feelings. Right now, she just wants to help him feel understood. And he did. Jeremy leaned over and gave his teacher a hug, took a deep breath and went over to play with the other children.

Children will also respond well to a fantasy wish when they are upset. Rather than trying to reason with the child, it can sometimes break the negativity by offering to solve the problem with fantasy. You tell the child how much you wish you could change things with a magic wand, or fairy dust, or a magic pencil or potion.

Finally, when accepting children's feelings, you might also have to stop their behavior at the same time. For example, Maggie was upset when she came back from recess which was held for about 20 minutes in a poorly supervised, small play yard alongside the school. She pushed Sophia as she stormed into the room, clearly upset about what happened during recess. Her teacher gently stopped her, saying, "Maggie, I can see how angry you are, but I can't let anyone get hurt. Go over to the Quiet Spot and practice deep breaths. I'll be over in a minute so you can tell me about your anger." Notice how the teacher accepted Maggie's feelings. There is no point in telling a child she shouldn't be feeling something. She is already feeling it. Instead, convey the message that all feelings are accepted, but inappropriate behaviors are not.

Responding to a Child Who is Upset

1. Put the child's feelings into words. *"You seem frightened by that noise."*

2. Encourage the child to talk by using "Oh," "Mmmm," or "I see," and not evaluating.

3. Use fantasy to help the child feel understood. *"I wish I had a magic clock that could make it lunch time right now!"*

4. Accept the child's feelings, even as you stop unacceptable behavior. *"You are so mad you really want to hit Danielle, but I can't let you do that. Let's sit in the Quiet Spot and you can tell me about being mad."*

Adapted from (Faber & Mazlish, 1995).

Resolving Conflicts

Minor conflicts between children are a natural and inevitable part of social relationships. Our goal is not to get rid of conflict completely, but rather to create a safe environment in which children learn how to manage and resolve minor clashes, arguments, and disagreements. Much can be learned about social regulation from conflict situations. If a child's behavior becomes chronically dangerous and disruptive, you may need to use more intense intervention for challenging behavior described later in this book. However, for less severe disagreements and conflicts, you can help foster problem solving skills that will create a more peaceful classroom and teach social skills that children will use throughout their lives.

Problem Solving Steps

Epstein (2009) provides a step-by-step process to teach children problem solving skills which includes the following:

1. ***Establish safety.*** Approach the situation calmly and stop any actions that could hurt someone. Your ability to stay calm and collected is very important in modeling social skills for the children and for being able to think clearly yourself. For example, first-graders Dylan and Matthew are arguing during center time. Matthew is grabbing a game that is in Dylan's hands. You gently put your arm on Matthew's shoulder and separate the two boys.

2. ***Acknowledge the children's feelings.*** Describing the child's feelings helps the children to be able to listen to you, identify his feelings, and learn how feelings lead to behaviors and consequences. "Matthew, I can tell you are very angry right now. And Dylan, you seem to be scared that Matthew will hurt you." As children get better at this process, you should ask the children to interpret others' feelings: "Matthew, how do you think Dylan is feeling right now?" "Dylan, how do you think Matthew is feeling?"

3. ***Gather information.*** Allow the children to explain their view points, even if you observed the actions. Do not take sides. You will be modeling for the children how to think through problems. "Dylan, can you tell me what happened?" Dylan begins and Matthew interrupts. "Matthew, as soon as he is done, you can tell me what happened, too." Dylan says that Matthew tried to take the game he was using and he had it first. "Okay, Matthew, it's your turn

to tell us what happened." Matthew says, "I really want to play with that. I didn't get a turn in forever. And Dylan won't share with me."

4. ***Restate the problem.*** Describe the problem without judgment. Do not use terms like inconsiderate, selfish, stubborn. Just describe what happened. This allows the children to know that they have been heard and understood, and it helps them to see the problem more clearly. "So, it sounds like Dylan was playing with this game and Matthew really wanted a turn with it. Dylan was not ready to share, and Matthew tried to take the game so he could have a turn."

5. ***Ask for solutions.*** Since the goal is to teach social-relationship skills, allow the children to generate possible solutions rather than just pronouncing a solution yourself. If the children come up with the ideas themselves, they are more likely to follow them, and to learn how to eventually do this on their own. "Matthew and Dylan, do you have any suggestions for how we can solve this problem?" Dylan says, "He should leave me alone. I had it first." "Okay, is that a good idea or not?" Matthew chimes in, "No, I want a turn too. How about I get a turn in five minutes?" "That's one idea. Any others?" Dylan suggests, "We could play the game together." Okay, that's another idea.

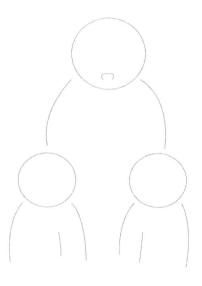

Which idea do you want to try? Matthew says, "Okay, let's play it together. But I get the game first tomorrow." How does that sound, Dylan? "Okay."

6. ***Provide follow-up support.*** After a problem-solving choice is made, check back with the children to be sure the solution is being followed and is working. Give positive feedback to let them know how well they've worked at problem-solving. "Matthew and Dylan, how is your solution working?" "Okay. Jesse wanted to play, too, so we're all gonna play it now." "Great thinking. You did a terrific job of solving this problem." In your feedback, focus on the good job they did with the process, rather than the good idea itself. We want to teach children that the problem-solving process is the important issue.

Setting Limits on Behavior

It is your job as a teacher to let children know when their behavior is not appropriate. This is sometimes difficult for new teachers because they are afraid of "being mean" to the children and not being liked. Perhaps we all have visions from our past of the teacher who screamed at children or punished them unfairly, and we don't want to fall into that persona. Rest assured, though, that children need boundaries in the same way they need good nutrition. When we insist that children eat healthy food, we are doing it because we know the child will benefit. When we set boundaries, we must keep in mind that we are doing it to benefit the child, not to be mean. In fact, children will appreciate knowing that someone will help them learn control because it is a frightening world when any behavior is allowed.

Most of all, keep in mind the foundation for all classroom management techniques is having a solid, caring relationship with the children. All misbehaviors in the classroom exist in the social context, and guidance strategies rely on teaching children to restore the social bonds that are strained when they misbehave. For consequences to be effective, the child must value the social bond with you and her peers and want to restore it.

Children learn boundaries by beginning to see the consequences of their actions. The ability to understand cause and effect relationships is a major accomplishment for young children and still limited, so it is important that consequences are concrete and experienced first-hand. In other words, young children are less likely to respond to lectures about their behavior. Instead, they need to experience developmentally appropriate consequences of their actions. Piaget points out that logical consequences are more appropriate in that they help children develop moral autonomy—that is, a personal understanding of what is right and wrong (DeVries & Zan, 1994).

Using Logical Consequences

The primary way that we figure out what works in interpersonal relationships is from the consequences. In minor conflicts, your first response might be to just observe to see if children can work it out themselves. Having the opportunity to do so builds competence, confidence, and maturity. Knowing when you need to intervene so that conflicts don't escalate out of hand is an art and comes mostly from experience.

Natural Consequences. Not all conflict needs your intervention. Natural consequences occur without teacher intervention. In fact, the most challenging part of using natural consequences is knowing when to allow children to experience the consequences. Of course, if children are in imminent danger of hurting themselves, other people, or school materials, you must stop the behavior immediately. Many times, however, children can and will figure things out themselves. For example, in her four-year old class, Ms. Price watched as Neisha, playing at the water table, tried to sprinkle water on Devon's arms. Devon shouted, "Stop that. You're getting me all wet!" Neisha stopped, and went back to pouring water into the buckets. She then said to Devon, "I've got lemonade. You want some?" In this interaction, Devon, a boy with especially good social skills, effectively set limits for Neisha. Neisha got the message and quickly tried a different approach at engaging Devon in her play.

In another example, you see Keon is working with a group of boys in the block center and he refuses to let the others use the materials. In an angry voice, Jason cries, "You're not gonna play with us when we go outside!" Keon frowns and his face shows anger and frustration, as he turns away, hoarding the materials. You wait to see what happens. The other boys continue talking, and a few minutes later, Keon pushes the materials into the middle of the rug so they can all use them. When you look over a while later, the group is working well without conflict. While certainly Jason's remark was painful, it seems that Keon was able to connect the cause and effect relationship of his hording the materials to Jason's outburst.

Natural consequences happen in real life on a regular basis and they can help children see how their behavior affects other people and themselves. It is important not to overuse this strategy. Be sure that the children are actually learning something from the consequences of their behavior, rather than just suffering frustration or humiliation. It is never appropriate for natural consequences to be harsh or unsafe.

Teacher-Applied Consequences. In addition to natural consequences, you can also apply consequences to children's actions to help them understand the effects of their behaviors. At the most basic level, this means choosing a sanction that is directly related to the misbehavior. These sanctions can include exclusion, deprivation, and restitution (DeVries & Zan, 1994). Any applied consequences, however, need to be used carefully so that children are not humiliated. The focus should always be on what the child can learn, otherwise, you are resorting to punishment which is not effective. There are two key pieces that ensure that an applied consequence works. First, be sure that you are emotionally calm and can deliver the message in a matter-of-fact tone. Second, always be sure to offer the child another chance to demonstrate positive behaviors. Here are different types of consequences:

- *Exclusion.* When children are not able to adhere to the behaviors needed to participate in social activities, you can exclude them as a way of teaching them the boundaries for the behavior. For example, if a child is throwing sand and you've explained and shown how dangerous this is, it would be appropriate to have the child move to a different activity and exclude him from the sandbox. Imagine this scenario: Keyana is sitting in the sandbox with three other children and she excitedly throws the sand up in the air over and over again. You rush over. "Keyana, you must stop throwing the sand in the air. When you throw it up in the air, it can hurt children's eyes. We don't hurt others." You walk away and a few minutes later you see Keyana return to her previous actions, throwing the sand higher. You say to her in a matter-of-fact tone, "Keyana, I see you are having a hard time playing safely with the sand. You will need to leave the sandbox so our friends are all safe. Tomorrow you can try again to see if you can play safely." At this point, you can help Keyana choose a different activity, even if it means gently guiding her out of the sandbox.

- *Deprivation.* An effective way to teach children how to treat materials is to take away the opportunity to use them for a short while. First, make sure that children know what behaviors are expected. They might need direct instruction and modeling to learn these expectations. Next, they need to know that you are serious about the expectations and that you will enforce them. For example, one teacher was having a difficult time getting Julissa to remember to put the covers on the markers. After repeated attempts to show her how to make sure the caps are on and click shut, Julissa was still tossing the markers into the bin on her table without the covers on. Her teacher approached her and said in a calm voice, "Julissa, I see you are having trouble using the markers properly. I can't let them be ruined since everyone enjoys them. Today you will need to use your pencil or crayons instead. We'll try the markers again this afternoon to see if you are able to take care of them." The teacher moved the markers away, and put down a pack of crayons next to her.

- *Restitution.* Teach children how to make amends when they have made the wrong choices in their behaviors. This is the essence of relationship-building and an important aspect of being a mature person. Rather than punishing a child for an action, it is a better learning experience for her to see that she has caused a problem and should then fix it. This strategy can be applied to a wide variety of situations, such as when one child hurts another child. Imagine that Annie has just knocked over Frankie's block structure as she dashed through the block area in his preschool. Her teacher gently stops her and points out that she has damaged Frankie's work. "See, Frankie is very sad that all his work has been knocked down because you rushed through this area. What can you do to make Frankie feel better?" Perhaps Annie will offer to help Frankie rebuild the structure, or give him a hug. The teacher asked Frankie what would work best for him and then guided Annie in following up on her restitution.

Restitution can also be used in conjunction with other strategies. For example, in addition to removing Keyana from the sandbox, the teacher might have asked her to help brush off the other children who were covered in sand to help them. Hannah's teacher might have also asked her to help soak the markers in water later in the day to try to revive them.

When you use consequences, be sure you use a calm, matter-of-fact voice and be sure that the child understands the cause and effect relationship. Never use sarcasm, humiliation, or harm. Your message must be that the behavior is unacceptable, but the child is cared about. Continue to work on building and maintaining a strong relationship with the child, even when using consequences. If you find that you have strong emotions building up, use a calming technique for yourself before intervening.

Helping Attention-Seeking Children

"Ignore him—he just wants attention!" How many times have you heard a teacher say something like this? Attention-seeking behavior has a bad reputation in our schools, and it can often lead to difficult classroom management challenges. Yet Maslow has helped us understand that seeking attention is a way of getting our love and belongingness needs met. The need for human interaction and affection is so strong that it is a kind of hunger—the more a child lacks these interactions, the harder he will try to get them. Any interactions, even negative ones, are better than none.

Some children, due to a lack of social emotional skills and competence, are hard to interact with. They might talk back, or whine. They may be pushy and demanding. They may lack manners, or constantly put others down. Naturally, teachers and other children begin to avoid them, or push them away. This reduces their chance to learn social and emotional skills, and thus begins a negative cycle. The result can be children who use challenging behaviors to achieve social interaction.

Notice what the consequences are when children act out inappropriately. Often the teacher gets close, touching the child (especially young children) by holding an arm, physically removing the child from the area, or even picking the child up. Often the teacher is at eye level, in very close proximity, and she is usually filled with strong emotions. In a way, the typical reprimand of a misbehaving child is intimate: close, physical, and emotionally intense. Often a child with frequent misbehavior is sent to the center director, or other disciplinarian, where he gets additional one-on-one attention in a more peaceful environment. In any case, the typical result of attention-seeking behavior is, not surprisingly, lots of attention!

So wouldn't it make sense to ignore these behaviors to stop reinforcing them? Yes, but only if you increase the amount of positive attention the child gets at other times. The child is hungry for a relationship with you and it can be difficult to develop this if you are angry and frustrated with the child. It's natural (but unprofessional) to ignore him instead. This is often why he is using challenging behavior that is so hard to ignore. What to do instead?

- Schedule time to spend with the child. Sit next to him at snack or invite him to read to you one-on-one. Greet him warmly when he arrives and spend an extra minute talking with him at the end of the day.

- Plan ways he can interact with other children in a successful way. Pair him up with a child who has excellent social skills for buddy activities.

- Rather than trying positive reinforcement with praise or other tangibles like stickers, think instead of providing rich interactions. Remember he's hungry, so he needs healthy "meals" of interactions, not "junk food" like quick praise.

- Have honest, authentic interactions. Find out more about his likes, habits, fears, and hopes. Think about connecting.

- Directly teach the child how to get your positive attention through modeling and practice. See the ideas in the next section for teaching children how to get attention in appropriate ways.

- Give it time. As his hunger for relationship is fed, you should see a reduction in the attention-seeking behaviors, but it can take a while to change deeply-engrained behaviors. Show him that he can get your attention more effectively with positive behaviors!

ↄ ↄ ↄ

Chapter 7: Understanding Challenging Behavior

In the preschool room, Miss Assad was wondering how to help one of her students. Christine, a petite 3-year old, was creating terror during work time at the centers. A few minutes before, Miss Assad stopped her in the middle of yanking on Stephanie's hair in order to get the pocketbook she wanted. Yesterday she didn't get the dress she wanted and she threw herself on the floor, screaming and kicking. Miss Assad talked with her after each incident, trying to explain to her that she must not hurt the other children. So far this wasn't working and the behavior continued. Chrstine's mother told Miss Assad that she was often a handful at home, too—demanding that she get her own way and kicking and screaming when she didn't. Miss Assad was meeting with her mom after school today in hope that they could come up with some strategies to help Christine.

Challenging behaviors in early childhood classrooms can be a serious impediment to adjustment to later academic and social achievement (Dunlap et al., 2006). It is very important to identify, prevent, and resolve challenging behaviors as early as possible in a child's development. Identifying challenging behaviors is a tricky topic because many of the inappropriate behaviors that appear in young children are considered part of the normal developmental pattern of young children, such as tantrums, biting, and physical aggression. Many of these behaviors disappear as the child matures and most children exhibiting these behaviors respond to developmentally appropriate guidance strategies that have been presented so far in this book.

A small percentage of young children, however, do not respond to our guidance or structure. They are considered to have challenging behavior when the behavior meets the following criteria (Kaiser & Rasminsky, 2007, p. 9):

- Interferes with children's learning, development, and success at play

- Is harmful to the child, other children, or adults

- Puts a child at high risk for later school problems or school failure

If we don't address challenging behaviors appropriately in the early years of a child's life there is a greater likelihood for poor academic outcomes, peer rejection, adult mental health concerns, and adverse effects on children's families and their communities (Dunlap et al., 2006, p. 33).

Let's take the case of Sheila, a four-year old in a Head Start program. When invited to participate in group activities she sits for a moment, then leaves the carpeted area and walks around the room playing with other materials. Her teacher, a seasoned veteran with good classroom management skills, has attempted redirecting her. This has led to screaming and kicking. During center time, Sophia enjoys the other children's company however she "claims" the materials as her own and hits or screams at the children who might want to use them with her. Her teacher recognizes that her typical guidance strategies are inadequate. Sophia is one of the few children who need more intensive individual interventions to address her challenging behavior.

Children with challenging behaviors also contribute to teacher burn-out, and feelings of helplessness. When you are faced with children's challenging behaviors, the information in this book can help a great deal; however, a team approach in which you have the support of the family, special education professionals, social workers, therapists, and others who are involved in the child's life is very important. This chapter provides only a brief overview of this process to help you gain a basic understanding of the ways in which we can help children turn around challenging behaviors and have a brighter future.

Personal Emotional Reactions

All of us have personal "hot button" issues that upset us when faced with certain behaviors of children. These come from our lifetime of experiences, the values we've adopted and inherited, from our fears, and perceptions of our own competence in restoring calm to the classroom. Some of us can't stand it when we perceive children being "rude". Others of us have our buttons pushed when children seem to defy us. Many student teachers are afraid that children's challenging behaviors will reflect badly on their abilities as a teacher. For all these reasons, and more, you can expect to often have an emotional reaction to challenging behavior in children.

These emotional reactions can be very strong and powerful in inhibiting our own ability to think clearly and rationally. Just like children, when our brains are flooded with the hormones released when we are anxious, we have less ability to think clearly and make good decisions. I think this is the reason why we occasionally see and hear teachers yelling at children, punishing them in harsh ways, humiliating them, and displaying anger towards them that disrupts their relationships with the children. Therefore, the first step in helping children with problem behavior is to take care of your own emotions.

How Can We Help Children with Challenging Behaviors?

The basic idea in helping children with challenging behavior is to understand that their behavior helps them get their needs met. All behaviors have a positive function for them (even if it seems like it couldn't have one) In order to help a child, we must understand the function of his or her behavior. Children are often using their challenging behaviors to get what they need because they don't have certain skills or abilities. Because the behaviors they are using are getting them what they need, they don't have much motivation to change them. This might not seem to be the case when you first think about inappropriate behaviors like throwing chairs, or pulling hair. How could this help a child get what she needs? We'll use some interesting strategies to figure this out!

Response to Intervention. The first concept to understand is that children need different amounts of support for maintaining appropriate behaviors (Hemmeter, Ostrosky, & Fox, 2006; Sugai et al., 1999). There are some lessons that will help all children, other activities are to help children who might be at risk of behavior problems, and some strategies you will use with only a few children. Researchers and policy-makers are using the *Response to Intervention* paradigm, originally designed to help support children with learning disabilities, to also help children with social behavior problems (Hawken, Vincent, & Schumann, 2008). This process can be conceptualized as a pyramid with different procedures at each level.

At the base of the pyramid are the actions we take for all children to prevent challenging behaviors. These are considered Tier One interventions that are available for all children and they include all of the strategies in the first section of this book. Unless these basic aspects to positive classroom management are in place, other interventions will not be successful. The Center on the Emotional and Social Foundations of Early Learning recommends that the Tier One interventions include nurturing and responsive relationships and high-quality, supportive environments (Hemmeter, Ostrosky, & Fox, 2006).

The next level on the pyramid is designed for the few children who will need additional support in learning social and emotional skills. In Chapter 3 there is an overview of social, emotional, and academic skills to use with the children who need more guidance in this area. These strategies are considered Tier Two interventions.

The top level of the pyramid, and the focus of this chapter, represents intensive individualized interventions. Very few children need these interventions—only those who have not responded to the other strategies. They are done only for specific cases and are carefully targeted to what the child needs.

Sometimes teachers are frustrated that some children need so much more energy than others. This is a reality of the classroom and a basic principle of positive guidance. It's helpful to come to terms with the fact that some children will need more of your time, energy, and emotional resources than others. If you get frustrated and angry about this, you will lose the joy of working with young children and become resentful.

Prevention. The first step in working with challenging behaviors is to review the strategies at the base of the pyramid. Are children's basic needs being met? You can start by asking the following questions:

- *Procedures.* Are my procedures smooth enough that they have become routine or do I need to re-teach my procedures? Do I need additional procedures I haven't taught the children? Do I need to change any of my procedures because they are not working?

- *Physiological needs.* Are the physiological needs of the children being met? Is the temperature okay? The lighting? Do the children get to be active enough? Can they easily get to the bathroom when they need to? Are the misbehaviors occurring when the children are getting hungry or tired? Are the children getting enough sleep at home?

- *Punishment.* Am I punishing the children, or criticizing them instead of teaching them positive behaviors? Do the children feel unsafe in our room because they are afraid of getting in trouble?

- *Physical environment.* Do the children have enough personal space? Are they too crowded when they sit on the rug for group time? Are they able to see easily what I am doing when I lead the class? Are there too many open areas that invite children to run?

- *Belongingness and positive relationships.* Do the children get enough of my attention? Do they feel accepted and understood? Do the children feel that they belong to the group and that the classroom is theirs? Have I taught children the social and emotional skills they need to live together in a classroom setting? Do I focus enough on promoting self-regulation?

- *Transitions.* Have I left enough time for transitions or are the children rushed? Am I giving the children enough of a warning before transitions? Do I have too many transitions? Is my daily routine giving the children enough balance between sitting and being active and between teacher-directed and child-directed activities?

- *Classroom climate.* Is the climate in my room positive? Warm? Inviting? Am I communicating in a way that encourages children to be collaborative? Do the positive comments I make to the child outnumber the negative ones?

- *Curriculum and instruction.* Are my lesson plans and activities appropriate for the age of the children? Are there plenty of active learning experiences or are the children sitting still for long periods of time? Are any of the children finding the class activities too difficult or too easy?

If you have reviewed all these questions and feel that your classroom structure works well to meet the children's needs, but you still have challenging behaviors then you can consider functional analysis and positive behavioral support. These strategies offer an alternative to punishment by helping us to change the classroom environment so that challenging behavior doesn't occur, and helping children learn new, more appropriate behaviors (Ryan, Halsey, & Matthews, 2003). This approach is research-driven and effective across various settings, ages, and behavioral challenges (Shippen, Simpson, & Crites, 2003; Sugai et al., 1999).

Understanding the Acting-Out Cycle

In order to understand children's challenging behaviors, it's helpful to take a closer look at what is going on when children act out in behaviors such as screaming, throwing things, fighting, or tantrums. It may seem like this behavior comes out of nowhere, but in reality, there are phases in this acting out cycle that are recognizable and predictable (The IRIS Center for Training Enhancements, n.d.-a). When you learn to identify the phases in this cycle, you can intervene earlier and help children learn new behaviors and skills, and adapt your teaching and classroom to be more supportive.

The figure below shows the seven steps of the acting out cycle, demonstrating how the intensity builds and accelerates into a peak and then subsides. Your goal is to help the child in the early stages of the cycle, preventing the full cycle from occurring.

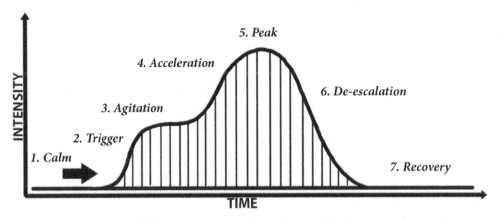

Your response to the child's acting out cycle will completely depend on what point in the cycle you are intervening.

The acting out cycle. (from The IRIS Center for Training Enhancements, n.d.-a)

Calm phase. Children who are in the calm phase are typically engaged in learning, able to socialize comfortably, focus attention, and respond to requests. Most of the strategies in this book are designed to help keep children in the calm phase, however teaching social and emotional skills are especially important. It is also critical to create a positive climate by building relationships and giving children plenty of attention. It's helpful to remember that some children may typically be in an anxious state on a regular basis and will need more support to achieve calmness.

Trigger. Children's behavior can change as a result of classroom triggers such as a change in the routine, a negative interaction with the children or teacher, confusion about an activity, or overwhelming stimulation. Besides the classroom environment, children may be triggered because of hunger, not getting enough sleep, oncoming illness, or stress at home. As you get to know your children, pay special attention to what their specific triggers might be.

The first strategy you can use is to help the child avoid or manage his triggers. For example, if you know that Kevin tends to get angry and hit children when the class is coming in from the playground, you can use some prevention strategies such as asking Kevin to come in for a special job ahead of the rest of the class. Or you can walk next to Kevin, engaging him in conversation as you enter the classroom. If you know that Jenny begins to have tantrums at the beginning of clean-up time, you can give her early notice that center time is ending, or get her to stop ahead of the other children and then give her a job to do—like watering the plants—that is away from all the movement during clean up time. When triggers are related to health issues or the home environment, you'll want to share information with families to help reduce triggers. For example, parents might not realize their child is tired or hungry during the day.

Agitation Phase. After a trigger occurs, a child will begin to get agitated. In my view this is the critical phase that requires your intervention. At this point, children's emotions and behaviors begin to gain energy. If you are attuned to this phase, you may notice nail biting, hair twirling, tapping, wiggling, inability to sit still, a lack of focus, or daydreaming. Some children will clench their fists, or their jaw, making a grimace or showing frustration on their face. It is critical to be able to recognize and intervene at the trigger or the agitation phase to prevent behaviors that end up being aggressive. At this point intervention by the teacher is most effective and most necessary.

Your goal in the agitation phase is to restore calm, otherwise the child will move into the acceleration phase and can become out of control. It's especially important not to yell at the child or add to their growing tension with lecturing or reprimands. Calming a child in the agitation phase can be as simple as moving your body close by, giving some focused attention on the child, or redirecting the child toward a different activity. Here are some examples:

- Carmen is playing in the housekeeping area and two other girls move close to her to play with the kitchen items. Carmen makes an angry face and starts to push their things off the table. You quickly walk over and engage Carmen in a conversation about her play. She starts to relax and smile so you make suggestions about playing together with the other girls.

- Tyler has been engaged and sitting quietly throughout the storybook reading time. Toward the end of the book, he begins to fidget on the carpet and starts rocking his body side to side. You notice this and call on Tyler to come up and point to one of the words in the Big Book that starts with the same letter as his name. He quickly gets up and bounces to the front of the carpet.

The most important thing to keep in mind is reducing the negative energy and restoring calm. If at this phase, for example, you lectured Carmen about sharing or yelled at Tyler to sit still, it could easily have pushed the child into the acceleration phase rather than restoring calm. You can talk to the child later about the problem behavior, or help her learn new coping strategies, but at this point, your only goal is to restore calm.

Acceleration Phase. The child increases his efforts to engage the teacher, often through arguing, refusing to do what was asked, and perhaps beginning to push or kick other children or things. During this phase children start to use negative behaviors to gain the teacher's attention. It is a form of communication which says "help me!" For novice teachers, this is often the first part of the cycle noticed as being problematic, which is why it is so important to practice recognizing triggers and agitation. It is much easier to redirect a child and keep a positive focus before the acceleration phase because young children's behavior and composure can fall apart quickly.

Once again, you need to cool things off and calm the child down, even if it means ignoring some of these behaviors for the time being. The worst thing a teacher can do at this point is engage in a power struggle. This adds tension and intensity to the child's emotional state and will push the child right into the peak phase. Imagine the child's behavior as a run-away train. We can either help put on the brakes, or add fuel to the engine that pushes it into worse behavior. Here are some examples:

- Kaylie, is working with two other children, putting together a word puzzle. She begins to get frustrated when she is not able to take over control of the puzzle, whining at the girls, and jumping out of her seat. The teacher is helping children across the room and doesn't notice this until Kaylie yells at the girls, "I wanna do it myself!" and sweeps some of the pieces off onto the floor. The teacher notices this and asks her to pick them up. Kaylie responds, stamping her feet, "No, I won't. You can't make me." The teacher calmly approaches her and, with a neutral tone of voice, she asks Kaylie to come for a walk with her. She takes her to the hallway and suggests she gets a drink of water. As Kaylie calms down, the teacher is able to talk with her about problem-solving strategies that might work with the other girls.

- Three-year old Jackson is playing with the blocks, trying to build a large tower. Mark comes over and places a block on top of his tower. Jackson screams, "Stop it! My tower," and the boy moves away. The teacher is in the art area, and doesn't notice Jackson's agitation. A few minutes later, Mark returns to the area, and tries again to place a block on Jackson's tower. Jackson screams, "Stop it!" and pushes Mark away, causing him to tumble backwards. The teacher quickly comes over and with a calm, soothing voice says, "Jackson, you've got a lot of blocks on that tower." She sits down next to him, between him and Mark and puts her hand on his shoulder. "It looks like you really want to work on this tower by yourself." As Jackson shows signs of calming down, she prompts, "Jackson, can you say to Mark, 'I want to work alone?'" He repeats this and she turns to Mark to help him find another activity.

- Jorge begins to wriggle on the rug while the teacher reads a story and asks the class questions. He begins to call out answers and his teacher reminds him to raise his hand. He continues to wriggle around on the rug, bumping into the children next to him. He calls out a few more times, but does not get the teacher's attention. He starts to poke the boy next to him who yells out, "Stop it! That hurt!" The teacher calmly asks Jorge to come sit next to her, and she decides to end the story quickly and start a movement activity. Jorge goes back to his spot on the rug with a smile on his face. Later she will work with him on ways he can let her know when he needs a break from sitting on the rug at reading time.

What do these examples have in common? The teacher stayed calm in both tone of voice and body language. She redirected the child each time, rather than tackling head-on the behavior problem. If the teacher had started to argue with Kaylie about picking up the puzzle pieces, or spoke in a harsh voice to Jackson about pushing Mark, or punished Jorge by making him leave the rug, these children would have likely ramped up their own behavior into full-blown outbursts.

The hardest part of this strategy is letting go of the idea that all inappropriate behavior must be corrected, punished, or dealt with immediately. When children are this agitated, the most important step is to cool them down so they can think and act more appropriately. The time to teach a child more appropriate behaviors is not when he is upset. When the child's anger is directed at us, rather than another child, this can be especially hard to do. With practice, being able to stay calm and redirect children's behavior during the Acceleration Phase will pay off in fewer severely inappropriate behaviors. You will also be more effective in teaching children appropriate behaviors to use instead.

Peak Phase. At this point in the cycle the child is out of control. You will now be unable to prevent the problem behavior and must try to reduce the harm as much as possible. Think of a plan ahead of time for out-of-control behavior so that all the adults in the room know how to respond. Check with your school or center to find out if there are preferred procedures for what to do when a child is out of control. This is often the point at which we get very stressed—even frightened of children's behavior. Practice ahead of time using breathing techniques, positive thoughts ("I can handle this"), or other self-calming behaviors. Using the STAR technique immediately can help: Smile, Take a breath, and Relax (Bailey, 2001). It is essential to stay as calm as you can because your anxiety and negative energy will transfer to the child. The child needs *you* to stay calm in order to regain control! Lecturing, admonishing, yelling at, or threatening the child at this point will only prolong the behavior. Try calming techniques with the child, and if necessary, move the child to a safe place away from the rest of the children. The peak phase is usually intense but short-lived—if you don't add negative energy to it.

First, act to ensure that everyone is safe from harm. You may need to gently but firmly restrain a child from hurting himself or others. Your focus is to help the child regain control in a respectful, caring way. It's sometimes hard to remember that a child is literally out of control and that he might not have the skills to calm himself down. At this point in the acting out cycle the child needs your help and care. This is often difficult because aggressive behavior often sends our own emotional stability into chaos. The best possible scenario is to move out of this phase quickly and restore order.

De-escalation. After an outburst, a child is often disoriented, confused and perhaps exhausted. He or she will usually respond well to your requests at this point and they need a few minutes to regroup. This is a good time to direct the child to the Quiet Corner and encourage her to put on headphones and listen to calming music, hold a comfort item, look at a book, or to just lay her head down. At this point, you will want to return your attention for a couple minutes to the rest of the class to establish order and ensure the other children are engaged again.

Recovery Phase. When you return to the child, sit for a minute or two and discuss the situation, trying to learn as much as you can from the child about what triggered his behavior. This is often difficult with preschoolers, but it can be helpful to hear the child's side of the story. Don't assume that you know what was going on in the child's mind. You might start by just saying, "You were very upset just then. What was going on for you?" Try to avoid asking "why" questions since they are often interpreted as accusations and that will just lead to denials and anger. If Jarene says, "He hit me first!" you could respond, "He hit you first? Tell me more about that." When children begin to realize that you are not interested in finding blame and sentencing them to a punishment, they will more likely open up to you. Then you can use this information to better help you identify triggers and agitation. During the recovery phase, you should also help the children make a plan for what to do in the future when the trigger occurs. Be sure to follow up on the plan by teaching new behaviors and having the child practice while he is calm.

Children who are repeatedly acting out are sending you a powerful message that they need more support. You can begin to use functional analysis—which is discussed in the next section—with children who consistently display challenging behavior in order to go into more depth in identifying the triggers of problem behavior and the environmental situations that reinforce it.

The Acting Out Cycle (The IRIS Center for Training Enhancements, n.d.-a)		
Phase	**Student Behavior**	**Teacher Response**
1. Calm	Children are engaged fully in learning activity; emotional stability and full cognitive focus.	Provide positive attention, work on developing relationships with children, provide safe, calm environment.
2. Trigger	Environmental stressors such as change in schedule, boredom, confusion, overstimulation, negative social interactions; internal stressors such as hunger, lack of sleep, illness, medication, stress at home.	Begin to recognize what triggers are and help to prevent them, change the setting, social interactions, offer positive attention.
3. Agitation	Disengages from activity or lesson; shows body movements of agitation—tapping, rocking, running around—or stares into space, walks around unengaged, stops participating.	Redirect child, change the way the child is working on the activity—offer choices; provide assistance, offer calming techniques.
4. Acceleration	Attempts to gain teacher attention in negative ways; argues, is non-compliant, testing limits, trying to provoke the teacher and/or other children.	Redirect child to appropriate behavior calmly, acknowledge feelings, make high-probability requests; give positive attention. Do not engage in argument, use sarcasm, or offer negative remarks.

5. Peak Phase	Child is out of control; verbal and physical aggression toward teacher and other children; crying, damaging materials.	Maintain safety, stay calm yourself, help child to regain control in respectful caring way.
6. De-escalation Phase	Child is disoriented, confused, tired, and often withdrawn; typically receptive to teacher requests; may blame others and try to reconcile.	Move child to Quiet Corner, provide calm independent activity; check on rest of class to restore order.
7. Recovery Phase	Child is subdued and has calmed down. May avoid talking about the incident.	Debriefing of incident is critical. Discuss what triggered incident and make plan for prevention in future.

Why Children Act Out: Functional Assessment

Functional assessment (sometimes called functional behavioral assessment) is a procedure used to figure out the reason, circumstances, and consequences of a child's behavior. This allows us to figure out how the challenging behavior is helping the child get what he or she needs. It is not effective to try an intervention for challenging behaviors until you have a hypothesis about the function of the behavior. Using the same strategies with all children is like giving all children the same medicine for a fever. First we need to know what is causing the fever. In classrooms, we need to figure out the function or purpose of the behavior. That way we can identify the conditions under which the challenging behavior is likely to occur and we can adapt the classroom environment in ways that reduces occurrences of the behavior and teaches the child behaviors that can be used instead (Sugai et al., 1999).

Although functional analysis is often used for children with special needs, it can be used with any child who exhibits challenging behavior (Hanley, Iwata, & McCord, 2003; Matson & Minshawi, 2007). In functional analysis, we examine challenging behavior in terms of the setting, the specific details of the behavior, and the consequences of the behavior. Next, we try to determine what need the behavior fulfills for the child before deciding what intervention to make. When our interventions are based on an analysis of the relationship between the challenging behavior and the child's environment, we are more likely to be effective (Dunlap et al., 2006).

Functional analysis can be adapted toward a more humanistic perspective by using Maslow's theory to help us understand the reasons, or function, of the behavior. Let's look at the steps in doing a functional analysis, often called an A-B-C Analysis (Ryan et al.):

A: Antecedents. Discover what happens just before the behavior occurs. This is often hard to answer without very careful observation. Having another person help observe can improve your ability to begin to anticipate when the challenging behaviors occur. Notice the setting and the activity. Typical antecedents might be gathering at the rug for group time, or lining up in the hallway, transitioning to new lessons or working independently at a desk. It can be helpful to discover antecedents by thinking about when there are times that the behavior does not occur.

The antecedents can also be influenced by setting events. These are circumstances that happen before the behavior that make it more likely that the antecedent will trigger the challenging behavior. For example, a typical setting event is that the child has not gotten enough sleep. This makes it more likely that the antecedent (let's say, moving to a group lesson) will trigger a child's behavior, such as pushing others out of the way.

B: Describing the behavior. Articulate the challenging behavior using a behavioral description that is clear and thorough. When we become emotionally upset by a child's behavior, trying to describe what we see without putting any meaning to that behavior helps us to be more calm and objective. For example, it is not helpful to say that a child is "being stubborn" or "difficult" or "is acting up." Instead you can use the same skills you learned for taking good observational notes: "Glenda throws herself on the floor, kicking her legs and screaming," or "Michael crouches under the table, curling his legs up underneath him and remains there for as long as 30 minutes at a time." It may be the case that some children have multiple challenging behaviors. It might be easier to work on one at a time, until you gain expertise.

Challenging Behavior	Behavioral Definition
Gabriella doesn't listen.	When asked to comply with a teacher's request, such as putting away the blocks, Katie walks away and ignores the request.
Prashad is disruptive.	Prashad calls out and makes irrelevant comments, and pokes other children during group time.
Logan is hyperactive.	Emma moves from area to area without engaging in any activity. She will sit at the table for about five minutes, then she gets up and walks around the room, even when redirected. She pulls materials out of the shelves and dumps them on the floor.

C. Consequences. Observe carefully to determine what happens immediately after the behavior occurs. What do the adults in the room do? What do the other children do? What happens to the child? For example, you observe that when Keisha rolls around on the floor kicking others during the whole-group story reading time, the other children move away from her, the assistant teacher sits down closer to her, puts a hand gently on her shoulder, and whispers to her. The consequences of the child's actions reinforce them, or make it more likely that they will occur again. Often we find that our own actions as teachers are maintaining the child's behavior. We will examine this more closely later.

Functions of Behavior

this is a test Once you've done an A-B-C Analysis you will make an hypothesis about the function of the behavior. We assume there are three possible functions:

1. ***The child gets something.*** This could be a particular object, like the dress-up clothes, or attention from peers or adults. Look carefully at the consequences of the child's actions to see what type of attention the child might gain. Even if the teacher is reprimanding the child, or the other children look on with anxiety or confusion, the child may still be getting social interaction that he or she desires. We can inadvertently maintain the behavior by our negative attention.

2. ***The child avoids or escapes from something.*** Children often get out of activities that are difficult or boring for them, such as clean up time or transitions, or avoid contact with other peers or adults. For example, many children act inappropriately during circle time and then get told to leave the circle. This allows the child to escape and strengthens the likelihood the behavior will continue. In other words, he got exactly what he wanted - to get out of needing to sit still and listen.

3. ***The child changes the level of stimulation.*** All of us adapt what we are doing to maintain our preferred level of stimulation. When John is overwhelmed by the noise and movement during clean up time, he curls up in his cubby and successfully lowers his amount of stimulation. On the other hand, when Karen is waiting in line to go to the bathroom, she tickles the girl in front of her, causing a ripple of commotion that instantly increases the stimulation she wants. In this way, the environment reinforces the behavior through a change in stimulation.

A-B-C Analysis Example for Leah			
A- Antecedent	B - Behavior	C - Consequences that maintain the behavior	Function
Transition Time. Children move from circle time to small group timie	Leah skips around the room, then goes over to the housekeeping area and sits down.	Teacher goes over to Leah, scolds her, and grabs her hand to bring her over to the table.	Leah successfully avoids transitioning for a few minutes, and she gains close attention from the teacher

Developing an Hypothesis

Once you have determined the function(s) of the behavior, the next step is to develop an hypothesis about the challenging behavior together with your colleagues, the child's family member or other professionals working with child. The hypothesis statement should include the following information:

a. Description of challenging behavior

b. Identification of the settings when the behavior occurs

c. Function of the behavior (Be specific - if you think the behavior is to get attention – who's attention? If it's to escape demands, describe what demands you think they are)

d. Responses that sustain and maintain the behavior

Example Hypothesis

During transitions to group time on the carpet, Adam crawls to the rug, knocks into other children, and rolls around on the carpet. This allows him to escape group activities since his teacher sends him to sit at his desk by himself.

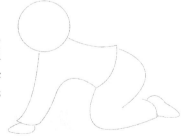

Positive Behavior Supports

Once you have developed an hypothesis, the next step is to develop plans to test it out and see if you were right about the function of the behavior. These plans are called Positive Behavior Supports (PBS) because they help the child in a positive way to develop new behaviors that are more appropriate. PBS is used frequently in classrooms with individual children, such as children with special education needs who are in inclusion settings, or it is used in entire schools, with a variety of children in many different settings (Wood, Blair, & Ferro, 2009; Conroy, 2005). In the next chapter, we will explore Positive Behavior Support plans in more detail.

Below is a form you to practice functional analysis until you are comfortable determining the triggers, consequences, and functions of behaviors you observe.

Functional Analysis Chart

Trigger (Antecedent)	Behavior	Maintaining Consequences
	Function:	
	Function:	
	Function:	
	Function:	

❧ ❧ ❧

Chapter 8: Positive Behavior Support Planning

Aiden is a 4 years preschooler in Miss Shelly's class in a community child care center. Although he is progressing well in most developmental areas, He verbally and physically interrupts both classroom instruction and other peer-interactions by screaming and darting through the room, squirming and fidgeting during seated instruction/work and touching or rubbing against other students inappropriately. Here are some excerpts from Miss Shelly's functional assessment observations:

10/5: During the transition from free-choice time to group time on the carpet, Aiden screams, runs in a circle, and then runs through brushing and bumping groupings of his peers as they clean up. Miss Shelly and her assistant, Miss Stephanie, call Aiden's name and reprimand him for running, not cleaning, and then remind him to sit on his circle spot. The function of this behavior seems to be to escape cleaning up and to get one-on-one interaction with the teacher.

10/6: When the children begin to clean up after free-choice time, Aiden first stands in place and screams, then darts to cubby. He buries himself amongst his and his peer's coats. Miss Shelly calls to Aiden to come help clean up. He stays in the cubby and Miss Stephanie goes over, takes his hand, and leads him to the block area. She guides him in putting some blocks away. The function of his behavior is to reduce the stimulation of clean up by escaping to his cubby, and gain one-on-one attention from the assistant teacher.

10/8: During group time when the children sit on the carpet together, Aiden pokes the child next to him, wiggles his legs, roll on the floor, and make sounds with his mouth. Miss Shelly first tells him to stop and reminds him to pay attention and sit with his legs crossed. Aidencontinues the behavior and Miss Shelly tells him to go sit at his table by himself. The function of the behavior is to escape group time and to gain teacher interaction.

Miss Shelly realized that her approach was not working and decided that she needed a more structured plan to help Aiden. She met with Aiden's parents to help develop a positive behavior support plan in order to help him learn the behaviors he needs to be successful, and to help the adults respond more effectively to his needs.

Children use challenging behavior because it gets them what they need. In these examples, Aiden gets the attention he needs from the teacher, while also escaping the situations (such as sitting still during group time, and tolerating the commotion during clean up time) that are too challenging for him. Like most children with challenging behavior, he is lacking important social/emotional skills so he substitutes challenging behavior. In order to help children with challenging behavior like Aiden, we need to know the function of the behavior, and then plan steps to help teach new, more appropriate behaviors. This process, called Positive Behavior Support, has the following steps:

1. *Analyze.* Determine the trigger and the function of the behavior by examining what happens before and after the behavior occurs.

2. *Prevent.* Change the environment, transitions, and task demands to make it less likely for the behavior to occur.

3. *Teach new skills.* Figure out what behaviors you'd like the child to use instead of the challenging behavior (using words instead of hitting, asking for a break instead of disturbing others). Systematically teach these skills through modeling and practice.

4. *Change your response.* If the behavior still occurs, change your response so that the behavior is not reinforced. If the child is obtaining intense interaction then provide less of a reaction. Provide attention and positive feedback when the child uses the new skills instead. If the child had been escaping activities, ensure the child must still participate or complete the work. Above all, stay calm and do not argue or lecture.

Remember that changing behaviors is a slow, gradual process that takes patience and plenty of time. Expect the changes to take weeks or months, although you should see some consistent improvement along the way.

Working in a team. Positive behavior support is most effective when done as a team so that the child can get support in many areas of his or her life and more ideas for support systems are gathered (Kaiser & Rasminsky, 2007). When the adults in a child's world are consistent, the child can learn new behaviors faster. If possible, include all the adults that regularly interact with the child on a regular basis, including the parents and family members, in both the functional analysis and the behavior support planning.

Preventing Challenging Behavior

One powerful way to help a child change his behavior is to change things in the classroom so that the child doesn't need to use the challenging behavior. You can think of prevention strategies as a form of scaffolding for the child.

Change the physical environment. Think about the triggers and consider what you can adapt to reduce the challenging behavior:

- Is the group area too crowded? Are the children so tightly congested on the rug that they bump into each other? How about giving each child a carpet mat to sit on to define his or her space?

- Is the child unable to stay focused because of distractions? Can the child's desk be moved to a quieter area? This should not be done as a punishment but as an offer to help the child.

- Are the materials too stimulating? Are there too many kinds of food in the house area? Too many blocks in the block area? Consider limiting the materials and rotating them on a regular basis, or limiting the amount of children in each area.

- Do the children have enough room to get to coat hooks or cubbies? If this area is tight, consider limiting the number of children in the area at one time, or allowing the target child to go into that area alone.

- Do children have a clear, defined place to line up? Consider putting a line on the floor, or marks where the children should stand to help them learn appropriate behavior.

Change transitions. Many children have a difficult time when changing from one activity to another. Changing the routine can often prevent those problems.

- Give plenty of advance notice to the child when transitions are going to occur. Two or three reminders that count down the time can be helpful.

- Use a visual schedule to show the child what the next transition is. These can be photographs glued to cards and made into a booklet.

- Allow the child to make the transition to the next activity before the other children. Get the child started cleaning up or finishing what he is doing, then get him settled for the next activity while you begin the transition with the rest of the class.

- Use a timer to help the child visually see when her turn will be ending, or when the next activity will begin. An old fashioned, analog timer is better than a digital one since it gives a concrete representation of the time.

- Be sure you teach all the children the appropriate procedures for a transition (how to push in chairs, how to walk across the room, how to put things away, how to sit at circle time, how to line up). Practice these procedures like a game for a few days in a row or every day until the transitions become smoother and more routine.

Change task demands. Children often use escape behaviors (pencil sharpening, drinks of water, talking to neighbors) because the task seems overwhelming. Change what you ask the child to do:

- Break the task into smaller steps and give positive feedback for getting through each step. For example, if a child puts away three blocks, acknowledge her hard work and give her three more.

- Give choices. What would you like to start cleaning up? Where would you like to sit at the circle? These give the child a feeling of power and control.

- Give the child frequent breaks. If a child can't sit still for all of circle time, ask her to sit for 5 minutes, give positive feedback and allow her to take a break and get a drink of water. Extend this time gradually.

- Teach the children how to work in pairs, sharing the work processes. Alternate between individual work and buddy work.

- Use high probability requests. This consists of asking the child to do something he is very likely to do, such as "Ethan, could you help me water the plant?" Once you've gained his compliance, you can then ask him to do the more challenging action such as putting his sheets on his cot (see for example Belfiore, Basile, & Lee, 2008; Jung, Sainato, & Davis, 2008; The IRIS Center for Training Enhancements, n.d.-b).

- Redirect the child when you notice her getting agitated by task demands. Be proactive. Before the child falls apart into a tantrum or other acting out, suggest she get a drink of water, help you with a task, or take a note to the teacher next door.

Use visual aids. Help the child to understand what behavior is expected by providing visual reminders.

- Take a photo of the child engaging in the proper behavior. Print it, glue it to a card and laminate it (such as sitting properly at circle, how to hang up a coat, how to stand when lining up). Remind the child to refer to the card before the inappropriate behavior is likely to happen.

- Post photos for the whole class showing appropriate ways to line up, put away items, hang up coats, wash hands, or sit at group time.

- Use visual markers for lining up, sitting on the carpet, and pathways to move around the room. Put footsteps or a solid line to show children where to line up for when they leave the room for other parts of the school. You can mark off specific areas on the line for each child to help maintain personal space. You can use mats with children's names on them to designate their personal space during group activities. If necessary, you can mark off an area of the block area to help the child stay more self-contained and focused.

Provide planned one-on-one interaction. Think about ways that you can make sure that the child can get adult or peer interaction in positive ways before the child uses challenging behavior. This is a difficult, but very effective strategy. Plan ways to give the child positive attention throughout the day so that the child will get all he or she needs. It's important that you plan for these interactions so that way the child will not be anxious that he or she won't have that time with you. The tricky part is that we are often angry or frustrated with children who have challenging behavior so it is hard to give positive attention. As always, reflect on your own emotions and see how you can keep a professional commitment to doing the best for children, even those who push your buttons.

Prevention examples. Here are some examples of how teachers have helped to prevent challenging behavior:

- Liam gets very agitated when he doesn't get to use the computer during free choice time. He pushes the child who is at the computer, screams, stamps his feet, and knocks things off the desk. His teacher has set up a chart of turns for the computer and the children place their name with their picture on it if they want a turn. There is also a timer at the computer to help children regulate their turn. At the beginning of free choice time, the teacher helps Liam put his name on the chart and help him count how many people until it is his turn. She then 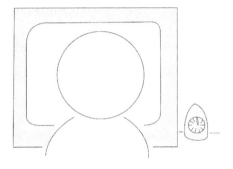 helps him to find another activity that engages his attention. She periodically reminds him that his turn will be soon.

- During clean-up time, four-year old Alexa typically sits down in the center of the group meeting carpet area, ignoring the request to put items away. When asked to help clean up, she rolls on the floor and screams. The functional assessment hypothesizes that she uses this non-compliant behavior to escape the demands of clean up time. Using High-P requests, the teacher asked her to come to the housekeeping area with her (her favorite area to play in), then asked her to pick up a cup on the floor and then to put the cup on the counter where it belongs. After she complied with these (which the teacher knew was likely), she then asked her to find the rest of the cups that match those and put them on the counter. In a sense, high-probability requests got the child jump-started and then she was more likely to continue the appropriate behavior.

- When the child is in a setting or situation that typically triggers the challenging behavior, you can step in ahead of time, using guiding statements to scaffold the child's interactions. For example, the teacher found that when Gabriella was heading over to the housekeeping area (a typical ante-cedent setting for aggressive behavior) she could scaffold her interactions by saying, "Gabriella, it looks like you want to play with the dress-up clothes. Jennifer, would you like to dress up, too? Let's figure out which outfits you will both use." This helps Gabriella get her needs met without her typical grabbing and pushing, and models social skills that she needs to learn.

Teaching New Skills to Replace Challenging Behavior

Many children use challenging behavior to get what they need because they don't have the skills to use more positive behavior. This is easily seen when young children grab a toy instead of asking for it, push a child rather than saying "please leave me alone" or knock down a block structure instead of entering the play theme. This can also happen when young children don't know how to seek attention in positive ways or how to express their strong emotions appropriately, such as sadness, fear, or anger.

Children who use challenging behavior often get less positive attention from other children and adults because we all tend to avoid people who are aggressive, annoying, extremely passive or violent. These are often children who are hard to connect to. Because they tend to get rejected or have few positive social interactions, they do not get as much opportunity to learn the social and emotional skills they need. If they also happen to have a more difficult time learning social skills in general, they can fall into a negative, downward cycle of inappropriate behavior.

What follows is a list and description of some of the most common skills that children will need to learn in order to replace their challenging behavior. These suggestions are similar to the skills discussed in Chapter 3, except you will need to teach them intensively and individually to the child. In order to give up grabbing, pushing, tantrums or back-talk, the child must get her needs met with the new skills more easily than with the previous challenging behavior.

Social Skills

- *How to get positive attention from the teacher.* The children we typically get along well with have learned ways to get our attention that are socially acceptable. They have learned social graces that other children have not. We can teach these strategies directly to children who need them. Mini-lessons with modeling and practice work well. Puppets can be a great way to show the strategies in action. Give plenty of positive feedback when a child first uses any of the examples.

- ***How to get positive attention from other children.*** This is especially important for the child who is being reinforced by other children's attention—typically the child who pushes, pokes, or grabs. Again, using modeling and practice, teach the child skills such as:

  How to say nice things to people

  How to join a group at play by adding to the play theme

  How to start a conversation

  How to ask for something instead of grabbing

  How to say "no" politely instead of pushing

- ***How to solve conflicts with others.*** Teach the child alternatives to using aggression. These might be walking away to take a break, getting a teacher to help, or using words to express emotions, such as "I don't like it when you say that!" or "Don't touch me. I don't like that!"

- ***How to ask for a break.*** Have a signal or teach the child what words to use to get a break. Allow the child a short break—getting a drink, standing and stretching, or sitting in the quiet corner for a few minutes. Remember that it is better to teach a child how to do this appropriately than to have them disturb others during group times, lunch, or nap. While they are learning to ask for a break, you can also work on helping them learn to stay involved in the activity for longer and longer periods of time.

- ***How to ask for help.*** During center time, teach the child a signal he can use to let you know he needs help, instead of yelling, calling out, or acting out in physical ways. Also teach the child how to get help from a peer.

Emotional Skills

- ***How to calm down and handle frustration.*** Life is inevitably frustrating, so learning how to handle these emotions is a critical skill. Teach the child how to use focused breathing to calm down. Have a "Quiet Spot" in your classroom that the child can use to get away from the group and compose herself. She might benefit from holding a favorite stuffed animal or blanket, or other attachment item to calm down. You can teach self-talk statements such as "I'm okay. I can calm myself down," Having a child watch the flecks settle in a snow globe can help her calm her breathing and body. The important point is that the child learns to eventually self-soothe rather than depend on an adult to help, but you will need to scaffold this a great deal until the child can learn to do it independently.

- ***How to control one's body.*** Games that require stopping movements like *Simon Says* and *Mother May I* are excellent for teaching self-control. Games in which children wait for a hand motion to speak, or wait until the music stops to give the answer are also helpful. Remind the child to look at his own body to see where he is in space. Many children are completely unaware of their bodies unless attention is brought to them. Designate a line or other marker that shows concretely where a child's personal space is during activities.

- ***How to stay focused during group activities.*** Teach the child how to track the speaker with her eyes, and what to do with her hands while she is listening. A fidget toy such as a squeeze ball, pipe cleaner, or play-doh can help with controlling the body during group times. Use a visual reminder, such as a photo of what the body should look like for the child to hold and refer to. Scripted stories about specific situations like circle time can help children learn what behaviors are expected.

- ***How to wait for a turn.*** Role-play and plenty of practice can help children learn to wait. Teach the child to use self-talk to distract himself with phrases such as, "I can wait. I don't need to have it right now," or "I can find something else to do while I wait." Have the child practice what she can do while waiting. Use visual reminders such as posting a name card to show who gets the next turn, or who will be called on next.

You might feel overwhelmed by this list, thinking, "How could I find the time to teach all those skills?" First, start with only one or two of the skills and engage an assistant teacher to help if you have one. Second, remember how much time you are currently spending focusing on the challenging behavior. Take this same amount of time each day to focus on teaching one of these skills and in a few weeks, you will see improvement!

How to Teach Replacement Skills

Teaching children new social and emotional skills requires some planning and commitment on your part. This doesn't work well unless you implement the following three steps:

1. Direct instruction through modeling, stories, puppets, videos, or other concrete ways to see the skills in action

2. Guided practice in which you coach the child while he practices using the new skills

3. Independent practice in which you "catch" the child using the new skills and provide positive feedback

Scripted Stories or Social Stories™. These small home-made books tell a story in the first person that models for the child the appropriate behaviors. Originally developed to be used with autistic children, research shows that these books can be very effective at helping children learn new skills (Gray, & Garand, J., 1993; Gray, 2000; Ivey, Heflin, & Alberto, 2004; Schneider & Goldstein, 2009). The story is written from the child's perspective and it includes various different kinds of sentences that provide descriptions, perspectives of others, and directives. The story should be written at the appropriate developmental and communication level for the target child.

You can write your own stories, or go to Carol Gray's website at www. thegraycenter.org where there is a wide variety of social stories, movies, and other information on social stories. The Center on the Social and Emotional Foundations of Early Learning also provides a similar version of teaching stories called Scripted Stories at http://www.vanderbilt.edu/csefel/resources/strategies.html. These can be adapted for individual children and specific social skill targets. For example, scripted stories could be written to help a child learn how to take turns, how to ask for help, what to do during circle time, how to line up, etc.

Here's a scripted story designed to help a child learn how to clean up

I Can Clean Up

I like to play during center time.

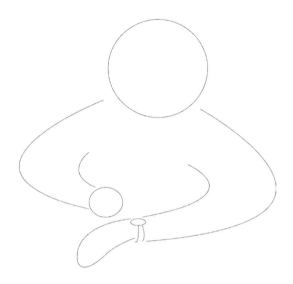

The teacher will tell us when
it's almost time to finish playing.

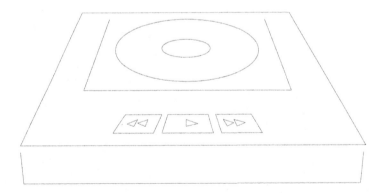

The teacher will play music to let us know it's time
to clean up. I don't like to stop playing, but I
will get to play again tomorrow.

When it's clean up time, I will pick up the things I've been playing with and put them on the shelf.

I can also help other children to clean up.

Once I've helped put some things away,
I can sit on the rug.

When everyone is done cleaning up,
we will have Circle Time.
I like Circle Time because we sing songs.
I can be a good helper at clean up time!

Least-to-most prompting. When teaching replacement skills, one form of guidance you can use is least-to-most prompting. This is a form of scaffolding in which you give the child the least amount of help and guidance he or she needs. If you see that the child needs more guidance in order to practice the target skill than you would provide it. For example, if you are teaching a second grader to use words rather than pushing or hitting when he is upset, the least amount of prompting might be a simple reminder, "words." If the child needs it, however, you could offer more specific suggestions, such as, "If you don't like that, tell him." Providing the least amount of prompting helps children to develop skills that they can use independently, without our help.

Providing positive feedback. When trying to establish replacement skills, it is critically important to provide positive feedback and attention when a child has used the new skills. This cannot be emphasized too much. When we are trying to help a child with challenging behavior, it is often easier to notice instances when the child does not behave appropriately. We need to train ourselves to be on the constant lookout for when the child is using his new skills so we can bring attention to this and help the child see his or her own growth and progress.

Changing Your Response to Challenging Behavior

We often reinforce the challenging behavior of children without realizing it. Look at the consequences for children's behavior and you will often see that they receive lots of attention and interaction from the teacher or the other children. There are two strategies to change this:

1. Respond in a way that makes the challenging behavior ineffective for the function it usually has.

2. Make sure the reinforcement for positive, alternative behaviors is better or more than the reinforcement for the challenging behavior.

These are easiest to explain through the following examples.

Nathan chooses the sand table each day then throws sand at any child who is there with him. The teacher rushes over, reprimanding him loudly and forcible takes his arm and leads him across the room. She continues to lecture him, face-to-face, leaning in close to him. Next she sends Nathan to play in a different area.

Nathan's teacher is reinforcing his behavior with her intense attention to it. In addition to using prevention strategies and teaching new skills, she needs to react differently—perhaps quickly and calmly sending Nathan to a different area without giving him much attention and giving him more attention when he is playing appropriately. Alternatively, she could go over to Nathan when he first starts working in the sand table, giving him plenty of attention, asking questions, discussing his work with the sand or other personal conversation before he throws the sand.

Latoya gets up out of her seat and runs to the door whenever the class starts group time. The teacher assistant catches her before she reaches the door, then Latoya throws herself on the floor, kicking her feet and yelling. Eventually the assistant takes her to the Director's office where she waits to meet with her. The director talks to her about staying in the classroom and sitting properly and brings her back to class once she's calmed down.

Clearly, Latoya is not only getting a lot of adult, one-on-one interaction, she is also escaping group time which she has trouble with. In addition to teaching her how to pay attention and sit still at group time, giving her choices, and providing visual reminders, the teachers also need to stop reinforcing the escape behavior through their reaction. When she tries to bolt from the room, the teacher can redirect her to the carpet to sit down. After she has stayed there for a 3-4 minutes, she can be allowed to go to quiet area for a short while and quietly look at books. The teachers should give her positive feedback for her success, and each day, extend the amount of time she needs to stay at group time before she can leave. I also recommend giving her plenty of one-on-one attention before group time to fulfill her need for adult social interaction. She should not be rewarded with a visit to the director's office since this is helping to reinforce the inappropriate behavior.

During calendar time Martin gets upset if he doesn't get a turn to put up the number for the day and lead the group in counting. He also has difficulty at other times during the day when he does not get to be the line leader, or to answer a question. He lies on the floor, yelling from his frustration, and slides his body around on the floor to comfort himself. Eventually, he ends up playing with toys on the other side of the carpet. Although

the teacher ignores him, the children pay plenty of attention to him, looking at him and talking to him. It creates chaos for the group activity.

In addition to providing more time for children to socialize during the morning, the teacher can also teach Martin better ways of getting the children's attention. She can also teach him how to deal with frustration and calm himself down. Finally, she can change her reaction and stop him from getting the children's attention by directing him to the quiet corner until he calms down. Alternatively, she can give Martin plenty of positive feedback when he manages to tolerate not having a turn.

The important strategy is to do something different than the way you typically react. If your prevention strategies and new skills are working well, you should have much less to react to. Above all, provide positive feedback constantly when the child is behaving appropriately. Children who have difficulty learning social and emotional behaviors need steady feedback in the beginning so that they know when they are doing things correctly and are meeting your expectations. Don't fall into the trap of assuming that they know they are doing well. Provide plenty of positive acknowledgements and you'll find a new, calmer environment is created.

Safety-net procedures. When children exhibit behaviors that are harmful to themselves or others it is necessary and appropriate to have a plan in place to maintain safety. This might involve holding the child gently but firmly or removing the child from the situation. Safety must always be our first priority, however, safety-net procedures are only one part of the behavioral support plan. They will not in and of themselves teach new behaviors or change the child's behavior.

Staying Calm

Perhaps the most important aspect of your response is your demeanor and tone of voice. Strive to stay calm, no matter what! First, you are a role model, and you have an opportunity to model mature emotional responses. This is a teachable moment. Second, you want to avoid adding negative energy to a tense situation. By adding negativity, you can easily push a child who is agitated into a full blown melt-down or aggressive response.

It can help to remember that this outburst is not about you. It is about a child not having the coping skills to handle her challenges. Do not take it personally. Think of yourself as a firefighter. There's no point in getting angry at the fire—you need to put it out as quickly as you can to minimize damage. You can't do this well if you are as agitated as the child. Also remember that children cannot learn new behaviors or concepts when their body is flooded with the flight-or-fight hormones. There's nothing to be gained in lecturing or trying to teach new skills until the child has calmed down.

Practice breathing techniques and body relaxation on a regular basis so you are prepared when you need to stay calm.

Putting it All Together

Once you have identified a hypothesis, prevention strategies, the replacement skills strategies, and new responses to challenging behavior, you and your team are ready to put the support plan together. Of course it is important to remember that when making the plan one of the most important aspects is practicality. We could all come up with wonderful plans, but we need to think through carefully who will do what steps and how we will manage the plan throughout the day. In summary, these are the Positive Behavior Support Plan elements:

- *Prevention Strategies:* What you will change so that the behavior doesn't occur.

- *Replacement Skills:* What skills does the child need to learn so that he/she doesn't need the challenging behavior. What strategies will you use to teach these replacement skills?

- *Change in Responses:* How will adults respond to the inappropriate behavior when it occurs that is different from how they have been responding which has been helping to maintain the behavior?

- *Evaluation plan:* Gathering data to determine if PBS is working.

Case Study: Aiden

Let's turn back to Aiden, whose behavior is described at the beginning of this chapter. The teachers and Aiden's Positive Behavior Support team developed an hypothesis and support plan for her, described below:

Hypothesis. During clean up time Aiden screams, pushes children, and hides in his cubby. During group time he pokes children, rolls on the floor, and makes sounds. In both settings, the teachers speak to him about his behavior, and often let him escape the activities he doesn't like. The function of the behavior is avoiding clean up time or group time, and receiving one-on-one attention from him teachers.

Positive behavior support plan. One strategy for helping to prevent serious behaviors from occurring is to intervene early in the acting out cycle because at that point, there is a greater chance of keeping the behavior from accelerating. With these thoughts in mind, the teachers discussed strategies that they felt would appropriately address the needs of this student. This plan includes prevention strategies, replacement skills, and changes in how adults respond to the student's inappropriate and challenging behaviors.

Prevention Strategies

- *Preparing for transitions.* Aiden will get extra warnings about finishing his work during center time. The teachers will give him a special job to do during clean up time, such as water the plants or put books away, which is away from the busy, noisy areas of the classroom. They will help Aiden get started with his special job before starting the music for clean up time. Once he has done this job he will be able to sit in his cubby until group time.

- *Changes to the physical environment.* The teachers will use carpet squares during group time so that Aiden will see clearly the space that is his.

- *One-on-one time.* The teachers will ensure that Aiden receives one-on-one time each day. This time will help meet Aiden's needs for adult social interaction. The teachers will ensure that during center time everyday one of them interacts for a sustained period of time with Aiden.

- *Fidget toys.* During group time, Aiden will hold onto a squeezable plastic toy in order to help him stay focused and keep his body calm.

- *Increase small-group instruction.* The teachers will be better able to help Aiden to focus and stay on task in a small group setting as opposed to a whole-group setting. Small group will allow for more student-teacher interaction which will help Aiden learn to focus and stay engaged in the activity.

Replacement Skills

- *Appropriate ways to receive attention.* The teachers will model appropriate ways for Aiden to receive attention without resorting to inappropriate behaviors. Aiden will be taught how to ask the teachers to read him a book, give him a hug, how to show the teachers what he has created, or to ask for help with an activity. This will be done daily for two weeks, and then reinforced and supported with reminders afterwards.

- *Self-regulation.* The teachers will help Aiden practice how to sit and look at the teacher during group time. They will show him what his personal space is and how to keep his body within the space, and how to use the fidget toy to keep himself focused. This practice will be done during center time on a one-on-one basis. They will also teach him how the timer will work during group time and how he can take a break once he has tried sitting still for short periods of time.

- *Calming down.* The teachers will bring Aiden to the Quiet Corner and show him how to relax. He will pick out a pillow or stuffed animal that will be his calming object and the teacher will show him how to use breathing to calm down. He will be reminded when he needs to spend a few minutes in the Quiet Corner.

Changes in Adult Responses to the Inappropriate Behavior

• The teachers will observe Aiden carefully to watch for early stages of agitation. They will redirect him at that point.

• If Aiden begins to scream or push children, the teacher will gently direct him to the Quiet Corner, tell him to calm down and walk away, giving him as little attention as possible. If he goes to his cubby, he will be ignored, and the next day, the teacher will try to intervene earlier, before Aiden is likely to escape to the cubby. He will be allowed to go to the cubby after he has done his clean up job.

• The teachers will provide positive feedback to Aiden immediately when she is exhibiting the new skills and responses.

Below is a form that you can use to practice functional analysis and positive behavior support planning.

Positive Behavior Support Planning Chart

Antecedent/Trigger	Challenging Behavior	Maintaining Consequences
Function:		

Prevention	New Skills	New Responses
		To inappropriate Behavior: To new skills:

ℰℬ ℰℬ ℰℬ

Chapter 9: Solving Common Behavior Challenges

Marlene had just completed her first year of teaching preschool. She had been an assistant teacher for a few years, so the transition was smooth for her. She felt that the basics of her classroom management were going well, although there were still some behaviors that puzzled her and created bumps in the smooth running of her classroom. She had a group of girls who teased each other frequently, and a little boy who loved using curse words that he learned from his older siblings. She also wondered about Chloe who was biting her nails all year, and Joey who wouldn't fall asleep at nap time. Marlene hoped she could get some ideas to help children with these common problems next year.

There is a wide range of challenges that teachers typically face on a repeated basis. This chapter offers some solutions that put together principles and advice from various parts of the book. In this way, you can see some examples of how you'd apply multiple aspects of guidance and classroom management to everyday problems.

Social Issues

Many of the common challenges in the classroom stem from the social community. Young children are still learning how to function in a group and are learning how to take other's perspectives, control their impulses, and put the needs of the group ahead of their own.

Name Calling/Teasing

If you find the children are calling each other names in hurtful ways, you can think of working on this problem on two levels: with the classroom as a whole, and with specific children. The first level is the classroom climate, which needs to be more caring, positive and accepting of others. This can be done by building cohesion in the group. Think of ways to help the children feel that they belong—perhaps by creating a class mascot, name, theme song, a secret handshake, getting-to-know-you activities, and celebrating being together as a group. You must make it clear that name calling or other forms of bullying are not tolerated and intervene immediately when it occurs. Be firm and gentle in your insistence and remind the children about the goal of creating a safe and accepting environment for everyone. You can bring up this topic at class meetings to get children's input on how they can help create this climate. A list of kind things to say might be posted on the wall, and at group times the children can add to the list or practice saying helpful or kind words.

You will also want to work with individual children who need extra support in developing social skills. Depending on the age of the children, this might be focused on how to make friends, how to join in play, how to say "no" kindly, or how others feel in reaction to unkind behaviors. Model these skills, perhaps using role play, puppets or scripted stories and then support the children by reminding them when to use these skills in everyday interactions. Be sure to provide positive attention and feedback to children when you observe them saying kind words. And of course, model kind behavior yourself. If you are sarcastic or react with anger and frustration, children will quickly learn that those behaviors are acceptable.

Summary:

• Create a positive classroom climate through group-building activities

• Have a no-tolerance policy for making fun of others

• Intervene when name-calling occurs

• Bring up name calling at group meetings and ask for solutions

• Teach children kind words and give positive feedback when children use them

• Model social skills training through role play, puppets, and scripted stories

• See Chapter 3 for social skills learning; Chapter 2 for building community

Swear Words/ Curses/ Bathroom Talk

Children learn at an early age that certain words are very powerful and get a huge reaction from adults. I have found that children use swear words in two different ways. The first is to get attention—either from peers or adults. The second use is by children who hear swear words in their environment and use them naturally as part of their general vocabulary. They might not even realize they are using anything inappropriate until they get a reaction.

The first step is to stay calm and not overreact emotionally. Children are not bad or come from terrible homes because they use words that might offend you. They are exploring their world and trying to figure out how things work, including the use of language. The next step is to let the child know in a matter-of-fact way that that word (or words) is not appropriate for school. Don't overdo the attention. If other children have brought it to your attention, tell them you'll take care of it and talk to the child privately.

If the child used the word in anger, then move on to helping her express her anger in other ways, including having a couple of words she can use instead. Model using these new words and have her practice. Remind her throughout the day, if necessary. If the child used the words to get attention from other children in a silly way, then you can try a similar approach in teaching him how to get attention in better ways. This might include making funny faces or drawing a funny picture. At the same time, you'll want to assess whether the child would benefit from other social skills development.

Often children use bathroom talk or other inappropriate words as a way of getting social interaction started. If children use inappropriate sexual references, you'll want to make it clear that such talk is not appropriate and look deeper into the behavior. Is this a pattern? Are there other instances of sexual play or references that are inappropriate? You may need to speak with a family member if you feel the situation is not the typical one in which children test out new-found phrases just to get a reaction. When children have difficulty regulating their own use of inappropriate words, you might put them in charge of monitoring the rest of the children. It is easier for children to learn to regulate others before they can regulate their own behavior (Bodrova & Leong, 2007). As always, when children use more appropriate behaviors or words, be sure to acknowledge the effort.

Summary:

- Stay calm and don't overact or give the speaker too much attention

- Teach children alternative words to use to get attention or to express anger

- Look more deeply into the circumstances of children who use sexual references to rule out abuse

- See Chapter 3 for teaching social and emotional skills

Tattling

Children tattle on each other when they are used to an environment in which children are punished for misbehaviors. The first step in reducing tattling is to create an environment in which children feel psychologically safe. This means it's clear that they won't be humiliated, put down, or embarrassed—especially by the teacher. Once you've created this environment, children will realize there's no point in tattling. But children will often enter your classroom without this understanding and may have come from a very punitive environment. In that case, there are some steps that will help you turn things around.

First, determine whether the complaints are valid and important or not. Perhaps there are misbehaviors occuring that you are not aware of. If however, the tattling is about trivial things, think hard about why the child is tattling and what they get out of it. Usually it is adult interaction and attention. So instead of giving much attention to this, be sure that you are spending some concerted effort on building a relationship with the child or children who are tattling. Give them your attention in positive ways: talk about their weekend, what they like to do, what their favorite foods are. Sit down and read to them one on one, or work with them side by side on an art project or writing assignment. Children who tattle can be annoying and it's somewhat natural to want to avoid them. Resist this urge! Instead give the child plenty of attention in ways that promote positive interactions.

In order to avoid giving the tattling itself much attention, you can encourage the children to write down their complaint on a piece of paper, or tell it to a stuffed animal that you've designated for this purpose rather than discuss it with you right then. If the tattling continues for more than a week or two, however, you need to assess how well you are building a positive community in your classroom. Check how often you say positive things to the children (compared to negative things such as reminding them not to do something) and be sure you are not using a punitive approach to problem behavior.

Finally, be sure that you have taught the children what an emergency situation is and when they should report unsafe behavior, even if it would be interrupting you.

Summary:

- Focus on creating a positive environment in which children are not punished

- Reduce the amount of immediate attention you give to the tattler

- Provide more positive attention and relationship-building with the tattler

- Ask child to write down complaint or tell it to a stuffed animal

- Teach children what an emergency situation is and what unsafe behavior they should report to you

- See Chapter 2 for building relationships with children

Talking Back

I've found that there is not one definition of what it means to say that a child is "talking back." To a large degree this depends on our cultural background and what we were taught about responding to adults. For people raised in families in which quiet obedience to adults was expected and demanded, it can seem very disrespectful when a child responds negatively to your request. However, in many cultures, children are taught to challenge what adults say, questioning their logic. In some families the expectation is that children deserve to have an explanation for why something has been requested. So my first suggestion is to take a deep breath and think through a professional response rather than reacting emotionally.

Children can sometimes talk back because they are feeling shame and anger. So when a child talks back, your first response (after taking a deep breath) is to reflect back the child's emotion: "I can tell you're very angry with me right now." At the same time, you can make it clear that certain behavior, such as using inappropriate language or physical aggression, is unacceptable. This is a teachable moment for all the children in your class; feelings are acceptable, but certain behaviors are not. The next step is to help the child regain his or her composure. Try to figure out where the child is in the acting-out cycle. If this is just agitation, you might be able to redirect the child and calm him by acknlwedging his emotions. If the child, however, is in the acceleration phase, he might need a few minutes in the Quiet Corner or help in practice some calming breaths. The important thing is *not* to argue back. This will just escalate the child's emotional response into the peak phase in which the child is out of control. Staying positive and keeping your own emotions calm is the key to a professional response.

Summary:

- Keep yourself calm with a deep breath or two

- Remember that talking back has various meanings in different cultures

- Acknowledge the child's emotions while setting limits on his behavior

- Stay positive to keep the child from escalating in the acting out cycle

- See Chapter 7 for the Acting-Out Cycle; Chapter 6 for Positive Time-Out; Chapter 3 for Teaching Children to Calm Down

Biting

An appropriate response to biting is highly dependent on the age of the child. Two-year olds and toddlers often bite as a way of exploring their world. They get sensory stimulation from using their mouth and it takes a while until they learn that some things can be bitten (such as certain toys designed for teething, or cookies and bagels) and some things can not be bitten (such as pets and other children or adults). In this situation, your job is to teach the child what can be bitten or not.

In other cases, however, children bite in order to communicate anger, when they get over-excited and lose impulse control, or to get attention. Because biting cannot be ignored, children learn quickly that they get a powerful reaction from doing it. It also feels good in sensory terms which makes this behavior a tricky one to change. A plan for helping a child to stop biting needs to be individualized based on what they get out of it. Be sure to read through Chapters 7 and 8 for carrying out a functional anlysis and behavior support plan. In a nutshell, it will important to teach the child more appropriate behaviors to get what he or she needs. For example, if the child is getting lots of adult and children's attention for biting, you can work on helping the child get attention in more appropriate ways and to give the child as little attention as possible when the biting occurs, focusing more on the victim. If the child is biting in anger, you can work on teaching him verbal skills and phrases to use to express anger (see Chapter 3). If the child is over excited and loses control, you can work on recognizing the triggers of this behavior and redirecting the child, while also teaching more self-control and calming skills.

Biting is an emotional topic and teachers as well as parents can get very upset about protecting chilren, spreading disease, etc. It is extremely important to stay calm and realize this is just another kind of learned behavior that can be changed through a thoughtful teaching approach. Punishment is not going to work. Form a team with the parents and other teachers to have a unified approach.

Summary:
- Consider the age and developmental level of the child and determine what he or she gets out of biting - exploration, attention, release of anger?
- Teach the child more appropriate behaviors to get his or her needs met
- Focus on calming skills, verbal request skills, expressing feelings
- Stay calm and be thoughtful rather than quickly punishing the child
- See Chapter 3 for teaching social and emotional skills; Chapter 7 and 8 for creating a positive behavior support plan.

Lying

First, it's important to examine your own emotional reaction to lying. Many teachers are particularly offended by lying and see it as a moral failing, usually because of the messages they were given throughout their own childhood. However, children lie primarily to protect themselves. Remember that children have a rudimentary understanding of what's right and wrong that is usually based on whether they get into trouble or not. It is our job to help them grow in understanding why lying might not be the best choice. Another thing to remember about young children is that their imaginative worlds and actions can seem very real to them. Many times when children are "lying," they are really using wishful thinking, which is a normal aspect of their developmental stage.

When it is clear that children are lying or creating their own truth, don't criticize and challenge them. Above all, don't argue. Consider this a very important teaching moment—not a time for punishment. If they are trying not to get into trouble for something they did wrong, then the best course of action is to help them make amends and fix the problem. If a child has pushed someone, for example, help her make that child feel better. If the child said they did something (like homework) when they didn't, then help him to make up the work. The next step is to help the child understand that lying is wrong because it breaks our trust. When we care about people, we trust them and when we lie, it hurts the people we care about.

If you find children lying frequently, carefully consider whether the climate in your classroom revolves too much around children getting into trouble. Children won't need to lie as much when they are accepted, cared about, and taught the social skills they need. Focus on creating a classroom where children care about each other and feel cared for. Lying is a wonderful topic for group meetings so children can explore their feelings and experiences, and you can offer a mature point of view in a calm setting.

Summary:

- Examine your own emotional reactions to lying and try to stay objective

- Remember that children lie to protect themselves

- Consider this a teachable moment and help the child make amends for lying or for whatever they were lying about

- Emphasize the importance of trust in relationships and model trust

- Discuss lying at a group meeting

- See Chapter 6 for sections on Guilt and Shame and other guidance techniques

Stealing

There are many reasons why children might steal, so the first step is to try to identify why. Once again, try to set aside any strong personal emotions about stealing. Young children do not steal because they are bad, but rather because they don't have the skills they need or the ability (yet) to make good choices. Always consider what you can be teaching the child when problem behaviors occur.

A child might steal because he wants something very badly and cannot resist the temptation to take it. Preschoolers may have very little impulse control. As we know, adults often have trouble with this too! There are two approaches that can help. The first is to help the child understand the social ramifications of stealing—that it hurts other people. Developmentally, children do not easily consider what others are feeling and need scaffolding to understand this. Also, some children might live in an environment in which adults or older children that they care about steal. It's important to emphasize that in your classroom, children are part of a community that cares about each other. Remind children of how important the rule is to not hurt each other, and that stealing hurts people.

The second approach is to help children develop impulse control so that when they are in the position to want something badly, they have the skills to resist. For example, you can teach children self-talk such as "I really want that, but it's not mine. I need to find something else to do." Children can role play being in such a situation and practice using the self-talk statements. You might want to help the children create a scripted story about resisting stealing because it hurts other people. You can put this together into a booklet and read it at group times and have it available for children to read on their own.

Summary:

- Examine your own emotional reaction to stealing

- Identify why the child is stealing

- Help child understand that stealing hurts others

- Help children to build impulse control skills using self-talk and scripted stories

- See Chapter 8 for scripted stories and other ideas for challenging behaviors

Damaging Property

Children will occasionally break or damage materials because of carelessness or lack of motor coordination. When that happens, the best route to take is to help the child make amends. That might mean having the child help to repair a torn page or cleaning up a broken flower pot. You can show your disappointment in the damage done, but keep this in perspective and be sure the child understands that while his behavior was inappropriate, he is still cared about. Be aware that young children might not understand cause and effect they way you and I do, so they will try to do things with materials that are damaging without being able to predict that the damage would occur. As much as possible, try to predict where children might need direct instruction in how to use materials. For example, many young children will tear pages in a book because they have not been shown how to do it in a gentle way. Likewise, children need instruction in how to carry things carefully, or how (and on what) to use scissors safely.

When children repeatedly damage materials, you need to consider more of an intervention. If the problem is not severe, you can try applying consequences such as not allowing the child to use the materials for a period of time, reminding her of proper use, and then giving her another try to use them properly the next day or later in time. If the problem is more severe, it makes sense to do a functional analysis. The first step is to determine what is going on in more depth. What triggers the behavior? When does it occur? Is the child angry? Is she trying to get a reaction from you or others? Is he impulsive and not aware of what he's doing until it's too late? What function does the behavior serve for the child? These different scenarios will need different approaches and you can formulate a positive behavior support plan to help the child learn new behaviors.

Summary:

- Teach children how to use materials properly

- When children damage property, have them make amends

- When children repeat damaging behaviors, use consequences such as deprivation, exclusion, or restitution

- If the problem becomes severe, complete a functional analysis and create a positive behavior support plan

- See Chapter 6 for applying consequences; Chapter 7 and 8 for functional analysis and positive behavior support plans

Fighting

Fighting can range from an occasional altercation to persistent aggressive behavior and there is a not a simple solution. If you have a child who is regularly fighting, you'll want to consider completing a functional analysis of the behavior and develop a positive behavioral support plan that will help prevent the fighting from happening, teach the child needed social and emotional skills, and change the adult reactions to the behavior. For aggression that happens sporadically, it's important to understand the acting out cycle. The most important strategy is to help calm children down when they are in the agitation phase and prevent the behavior from accelerating. Once a child is out of control, you can do nothing but maintain safety. However, if you can intervene early on, when the child shows the first signs of agitation, you can help support the child in developing better social and emotional skills.

In general, children who are fighting do so because they get what they want (toys, materials, attention) better with fighting than they can with other skills. So a long-range solution is to systematically teach children social skills throughout the day and throughout the year. Although this takes time away from other academic activities, in the long run it will improve the learning of all the children in your room. If you have a lot of aggression, also review your daily schedule and format of your activities to be sure that you are meeting children's basic needs. Are things too rushed? Are the children sitting for too long? Do they have ample time for social activities? Are the children frustrated by the academic demands? Also consider ways you can reduce stress in the whole classroom, such as having a few moments of breathing exercises when the children come back from lunch or outside play, or having five minutes of yoga before moving to center work. Check to see if the noise level in the room can be lowered, and make sure you have a quiet corner that children know they can use whenever they need to take a break.

Summary:

- Children who are frequently aggressive will need direct intervention through functional analysis and positive behavior support—See Chapter 7 and 8

- Teach children social skills as direct lessons and through teachable moments throughout the day

- Reduce the stress level in the classroom by reviewing your schedule and types of activities

- Use relaxation exercises and have a quiet corner in the classroom

- See Chapter 3 for social emotional learning strategies

Rejecting/Rejected Children

When children are rejected, the whole class suffers because the other children realize they are unsafe and could be rejected, too. This breeds a hierarchy in which children struggle to be on top of others. This situation does not have to happen if you make it a priority for everyone to be accepted and included. Of course this is not as easy as it sounds. Focus on building positive group spirit, and talk with the children during group meetings about rejection. Solicit their ideas for what can be done so no one feels left out. Make your feelings clear that you want a classroom in which everyone is kind. You might want to read Vivian Paley's book, *You Can't Say You Can't Play* in which she established this rule in her kindergarten classroom (Paley, 1993). You can share the ideas in this book with the children in your class and see how they react. Would they like to have a similar rule?

Another important step is to work with the child or children who are being rejected. Also refer to the section on teasing and name calling in this chapter and work with those children, too. Many children will benefit from some direct instruction in social skills such as making friends, asking to join in, listening to others and carrying on conversations, and taking initiative. If the child is being rejected because of aggressive, bullying acts, then more skill instruction will be needed in how to say kind things, how to help others, and how to control anger or impulses. Having children work in pairs will provide practice with these social skills and help them get to know each other in a more structured way. You might want to encourage parents to invite another child over for a play date to help the child get social skills practice in a different setting.

When you observe children using rejecting behaviors such as telling children they can't join in, or you see children left alone to work or play, use these opportunities as teachable moments to point out to children that what they've done is unkind, or that they are leaving others out. For the rejected child, this is a good time to scaffold the use of the newly developing social skills.

Summary:

- Focus on creating a climate in which children rejecting each other is not accepted

- Come up with a plan for not rejecting others during class meetings

- Teach withdrawn children how to make friends, and initiate and join social situations

- Teach aggressive children how to use kind words, help others, and control emotions

- Pair children up for activities to help them practice skills and get to know each other better

- Suggest that parents arrange play dates or provide other social opportunities for the child

- See Chapter 3 for social skills development

Apology-in-Action

Should we force children to apologize? This is a tough question, and I think the answer lies in what we are teaching children when we make this decision. If we insist that a child apologizes, even if she is not at all sorry for her actions, we run into a problem. Children learn that we should say "I'm sorry" even when we don't mean it or when we don't know what we did wrong. It becomes a hollow action that can make the child more resentful.

Young children have a hard time understanding the effects of their actions on other people, so it's better to offer a more concrete solution. Instead of saying some empty words, encourage the child to make amends instead. Think of this as an apology-in-action. First, the child will need some time to calm down so she can process information. Next, review with the child what she did that was hurtful and why. Help the child to understand how the other person is feeling right now. Next encourage her to think of ways she can make that person feel better. At the bare minimum, a child should give back something they grabbed or took, but beyond that, encourage her to think of a way to make the other child (or adult) feel better as well. Here are some ideas:

- If the child hurt someone—give a hug, or make a picture, or say something nice about the person who was hurt

- If the child broke something—help to fix it

- If the child made a mess of something—help to clean it up

- If a block-building was knocked down—help to rebuild it

Of course, a child can also choose to say, "I'm sorry." But this should be a choice that is not coerced. Try to have the child generate some ideas and you can add a couple of choices, too. When a child has made a choice and has carried out an effective apology-in-action, be sure to offer plenty of positive feedback. As time goes by, children will get used to this idea and with enough practice, they will not need as much guidance. Remember that the ultimate goal is to develop a classroom in which the children care about each other and feel that they are cared for too, so the goal should be on repairing relationships, rather than an insincere, mumbled apology.

Summary:

- Focus on having the child make amends for what she did, rather than a verbal apology

- Encourage the child to think of ways to make the other child feel better

- See Chapter 3 for teaching social skills as needed

Instructional Issues

Some behavioral challenges are related to classroom activities and lessons. Many children, especially those with poor impulse control, can easily get off task or find ways to avoid appropriate activities.

Paying Attention at Group Time/Circle Time

A common challenge for new teachers is trying to keep a whole group of young children engaged during circle time or other group times on the carpet. This is challenging because young children have a high need to move around and they are just learning how to control their bodies and their attention. Because of their temperament, learning experiences, and age, some children can do this better than others. First, keep your expectations appropriate for the developmental level of the children. There is not a set amount of time that children can sit and pay attention based on their age, because their focus will depend greatly on what the activity is and their interest and understanding. Instead, learn to pay careful attention to children's body language. When many children are beginning to wiggle and fidget, you need to wrap up or move on to a different activity.

There are specific techniques that you can use to help children be successful in paying attention. Make sure that the physical environment of your meeting area is large enough so the children don't have to touch each other. I prefer to have the children in a circle around the edge rather than bunched into the middle so that children can see clearly and not be in front of each other. Carpet squares can be used to help define the child's personal space. Next, teach children what behaviors you want them to use. You can have them practice how to sit, where their bodies should be, and what it looks like to pay attention.

You can also help children stay engaged and focused by using plenty of interactive activities in which they can answer, move or participate in some way. Sometimes when I observe teachers I find it hard to pay attention because the lesson itself it not engaging. Be sure to keep the pacing of the lesson quick enough to move things along without being so fast that you lose the children. This takes practice, of course. When you notice a child losing attention, try to engage him by calling on him to participate, or moving close to him. Do not stop your lesson to ask for children's attention. By the time you do this, you've broken the pace of the activity and you'll likely lose the attention of other children. Instead, remember to give positive attention to children when they are focused and acknowledge when children are participating well—especially those children for whom staying on task is a challenge.

Summary:

- Have appropriate expectations for how long children can pay attention

- Watch children's body language for signs that you need to move on to a different activity

- Keep your group activities engaging with opportunities for active involvement

- Be sure your meeting area is large enough

- Sit children in a circle with enough room so they don't touch each other

- Keep the pace of the lesson going when redirecting children

- Teach appropriate behaviors and acknowledge when children use them

- See Chapter 1 for teaching procedures; Chapter 4 for keeping children engaged

Clean Up Time

It seems that there is at least one child in every classroom that has difficulty with clean up time. A child will go hide in her cubby, another might continue playing with the materials, and yet another might start to throw things around instead of putting them away. Before you begin any kind of individual intervention, make sure that your clean-up time routines are well planned. First, keep the atmosphere pleasant and game-like. Do not yell at the children to get going, or work harder, or chastise them for not getting much done. Keep your expectations realistic. Often children cannot reasonably put everything away in the time you've planned for this transition. Some children will be able to easily sort the dishes into the cabinet, while others might only be able to pick a few things up off the floor. Be sure to give positive feedback to children who are putting things away well and meeting your expectations. This is a good time to monitor how many positive comments you are giving compared to how many negative.

After a couple of warnings that choice time is almost over, some teachers play music or have a "clean-up time" song to cue children. It can be helpful to assign children to specific jobs. "Jacob, could you put all the square blocks on the shelf?" "Paola, would you hang up all the dresses?" Sometimes children like to be the "boss" of that particular job. Check your classroom environment to make sure it is easy to put things away. Are the shelves labeled with where everything belongs? Can the children easily reach the shelves? I have seen classrooms where there were so many materials available, I was overwhelmed myself at clean up time.

Finally, once you've tried improving your clean up time routine in general, you can look more closely at the children who are having trouble. I've seen some children overwhelmed by the noise and activity level in the classroom—especially in the block and housekeeping areas. You could offer that child a job in a farther corner of the room. Some children don't know where to start and need some direct guidance in what to put away. Other children have difficulty transitioning from one activity to another and might need more individual attention to get them ready for the transition. You could start 5 or 10 minutes ahead of time to get the child prepared, perhaps pointing out the pictures of the daily schedule, or giving the child her own copy on small cards. In the end, I think the important thing is that all children help in some way, although the child's contribution could be adapted to meet her own needs and doesn't have to look like all the other children's work.

Another strategy is to turn to the class for their suggestions to make clean up time fair and effective. At a class meeting, explain the problem and see what solutions the children can generate and which ones they think are worth trying.

Summary:

- Be sure your clean-up time routine is well planned by preparing the children ahead of time, being clear in teaching them how to put things away, and being reasonable in your expectations

- Offer children who are overwhelmed the opportunity to clean up something in a quiet area of the classroom

- Help prepare individual children who need more time for transitions

- Prepare the physical environment to ensure shelves are labeled and easily accessible to the children

- See Chapter 1 for planning routines and transitions; Chapter 6 for guidance strategies

Passing Out Materials

Ms. Davison has just passed out musical instruments to her class. Some of the children are banging away, others are grabbing their neighbor's instrument, and a few children are whining that they want something else. In Ms. Karen's room, she explains to the children that they will be using the instruments today and if they don't get the instrument they want, they can use them during center time later in the week. Each day she puts out two or three instruments in the music corner so the children can experiment without a great deal of noise. As she passes out the instruments the children all chant: "You get what you get, and you don't get upset." The children calmly start to try out their instrument.

The difference between these classrooms is preparation. Children need to know what to expect and be prepared for what the procedures are for that particular activity. During your weekly or daily planning, think through how you will pass out materials. Not only will you need to prepare the children, but you'll need to prepare yourself. You don't want to spend a lot of time passing out materials or the children will become restless, and you'll also lose out on instructional time.

There are a few options that seem to work well with young children in passing out materials. First, you can pass them out yourself if you can do it quickly. Be sure that the children know what to do with the materials once they have them. Should they sit quietly? Use this very sparingly because it's difficult to do and wastes learning time. Can they begin using them? How do they use them? You'll want to review the procedures first. Another option is to have the materials in one place and guide the children to go individually or in small groups to get them. Let's say you have the writing journals in a box on the side of the room. Once you've explained the activity, two or three children could go at a time to get their journals, then sit down and begin working. The third option is to have a few children help you pass out the materials. This makes the job go more quickly and gives children the added benefit of taking responsibility in the classroom. The challenge is to make sure that the helpers have also had instruction in how to pass out the materials.

The bottom line is preparation. Have the materials ready. Be sure the children know the procedures for getting the materials (choice or no choice) and what to do with them once they get them. The more you keep children waiting, the more likely it is you will have behavior problems. Finally, have yourself prepared. Know what the next step is that you want the children to do, especially if you are leading a group activity.

Summary:

- Prepare the children ahead of time for whether they will get a choice of materials or not

- Have the materials ready, and explain and model the procedures before passing out materials

- Choose a method for passing out materials: you pass them all out, children go and get their materials, or other children become helpers to assist you

- Think through all of your procedures before getting started

- See Chapter 1 for teaching procedures and managing transitions

Physical Issues

Individual children can often have challenging issues related to their understanding of social rules and norms, and their self-control. It helps to keep in mind that children with inappropriate behaviors have not yet learned the skills they need to act in more acceptable ways. Always keep in mind the child's developmental age in deciding whether or not there is even a problem.

Thumb Sucking/Pacifiers

Children naturally suck their thumbs—often from the time they have enough coordination to get their thumb to their mouth. This is a human reflex that babies learn to associate with the pleasure and calming of being fed and held. It is no wonder it is such a powerful habit that often continues through childhood. Some children have learned to use a pacifier in the same way. It is a cultural choice that a particular society makes as to when a child should stop this behavior. For some families, thumb-sucking is encouraged and it is not considered a problem for older children to still suck their thumbs. In other cultures and families, children are expected to stop such behavior as a toddler. It might be helpful for you to examine your own beliefs about thumb-sucking and where and when you learned them.

Depending on the age of the child, you might decide that the thumb-sucking is helpful to calm the child and does not interfere with learning. For example, many of us would accept a preschool child sucking his thumb at naptime, or even a first-grader quietly sucking her thumb during a movie. At the same time we might feel that thumb-sucking during regular classroom activities interferes with the learning opportunities. It might also be helpful to have a discussion with family members to see how they feel about it.

If you eventually decide that you'd like to help the child reduce this behavior, you can use the same techniques that help break any habit. This means helping the child find other ways to self-soothe and make different habits. Because thumb-sucking is so sensory, a cuddly blanket or cloth can be a logical choice. Gradually have the child include the cloth whenever she might suck her thumb or use a pacifier, then gradually encourage the child to stop the thumb-sucking (or pacifier) and use the cloth instead. Do not make demands, because the fear of having to give up the habit will cause more stress and the child will need the thumb-sucking more. You can also teach the child other relaxation exercises such as breathing or self-talk. Remedies such as bitter ointments or gloves generally do not work because they cause more stress and don't offer the child a replacement for the soothing they achieved from thumb-sucking.

Summary:

- Decide whether thumb-sucking is really a problem or not—many children stop the behavior on their own when they get older

- Choose a replacement behavior for the thumb-sucking, such as soothing cloth or blanket

- Gradually replace the thumb-sucking with the other behavior

- Teach the child self-soothing techniques

- Don't focus much attention on the behavior because it will increase stress

- See Chapter 3 for relaxation exercises and other emotional skills

Nail Biting/Hair Twirling/Biting Lips, etc.

Nail biting and other behaviors like it are typically a habitual reaction to stress and anxiety. Because they can hurt the child physically, it's usually important to help the child stop these behaviors. This can be done in similar ways to thumbsucking described previously. The important thing to focus on is reducing stress and helping children cope with feeling anxiety. Help children recognize and label their feelings. At the same time, teach them relaxation techniques to use instead of the nail biting. Just like thumb-sucking, it is not advisable to use bitter lotions or gloves or other drastic measures. These greatly increase the child's anxiety which is, of course, counterproductive. Try to convince the child that you are on the same team and you will support him in learning how to calm down in better ways.

Summary

- Help child learn to label and recognize their anxious feelings

- Teach relaxation techniques

- Avoid harsh remedies that increase child's stress

- See Chapter 3 for relaxation exercises and other emotional skills

Nose Picking

Children will do a variety of things that we might consider disgusting. First, remember that children naturally explore their own bodies and their nose seems to be particularly interesting at times! You can help children understand that when they touch their nose, especially the inside, it makes other people uncomfortable and it spreads germs. Don't assume they know this. Even with this knowledge, children will need reminders. This can be done by offering a child a tissue, or a quick non-verbal signal to stop. Do not shame the child by saying things like "that's disgusting" or draw much attention to it. You can quietly and privately talk to the child about the need to use a tissue. If the behavior continues over time, be sure to mention it to a family member so they can check to be sure there are no medical issues. The child may have allergies or some other type of physical discomfort.

Sometimes children get stuck into a habit of touching their nose as it calms them down or gives them something to do when bored or not engaged in school activities. Habits are hard to break because they fulfill a need we have. Instead of just expecting a child to stop a habit, help her replace it with more acceptable behavior. For example, a child can keep a special object in her pocket, like a sensory toy or piece of fabric to touch instead. Also be sure the child has a supply of tissues close by. Reflect on your instructional methods to make sure this child is fully engaged in the learning activities and not bored or frustrated. Most of all, have patience and keep offering support until the child learns new behaviors.

Summary:

- Without shaming the child, teach her to use a tissue instead of picking her nose

- Speak with parents if the behavior continues

- Help the child break the habit by adopting other self-soothing behaviors

- Be sure your learning activities are engaging the child

- See Chapter 3 for relaxation and calming activities

Overexcitement/High Energy

It is important to recognize that a high activity level can be completely normal for many young children, even if it does pose challenges in the classroom. Gender and cultural backgrounds can also affect families' expectations for children's behavior and these interact with the child's biological temperament (Rothbart & Bates, 2006). This can result in a more typically high energy level, distractibility, and impulsiveness (all of which are defining features of young children). First, make sure that you have scheduled enough time during the day for children to be physically active. If at all possible, ensure the children get outside recreational time. You can also provide plenty of inside movement activities within your classroom.

Next, consider prevention strategies such as seating the child close to you during group activities, or in a location in which fidgeting will not bother other children. During activities, give instructions one at a time, repeat as needed, and use visual aids, charts and color coding to guide the children as much as you can. Examples include a small card with a photo showing how to sit at circle time, a sheet that shows visually how to hang up a coat, or a photo showing how to use geoboards. Also provide extra time as needed for the child to get his belongings organized at transition times throughout the day, especially first thing in the morning, at nap time, and before going home.

You can also help all your children learn self-regulation strategies, such as body awareness and impulse control. A great way to start is by asking the high-energy child to monitor the behavior of other children, since developmentally, children can do that earlier than they can regulate their own behavior (Bodrova & Leong, 2008). For example, you might have the child raise her hand or come tell you when she notices other children running, bouncing, rolling around, tipping a chair, or getting up at the wrong time.

Throughout the day, you can lead calming activities for all the children, such as yoga and patterned breathing, or offer these to the particular child as needed.

If you have a child who has been diagnosed with ADHD (Attention Deficit Hyperactivity Disorder) and has severe behavioral challenges you'll want to work with the family and other treatment providers in creating a positive behavior support plan as described in Chapter 7 and 8.

Summary:

• Be sure children have plenty of opportunities for movement throughout the day

• Provide space or seating for high-energy children that prevents them from bothering others and reduces distractions

• Use visual aids to provide behavioral guidance

• Teach self-regulation strategies

• See Chapter 3 for social emotional skills and self-regulation; Chapter 5 for cultural considerations; and Chapter 6 for guidance techniques

℅ ℅ ℅

Part III: Working with Others as a Professional Community

Chapter 10: Partnering with Families

Tatiana is teaching in a preschool classroom in an urban public school. Many of the families in her school are recent immigrants and barely speak English. Tatiana remembers her own mother, who rarely came to her school or met with her teachers. Since her mother spoke only a basic level of English, she was too embarrassed to try to talk to the teacher. Tatiana knew, however, that her own mother cared a great deal. Education was very important in her family. Now that Tatiana is in the position of the teacher, she wants to make things different for the parents. She wonders how she can help all her families to get involved and what the best way is to reach out to them.

Robert is in his first year teaching preschool after moving from teaching middle school to this position. He is nervous about working with families since there is so much more demand for collaboration with parents at the preschool level. How will he communicate best with families? What will he do if a child is having a problem? How will he make sure the parents feel connected and welcome in his class?

Ms. Jones has a child in her class whose parents have recently seperated. She was a young child when her own parents divorced and she remembers it being a difficult time with lots of stress. Ms. Jones hopes that she can help the children to have a stable, positive experience at school, and she wonders how she can reach out to parents to help them with this transition in their lives. How can she keep both parents involved and in the loop even though they are barely speaking to each other?

In this chapter, we will explore ways to manage your classroom to more easily support and empower families, develop reciprocal relationships, and help involve families in their children's learning and development. This is challenging work. Too often new teachers enter an environment in which families are sometimes seen as "the enemy" or at least a frustrating part of the job. Not surprisingly, when I ask parents about their experiences in collaborating with their children's schools, many are disheartened and cynical about being a partner in their child's education. However, there are better ways to work as a team and you have the opportunity to make a big impact in your work with families. What you do and the way you do it does matter.

First and foremost, provide a sense of welcome. If you can develop a school-family partnership that is characterized by a sense of welcome, this will foster the relationships that will allow family members, no matter their background or ability, to support their child's education in meaningful ways. (Ferguson, Ramos, Rudo, & Wood, 2008). The very first interactions you have with family members will set the tone for your relationships. When parents have positive experiences with you, they will feel more trust, will be more likely to engage in school activities, and be more involved in their child's education.

In all of your interactions with family members, building trust should be a primary goal. Parents' trust in the teacher or caregiver influences their beliefs that their child is well cared for, and it increases their tendency to be responsive to teacher-initiated interactions (Knopf & Swick, 2007).

School- and Classroom-Level Involvement

Encouraging involvement is the most obvious way that you will interact with families in your work. You can think about the ways you interact on two levels: The first is the school, center, or classroom level and this will include activities and programs that are planned for all parents, such as Open House, Back-to-School Night, Family Nights, and Family Gatherings. As a new teacher, these programs are often planned and controlled by others in your school. The second level includes interactions and communications with each family individually.

Open House or Back-to-School Night. Most schools or centers have some type of open house in the fall each year when families are invited to meet you and learn a bit about the curriculum and activities of the class. Participation by families can vary greatly from school to school. In some schools, you will have a room full of eager parents wanting to learn about you and what goes on at school. At other schools, only a handful of parents might show up. Do not take this personally, or as a sign that parents don't want to be involved. There are many reasons parents don't come to open house, which will be explored later. If you are in a school in which the open house is not well-attended, this is a clear message to you that the needs of the families are not being met. Try to come up with an alternative way of communicating with parents and encouraging involvement on an individual basis. As you gain more experience in your school setting, you may become more involved in the school-wide or center-wide planning to improve the way the open house is planned and increase attendance.

When you are planning for an open house or back-to-school presentation, you have an opportunity to communicate to parents what is important about your daily activities, curriculum, and the philosophy of your classroom. This helps build their trust that you are competent in helping their children learn. It is also an opportunity for the parents to get to know you, which is an important part of building a collaborative climate. Family members know that you have a huge impact on the life of their child. Your actions affect their child's happiness, well being, and learning so naturally, they are anxious, curious, and deeply interested in who you are. If you are working with an assistant teacher, or other paraprofessionals, be sure to include them in the introductions and activities.

In many open house situations, only adults are invited. Teachers often provide a slide show of the daily schedule, showing what children do throughout the day, or they may have an activity that parents can participate in, such as writing a note to their child to be read the next day. Often teachers will give a handout with important information about classroom processes such as being absent, having a change of clothes on hand, or class field trips. If you have a parent handbook, briefly review the main points. Make it clear to parents how to get in touch with you, and to find out from them how to best communicate information.

If your school or center has an open house in which families attend with their child, you will need a different plan. The best course is to set up activities that children and parents can do together, but that also help the parents see what kind of learning is taking place. For example, you could set up a table with play-doh and various cutting and shaping implements and have a sheet at the table which explains the types of learning taking place. You could include math manipulatives, books from your reading curriculum, or planting seeds that can be left in the classroom to observe (or taken home as a gift).

Here are some other things to consider in planning an open house:

- Have name tags available for family members

- Keep a camera on hand to take digital photos and then make them into a class book

- Have a sign-in sheet for attendance that includes updated contact information: phone, address, email

- Be firm that you will not discuss concerns about individual children and instead offer a date and time for an individual conference if needed

- Display children's photos, artwork, projects, books that are currently being read, other textbooks, etc.

- Have pictures of other staff members posted so that families get to know all who are involved in their child's time at school.

Family Activity Nights

Some events are planned to encourage families to be directly involved in their child's learning and development. Parents, children, and other family members are invited to the school to participate in an evening activity together. Often these family nights have themes, such as Family Science Night in which the center or school is set up with various science activities that families can do together. Similar to the choices about centers you make in your classroom, you can also make choices about Family Night centers. There can be a large variety of centers and families can move from one to another at their own pace and stay as long as they'd like, or families can be assigned to a specific room or activity and then told when to rotate to the next activity location. Some schools offer these family events as a 6- or 8-week series in which the family member and child come each week. Here are some other suggestions for family nights:

- ***Family Math Night.*** Set up stations around the room (or a larger area like the cafeteria or gym) that allow families to solve mathematical problems or experiment with mathematical materials such as blocks, geoboards, Cuisenaire rods, unifix cubes, LEGOS or other building materials. You can find more family math activity ideas from *Family Math* (Kerr, Stanmark, Thompson, & Cossey, 1986), and ideas for planning in *Family Math Night: Standards in Action* (Taylor-Cox, 2005).

- ***Family Write Night.*** Family members can work together on any type of literacy project such as creating a home-made book in which they can write a story about their family, a poem, family memories, or other themed writing. Families can write in their home languages to support the cultural identity of the children.

- ***Family Reading Night.*** Bringing families together to enjoy reading emphasizes the importance of this experience. These reading events can be held monthly, or a few times throughout the year. Some schools have children come in the evening in pajamas. Other schools hold events during lunch to encourage parent involvement. Books can be provided in a variety of different languages. For more ideas, see *Family Reading Night* (Hutchins & Greenfeld, 2007).

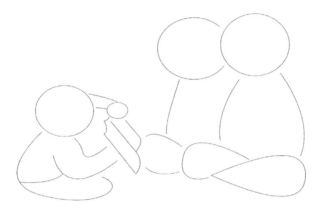

- *Family Science Night.* Although science activities take a good deal of preparation ahead of time, they are very popular and quickly get family members actively involved. Focusing on science also helps families to see their children exploring and discovering, and highlights the importance of hands-on learning. For more ideas see *Science Night Family Fun from A to Z* (Sarquis & Hogue, 2000) which is also available with a Spanish supplement.

Educational Workshops for Families

The purpose of this type of workshop is to teach family members skills and activities that they can use at home to help their children learn, a strategy shown effective in a variety of research studies (Epstein & Sanders, 2002; Henderson & Mapp, 2002; Starkey & Klein, 2000). Such workshops can range from parenting skills to more academic-based workshops. Here are some possible topics:

- How to help your child with homework

- Alternatives to punishment

- The importance of play in children's learning

- Teaching children self-help and organization skills

- Simple mathematics games to make at home

- Reading at home and other ways to support literacy skills

- Everyday art projects

- Science experiments in your kitchen

- How to choose a quality child-care program

- Preventing your child from being bullied

- Getting your child ready for kindergarten

- Community activities for families

Family Gatherings

Your school or center may hold picnics, ice cream parties, holiday celebrations, and pot-luck suppers so that you can get to know families and help them get to know each other. These provide an excellent setting to have informal conversations with parents and other family members without the pressure and possible anxiety of parent conferences. It is easier to approach a family member in the future with any concerns or with good news if you have already made a personal connection. These settings also provide an opportunity for families to get to know others in their community which can be an important source of support.

Individual Family-Level Involvement

The second level of interaction is at the individual family level and includes what you do with all the families in your classroom, such as newsletters, classroom parties and events, informal greetings, check-ins and notes home, and formal parent conferences. You will have more control over this level of interaction. Whether this involvement is positive and fruitful will depend to a great degree on how well you can establish a good relationship with the family. Think for a minute about how we establish and maintain good relationships with any of the people in our lives—by spending time together, being accepting, communicating well, and sharing something of ourselves. This can be difficult with families at times because they can be very different from us and spending time together is rarely built into the educational system.

Communication Strategies

Communication is at the heart of good relationships and it usually occurs in two ways: informal communication, such as exchanges at the end of the day, and formal communication, such as newsletters and parent conferences. If you are fortunate enough to see family members on a regular basis, short talks can be extremely helpful in building a relationship and exchanging information. You can share anecdotes about the child, talk about class activities, ask about what's going on at home, or just listen and learn more about the child. These exchanges make it easier to communicate with the family when a longer conversation is needed. Unfortunately, in some settings and circumstances, you will rarely see family members—perhaps the children at your school or center take a bus, or the babysitter or sibling drops off and picks up the child. If this is the case, you will need to rely more on formal communication strategies

Newsletters. In order to provide family members with more information about the curriculum and activities in your classroom, send home regular newsletters. Some teachers find the time and energy to do this weekly, others send monthly newsletters. This is a good choice for sharing information with all the families in an efficient way, and they can help to educate families about developmentally appropriate practices. It's important to be consistent in how often you send out newsletters because families will come to expect them and look forward to hearing from you. They can be sent home with the child, mailed to the family, sent by email, or posted on your classroom website.

Notes and calls home. It is well known that most teachers only contact parents when there is a problem at the school. This is, of course, unfortunate, and an easy trap to fall into. In order to be more proactive and share positive information, you'll need a system in which you regularly contact families. This could be weekly or monthly phone calls that you make to all the families on a rotating basis. For example, you could set aside time during nap, a planning period, or after dismissal (perhaps an enlightened director will provide this time if you ask for it) to call one or two parents each day. In some settings, parents will not be reachable by phone, and notes will work better. One possibility is to have a family notebook that the child brings home each night. You can jot down notes to the parents, and encourage them to communicate with you by writing back in the notebook. Email offers an excellent alternative since it is immediate and easy to respond to. Even if you don't think your families will use email, still give them your contact email contact information. Don't make assumptions that families will use email—but don't assume that they won't either. Another big advantage to using email is that you can send out one message to the entire class easily—such as reminders about events coming up, materials that you could use in the classroom, or other classroom news.

Family/Parent conferences. The first step in family conferences is to set up times for parents or other family members to come. Your school or center might have specific procedures to follow, but as much as possible, try to be flexible and offer parents a choice. This can be done through notes sent with the children, but is more likely to be received if it is mailed home. If possible, communicating with family members through email is more immediate and easier to answer back and forth. If you haven't heard from any parents or guardians, try telephoning. It's important to communicate how much you'd like them to attend.

Also consider inviting other family members or people who might be involved in the child's care, such as a grandparent. Be sure to let families know what special services will be available such as childcare, transportation, an interpreter, or a specific conference time. Base the length of the conference on the time you'll need to have a fruitful discussion. If your school or center allots only 10 or 15 minute slots, then schedule families for as many slots as necessary. Always provide privacy. Families who are waiting to meet with you should never be able to overhear your conversations with other families. Set aside a seperate waiting area, or spread out the scheduled times.

Provide families with information about your curriculum or any school handbooks before the conference so they can come with questions or suggestions. Let them know ahead of time that you would like their input by sending a form for them to fill out with information and questions. See the following for an example.

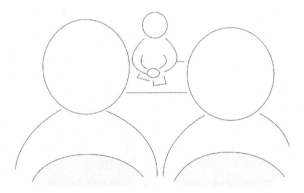

Family Conference Invitation and Questionnaire

To the family or guardians of _____.

You are scheduled for a teacher conference on _____ at
_____ in room _____. Your feedback and information will be very helpful
in working with your child together as a team. Please fill this form out as much as you
can and bring it with you to our conference. I am looking forward to meeting with
you!

- What are your goals for your child this year?

- How does your child learn new things best?

- What questions do you have about what your child is currently learning
  or will be learning this year?

- What types of things does your child like to do when he or she is not at
  school?

- What does your child say he or she likes about school?

- Doesn't like about school?

- What concerns, if any, do you have about your child?

- Is there anything else you'd like to share that will help me work better
  with your child?

Greet family members at the door and have adult-size seating available. Try
to make the room look as inviting as possible with the children's work displayed. Too
often I have attended parent conferences in classrooms where the children's chairs were
upside down on the tables from cleaning the floors. It left me feeling strange, like being
in a store afterhours. Have photos or examples of the child's work ready to share with
the family, and if you are also using formal reports, a copy of the child's grades and/or

progress. Always start out by sharing something positive about the child, and the more personal and authentic, the better. An anecdote about something their child recently did can help break the ice and establish rapport. Your goal should be to convince the parents that you care about their child and want to collaborate.

    A simple "conference record" can be created to document the information shared, such as in the following example (Starr, 2005):

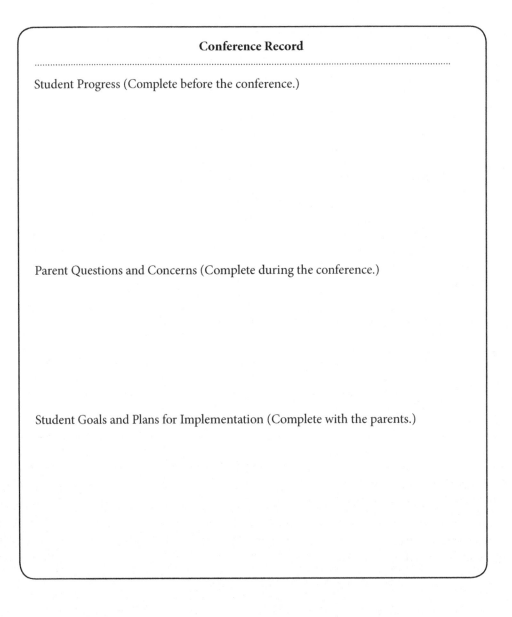

Conference Record

Student Progress (Complete before the conference.)

Parent Questions and Concerns (Complete during the conference.)

Student Goals and Plans for Implementation (Complete with the parents.)

Leave at least half of the conference time to listen to parents. This can be time in which you encourage questions, or let them tell you more about their child. At the end of the conference, plan next steps and what goals you will all be working towards.

Class web-sites. Many schools and child care centers have their own websites with links to pages for specific classrooms or teachers. This is a wonderful opportunity to share information with families related to your curriculum and the activities the children are doing in school. Since we all occasionally struggle to explain the value of the activities young children do, a website can be a great way to explain the goals and academic learning which is taking place. If you have permission from parents or guardians, you can post photos or videos of the children throughout the day, or when participating in special events. For security, it is also possible to password protect your website so that only parents of enrolled children have access.

Sharing decision-making. If parents are to truly be partners with us in educating their children, we need to provide opportunities for shared decision-making. This might happen at the school level with a parent advisory committee, or parent representation on the school governing board, but it is just as important at the classroom level. Family members should share in the decisions about their own child to the extent that is reasonable and productive. The best way for this to happen is to ask parents or other family members what they want for their child and then take the time to really listen. At parent conferences, or other more informal times, you can share assessment results or your own observations and ask the parents what they are pleased with and what they'd like their child to achieve. Simply being asked is very empowering, but you can also follow up throughout the year on the goals that you have jointly set with the family members.

Common Challenges

Despite your best efforts, there are some situations in working with families that are particularly demanding. In this section, we will consider some of the more typical challenges. Many of us spend our lives with people who are very similar to ourselves in terms of social class, ethnicity, values, and interests. It can be surprising, therefore, when you start working with families of the children in your class if they are very different from you. The first hurdle to overcome is our tendency to think that we need people to act or think like us in order to relate to them. Spend some time reflecting on your own feelings about the families in your class. Notice your judgments about who is a "good" parent and who is not. This kind of judgment is natural—but it can seriously harm your relationship with families. How will you possibly relate in a caring or professional way to a mother whom you think is parenting poorly? How can you create a positive relationship with a father who you believe is uncaring? Even when parents are behaving poorly or do not do what you think is best for their child, they need your respect and support—not your judgment. Remember that you can disagree with parents, their values, and their actions, but you can still be professional and supportive in your relationship with them. Respecting someone does not mean you agree with them or condone their behavior. That being said, you must take appropriate action if you ever suspect that a child is being abused or neglected.

Suspecting Abuse

A child's welfare must come first, and you should not let your relationship with a family prevent you from contacting authorities if you suspect abuse. If you have not had an orientation which covers the legal and practical aspects of reporting abuse, be sure to find out what procedures are used in your state or locality. In approximately 48 states, teachers are legally mandated to report suspected child abuse (Child Welfare Information Gateway, 2008). Remember that this is an important responsibility and if you report the suspected abuse to a supervisor or administrator who does not act on it, you should still take personal responsibility for the reporting.

The Child Welfare Information Gateway (2007, p. 2) provides the following list of signs and symptoms of possible abuse and neglect:

The Child:

- Shows sudden changes in behavior or school performance

- Has not received help for physical or medical problems brought to the parents' attention

- Has learning problems (or difficulty concentrating) that cannot be attributed to specific physical or psychological causes

- Is always watchful, as though preparing for something bad to happen

- Lacks adult supervision

- Is overly compliant, passive, or withdrawn

- Comes to school or other activities early, stays late, and does not want to go home

The Parent:

- Shows little concern for the child

- Denies the existence of—or blames the child for—the child's problems in school or at home

- Asks teachers or other caregivers to use harsh physical discipline if the child misbehaves

- Sees the child as entirely bad, worthless, or burdensome

- Demands a level of physical or academic performance the child cannot achieve

- Looks primarily to the child for care, attention, and satisfaction of emotional needs

The Parent and Child:

- Rarely touch or look at each other

- Consider their relationship entirely negative

- State that they do not like each other

Uninvolved Parents

In urban areas, and other areas with a high concentration of families living in poverty, the most common complaint teachers have is parents who seem uninvolved in their child's educational experience. Unfortunately, teachers hold many misconceptions about when, how, and if families are meaningfully engaged in their child's education and these misconceptions can make the situation worse by creating mistrust (Ferguson et al., 2008). For example, many teachers complain that parents do not attend the open house at their school. They might interpret this as not caring about the importance of coming to school, and even take it as a personal affront as a teacher. Perhaps families are not attending school events because of their work schedule. Many people in low-wage jobs do not have the option of taking time off from work and if they do, they might lose their job. Perhaps families are not comfortable coming to the school because of their own negative experiences in school or because they are unsure of their English conversation skills. Perhaps the school does not offer child care and they have no one to care for their children. Perhaps a family member is physically or mentally ill and their needs take precedence over the open house. It is dangerous to make assumptions about families who seem uninvolved, and it is futile to keep trying the same strategies that aren't working.

Many teachers have a stereotype of the "involved parent" which includes attending school functions, helping out with class activities, and teaching their child letters and numbers. This is a very narrow definition of parent involvement and it misses the many other ways that parents can be involved in the education of their children (Pomerantz, Moorman, & Litwack, 2007). For example, family members might be providing wonderful literacy experiences by reading the Bible or telling oral stories. Parents might be cooking with their children, or taking them to the market for food. It is a mistake to think that the amount of times parents attend school functions indicates how much they care about their child's education or how involved they are in their education outside of school. In some cultures, is it considered inappropriate to encroach on the teacher's domain. Asking questions, checking-in with the teacher, or trying to teach the child themselves at home would be considered a violation of the teacher's role and the trust given to her. Be clear in communicating that parents' input is valued.

In order to reach out to parents who seem uninvolved, use as many informal communication strategies as possible to try to establish a relationship. By building this trust, you will learn more about the family and gain insight into ways that family members could be more involved. Here are some strategies that family relationship experts, Knopf and Swick (2007, pp. 294-295), advocate for building stronger, positive relationships:

- Decide that you will actively pursue meaningful relationships with all families in your classroom

- Make sure your initial contact with parents is positive and early in the school year

- Communicate with parents consistently through a variety of means

- Share the small accomplishments and meaningful interactions that children have during school

- Learn individual parent needs and communicate how you are trying to meet them

- Listen to parents' concerns and respond to them

- Ask for assistance when you really need it (rather than just to give parents something to do)

- Explicitly convey the message that the parents are important

With a little bit of creativity, you can help make bridges between children's classroom and their home life and community. If the parent is unable to leave work to come to school, perhaps you could have regular phone conversations. Some parents might be able to stop by early in the day before leaving for work. Perhaps a family member is incarcerated; you might help the child write letters as a language arts activity. Suggest ways that parents can support their children's learning during community activities, such as going to church or playing at the park. This is an opportunity to use creative thinking to find ways to connect, rather than criticize or lose hope because the traditional parent involvement methods have not worked well.

Highly Involved Parents

You may find yourself in a classroom in which some parents are highly involved and demand too much of your time and attention. The first step is to monitor your own feelings. For example, imagine a mother who is constantly showing up at school, calling you, and making special requests for her daughter. She's driving you crazy and you begin to think, "She needs to get her own life and back off, for her daughter's good." If, however, you found out that this same mother was diagnosed with a terminal disease and might not live to see her daughter make it through kindergarten, you would probably have more sympathy and try to work with the mother to find the best way for her to be involved. We all tell stories to ourselves about why parents are the way they are. Our stories might not be accurate and they will color the way we interact with the families.

When parents are overly involved, there are a couple of approaches you can take. First, you can try to redirect their energy and see it as a positive situation. Perhaps this mother can type up and print out the newsletter for you. Perhaps she can serve on a parent committee, or help to organize your next field trip. You might find an ally that can make your life easier. On the other hand, you should also be clear about your boundaries. If you cannot spend 15 minutes at the beginning of every day speaking with a parent, then be sure to politely say so. "I'm sorry, I'd love to talk more, but I need to get back to working with the children now." Be firm, polite, and don't feel badly for walking away or cutting someone off if you need to.

Boundary Setting

New teachers can often worry about when to say "no" to parents, how to handle disagreements with family members, or how to assert their authority in the classroom. This is usually anxiety provoking because we want to please parents and be on good terms with them, and yet, there are times when we must stand up for our own ideas and beliefs and do what we believe is best for children. There are a few things that can help you establish your boundaries with family and communicate what decisions are part of your authority.

Stay calm. This is easier said than done, but messages that are delivered in a calm, matter-of-fact way are more effective. Take a deep breath, smile, relax your shoulders, and tell yourself you can stay calm and professional. Don't ever get into a shouting match or defensive arguing. Instead, calmly say, "I can't discuss this anymore today. I will contact you for another time to talk about this issue." If a parent is being abusive or out-of-control, walk away or ask them to please leave. Do not continue to defend yourself or try to get your ideas across. It will make the situation worse.

Be prepared to listen. Many parents just want to be heard. Take the time to fully listen to what they have to say and repeat back to them what you understood as their request or complaint. Once you've acknowledged their feelings and ideas (and *not* before then), you can share your own feelings and ideas and explain why you are making the decision you are making. Be firm, but maintain a professional demeanor.

Stand firm when appropriate. Remember that you are the authority on curriculum and instructional decisions. Certainly it is important to listen to parents' concerns, however, when parents are asking for changes that you feel are not educationally appropriate, stand firm and calmly explain your reasoning. There are some parent requests that you would not honor, such as having children complete tedious worksheets; however, other requests might be possible with some compromise, such as ensuring a child wears a smock when painting. Disagreeing with parents is more difficult when issues involve cultural values, such as having a parent ask you to not allow their boy to play in the housekeeping area. This situation takes patience and plenty of understanding to reach a shared goal. Always emphasize that you understand the parents want the best for their child, and see if you can both find common ground. Perhaps the parent would agree that preparing for fatherhood might be an adequate goal for her son and a short amount of time would help him to do that. Perhaps you can help the child achieve the benefits of dramatic play with more typically male costumes. Try to fight the urge to see the family as completely wrong—there's often plenty of space in between both of your views to find some common ground.

Look for support. Before a challenging situation arises with families, be sure to speak with your supervisor, principal, director or other person that you report to about what procedures to follow if you cannot resolve a problem. It is important for families to also know that there is someone else to speak with about a problem if they are not satisfied. In the ideal situation, your supervisor will work with you and the family members as a team. If your supervisor does not agree with you, it's important that he or she speak with you in private, and not in front of family members. It's best if you can both agree on the principles involved before meeting with the family. Teachers need to feel like someone "has their back" and will support them when difficult situations arise.

Separation Anxiety

A special challenge for teachers of young children is helping anxious, crying children separate from their caregivers. When I first started teaching preschoolers, I was overwhelmed by a handful of crying children, clinging to their mother's legs. I couldn't get the parents to leave and I couldn't help the children calm down. I'm happy to say I've since learned to understand this common response and I've developed some effective strategies.

First, understand that the separation reaction is as much about the mother, grandmother, or the caregiver who drops off the child as it is about the child himself. Many caregivers are embarrassed by their child's reaction, worried about the extra work it creates for the teacher, or frustrated by their lack of control. I think most are distressed by their child's sadness, fear, and intensity - feeling those emotions themselves. You can help the caregiver by reassuring him or her that this reaction is common, that it doesn't bother you, and that you have a plan to help.

Separation Plan. Create a drop-off plan together with the caregiver that includes clear routines which will be used every day. Keeping the routine exactly the same is very important for helping the anxious child to be able to predict and trust what will happen each day. For example, the plan might be as follow:

1. Caregiver and child come into classroom and put things away.

2. Child spends 5 minutes showing his caregiver one of the activities he's going to do that morning.

3. Teacher joins the caregiver and child while they say good bye with a hug or other gesture.

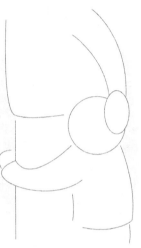

4. The child remains with the teacher (perhaps being held if he won't voluntarily let go of the caregiver) and waves goodbye as the caregiver leaves.

5. The teacher consoles the child as needed, acknowledging how sad it is to say goodbye and reminding him when his caregiver will return (in concrete terms such as "after small group time")

6. The teacher helps the child find a favorite activity to get involved in as a distraction.

7. The teacher calls the parent after 10-15 minutes to let him or her know that the child is okay and has calmed down - or is calming down and doing better.

Prepare the caregiver ahead of time that this plan will take a little while to work. Some children need a couple of days. Others need weeks to begin to calm down and have some trust in the process. There are a couple of important aspects to consider in developing your plan. Make sure the caregiver ***never*** slips out without saying goodbye to the child. Some caregivers will want to do this because it helps them avoid the clinging and crying. However, this is counter-productive and it will make the children more fearful of the parent leaving in the future. Be sure to build into your plan a clear process for saying goodbye and waving or watching the caregiver leave. You might want to have a special place in your classroom that is the "Saying Goodbye" spot, such as a window or location by the door that prevents the child from escaping, but allows him to wave goodbye. Finally, remember that the separation is as hard on the caregiver as it is on the child. Calling the caregiver (or having her call you) for reassurance after a short period of time can help this adaptation process go much more smoothly!

Separation/Divorce

Families in which the parents are separated or divorced often can use some simple accommodations to help make things smoother for the child. First, don't assume that children with parents who are not together are necessarily traumatized or upset by it. The degree to which children suffer in such circumstances is related to how well the parents continue to get along more than anything else. Therefore, you need to be very careful not to take sides or be persuaded to help one parent over the other. This is not easy, because in many situations, separated or divorced parents do not get along well. Parents will often share horror stories about what the other parent does, blame the other parent for teaching or allowing the child toget away with inappropriate behaviors, or trying to prevent the other parent from getting information or having contact. The first step is to find out if there are any legal restrictions pertaining to a parent picking up a child. This needs to be in writing, and try to get clear information about custody and the child's typical schedule of spending time with each parent. Remember that your first responsibility is for the child's welfare, and helping to inflame the relationship between parents is never in the child's best interest. On the other hand, you do not need to play therapist to try to help parents get along. Keep a professional distance and focus on what is best for the child. In general, here are some ideas for making life easier for separated or divorced parents and their child:

- *Anxiety.* The most difficult time for a child is at the very beginning of a separation when there is often high anxiety, many unknown variables, and little stability. Perhaps the most helpful thing you can do is to provide time to listen to the child and teach her ways to calm down, giving her time and space to be quiet and alone if it helps. As children get more settled after a separation or divorce, the family might settle into more of a patterned (if still anxious and tense) way of life. Some children in your care may have lived for a long time with their parents separated and it will seem the norm in their eyes.

- *Information.* Send information, such as newsletters, notices, forms, etc to both parents. This might require a little bit of work to get the contact information if it's not listed on the school forms, or to hold onto papers until a parent comes to school. It is typically the non-custodial parent that can get left out of the loop, especially when it is the father who has not been empowered to be involved in his children's school life. His child will benefit greatly if you make the extra effort to help him stay involved.

- *Shifting from home to home.* Be sensitive to the child shifting from one home to another. Items might be misplaced, books at the wrong home, and so on. Most young children do not have the cognitive skills or self-regulation ability to remember all the things they need a day in advance and bring them to the other parents' home. And this is worse if the custodial parent is actively (or inadvertently) subverting the involvement of the non-custodial parent.

- *Conferences.* Try to invite both parents to conferences. You can ask whether they would prefer separate ones or whether they want to come together. Try to reach out to the non-custodial parent (and not rely on the custodial parent to send the information) since he or she might not even know you are scheduling conferences at that time. Although it takes more of your time to hold separate conferences, it is very important for the child's welfare to have both parents involved and knowledgeable and you can learn a great deal about the child by meeting with both parents.

Sharing Difficult Information with Families

One of the most difficult aspects of being a classroom teacher is opening discussions with parents or family members when you have a concern about a child. The first step is to remember that the goal is to help the child. It is not to find blame, complain, or push the problem onto the family. Instead, our goals will include creating a team approach, treating family members with respect, and being treated with respect ourselves—while problem solving. This is a tough job!

Here are three powerful strategies that will help:

Empathize. It is very difficult for parents to hear that their child is having problems, and if this is a repeated issue, the parents may very well be angry, defensive, and exhausted. Show caring, kindness, and understanding. How? The easiest way is to listen. Ask the parents what their experience has been, and how they are understanding the problem. Let them know you have heard what they are saying, even if you disagree with them. Understanding and agreeing are two different things. In order for the parents to listen to you, they must feel like they've been understood. You are both on the same team so don't try to "make" a parent listen or see your points.

Here's an example: "I can see that it's been very hard for you to deal with Daniel's tantrums. It sounds like you feel that they are happening because other children are bothering him." Even if you know other children are not bothering him, you can address this later. The important issue is to build a team first.

Share information. Keep yourself calm and neutral while describing the behaviors you are concerned about. Do not use a judgmental tone, and give clear examples. Avoid drama in statements such as, "I can't tolerate Daniel's tantrums anymore. He's disrupting the whole class!" This meeting is not about your problem or emotional needs, it's about the child. Focus on when the behavior happens, where, and how often. "Daniel has been throwing himself on the floor at the beginning of group time. He does this almost every day, and it takes him about 15 minutes to gather control again. We have him go to the Quiet Corner to calm down."

If it's a developmental problem, show examples of the child's work or describe the skills or behaviors that the child is having trouble with. Remember that the family may not be able to process this information if they are anxious, afraid, or emotionally agitated. Some denial is normal and works as a powerful coping strategy for us all when we are emotionally overwhelmed. You can offer the information again at a later time. Don't push.

Offer hope. The most important step is to offer hope. Share with the parents the strong belief that, working together, you can help the child. Let them know you have some ideas for what steps can be taken, and how you will get started. This is the part of the process that will solidify the team approach and help the parents to stop being defensive if they have been previously. If parents are very emotional and angry you might want to start out with the hope step: "Mrs. James, I'd like to talk to you about Daniel's behavior because I have some ideas for how to help him. Can you meet with me later this week?"

If you can't offer any hope, then you should not be having the meeting with the family. First, do your homework and find out ways that the child can be helped, even if it is a referral. If you can't offer hope because you are so angry, frustrated, and exhausted, then do not have a meeting with the family yet. Wait until you can pull yourself together and be professional. We can often forget how damaging our angry words can be to a parent. If you suspect problems that are beyond your abilities or need intervention beyond your setting, be sure to speak with your director or supervisor. This information should be shared in a team approach with other professionals.

Homework

When I speak with parents from a variety of backgrounds and social classes, many parents expect homework, even in preschool. The value and use of homework is controversial (Cooper, 2007; Cooper, Robinson, & Patall, 2006; Voorhis, 2004). Many of the reasons that educators have advocated for homework—such as promoting higher achievement, reinforcing learning, teaching study skills and responsibility—are not fully supported by research with young children (Kohn, 2006). If we count on using homework for learning certain parts of the academic curriculum, then those children most at risk (especially poor children) will be hurt by the fact that they are living in homes in which family members can't help with homework assignments (Patall, Cooper, & Robinson, 2008). This causes a greater gap between the learning opportunities of affluent and poor children.

Many parents will ask you to assign homework to their child, making the assumption that homework is one of the ways that they can ensure academic success for their child—certainly a reasonable goal. For many parents, especially those who are Latino and African-American, homework represents an important way that they participate in their child's education, and a method of being informed about what their child is learning in school (Pomerantz et al., 2007). One national survey showed that most parents are satisfied with the amount of homework assigned to their children and only 10% felt their child had too much homework (Public Agenda, 2000).

So how do you respond to this pressure for homework while also realizing that typical homework is not appropriate for young children, may increase stress in the home, and provide an unfair disadvantage to children living in difficult family situations, including poverty? If you would like to meet the expectations of parents for homework, consider reframing this and offering home learning activities instead. Here are some issues to consider:

- ***Developmental levels.*** Consider the age of the children. Preschoolers learn best through active exploration and interactive experiences with other children and adults. They do not learn best by completing worksheets or written assignments. Consider having a lending library of home quality children's literature, science kits, or math materials in boxes.

- ***Family Time.*** Preschoolers are better served by offering families suggestions for interactive hands-on activities, such as playing together in the sink with water, encouraging parent-child reading in their home language, or creating art with simple materials like torn paper collages. Drilling children on the alphabet or other academic-looking activities as not as effective for learning as interactive experiences. Be a strong role model for parents in offering high-quality suggestions for home activities rather than worksheets.

Think of homework or home activities as "extra" learning that may or may not happen, rather than required work. Provide positive feedback to those who have the privilege of a supportive family, encourage learning at home, but do not be punitive to those who do not complete work at home.

Cultural Considerations

Parents' expectations, hopes, and dreams for their children vary by culture. In the United States, there tends to be a focus on children's independence, self-reliance and self-assertiveness. In contrast, many Asian and Latino cultures are more likely to emphasize interdependence, cooperation and collaboration (Okagaki & Diamond, 2003). In the classroom, you might find that families have different goals for socialization than you do. For example, in one research study, Cambodian, Filipino, Mexican and Vietnamese parents or Kindergarten, first- and second-graders expressed more value for their children developing obedience and conformity to external standards rather than independent thinking and problem solving skills (Okagaki & Sternberg, 1994). Researchers have also found that Chinese mothers are more favorable than Canadian mothers of a child staying close to their caregiver in an unfamiliar situation without exploring the environment (Chen et al., 1998).

These differences suggest that teachers cannot assume that children or families hold the same expectations for children's behavior. When a child's family holds values and expectations that are similar to that of the school and the teacher, the child will have an easier time learning appropriate behaviors and adapting to the social setting.

When children come from homes whose expectations and values are different, however, the child has a more difficult task in having to learn the rules and expectations of a particular classroom that might not be made explicit. For example, Ms. Young, puts a high value on independence and expects the children to feed themselves at lunch. She was frustrated with three-year old Ling who insisted on having the teacher help him eat, inlcuding holding the spoon. After a discussion with his mother, Ms. Young learned about this mother's values and the importance she puts on her children learning to accept help and be interdependent. Ms. Young was able to share her own views and reach a compromise. Ling would learn to use a spoon and fork in school, but would get any other help as he needed it.

In order to help children successfully transition from their families' expectations for their behavior to the school's expectations, you will want to understand the parents' expectations and goals for their children. This will require a great deal of trust and understanding, especially in restraining yourself from wanting to educate parents about what are the "best" strategies for young children. Being able to see the value in different goals and expectations will also model for the children empathic relationships between people who are culturally different.

Language Challenges

One of the most common and frustrating challenges is trying to communicate and establish a relationship with family members with limited English proficiency. One study done in California showed the following barriers that parents with limited-English proficiency face (Chinese for Affirmative Action, 2006, p. 4):

- Limited-English proficient parents lack critical information about their children's education and often have no effective means of communicating with teachers and school site administrators. 96% of respondents indicated that they did not know whether there was anyone at the school who could speak their primary language.

- Many parents do not receive school documents translated into their home language.

- Parents want more oral interpreters and other opportunities to communicate with teachers and administrators. More than 50% of LEP parents say that they need better language assistance to participate fully in parent-teacher conferences and other in-person meetings related to their child's education.

- Parents are largely unaware of existing parent involvement opportunities.

Although overcoming some of the barriers is out of the reach of a classroom teacher (such as offering English language courses), many others are not. You can work as an advocate for parents who have limited-English proficiency in trying to provide oral interpretation and translation of written materials. Perhaps the most important role you can play is to develop a trusting, non-judgmental relationship in which parents are more willing to communicate and get involved (Bermúdez & Márquez, 1996). You may also be able to create partnerships among the families in your classroom to provide support for language and cultural differences (Finders & Lewis, 1994). Think carefully about the assumptions you might have about your own ability to communicate with parents who are not proficient in your own language(s). You may find you are nervous, unsure, or confused about how to proceed. These are all normal reactions and instead of the natural tendency to avoid putting yourself into an uncomfortable position, you may need to push yourself a bit more to reach out to parents to overcome the language barrier.

Working with families is challenging and complicated, however, it can also be one of the many rewards of being a teacher. You can make a positive difference in a family's life that will last long beyond the time that their child is in your care.

∽ ∽ ∽

Chapter 11: Collaborating in the Classroom

Francine eagerly started her new job as the teacher of a 4-year old classroom in a community child care center in a predominantly African-American neighborhood. She felt well-prepared after completing her bachelor's degree and state certification at the local state college. In the first few weeks, she worked on getting the physical environment just right. She planned exciting activities based on the centers' themes, and she had gotten to know the children and families well. However, one problem remained. She didn't know how to work with the teacher aide assigned to her classroom. Having grown up in a white, middle-class Italian family, Francine had little knowledge or understanding of Shawanda's African-American culture. Shawanda, a very friendly, middle-age woman, had been at the center for five years and had worked in early childhood education for 20 years. Francine was a bit intimidated by her experience. She also wondered if Shawanda might have resented her coming in and making all the decisions. Francine and Shawanda had a very different interaction style with the children and Francine felt that they might be giving mixed messages to the children. She also worried that Shawanda wasn't doing all the things that needed to be done in the classroom. Sometimes Francine would find that lunch wasn't set out on time, or when she needed Shawanda at circle time she was busy cleaning the tables. Because Shawanda had been doing this for years, she just went about her work, not consulting with Francine or asking her for direction. Francine knew she needed to address how they were working together, but she was anxious and unprepared. No one had taught her how to manage adults—only children!

Diane has taught three-year olds for four years, long enough that she was finally getting comfortable with the curriculum, the assessments, and her classroom management. This upcoming year, however, she was selected to be a teacher in one of the preschool inclusion classrooms. In September, there will be 15 children in her class, with five of the children classified in special education with IEPs. Diane will also be working full-time with a special education paraprofessional in the classroom with her. Her head is spinning with questions. How will she modify instruction? How will she ensure that all the children are accepted and she creates a caring community? What will the paraprofessional's responsibilities be? How will they decide who does what? How much training does the paraprofessional have in working with children with disabilities? Just when she thought teaching would get easier, she realizes that she has a great deal still to learn!

One of the things that makes teaching young children different from other grade levels is the likelihood that you will be working with a teacher assistant, teacher aide, or other type of paraprofessional. Paraprofessionals are typically hired from the local community, vary greatly in the amount of training and education received, and in urban areas, up to 75% are women of color (Gerber, Finn, Achilles, & Boyd-Zaharias, 2001). While in the past, paraprofessionals spent most of their time on clerical and administrative duties, recently, they are more likely to be involved in instructional activities in the classroom such as tutoring individuals, leading small group activities, or instructing children with special needs. It is usually your role as the classroom teacher to make decisions about the tasks that paraprofessionals will carry out. In essence, you are the instructional team leader (Morgan & Ashbaker, 2001). This leadership role will include the following different responsibilities which research has shown to be important (Wallace, Shin, Bartholomay, & Stahl, 2001, p. 525):

Communication with Paraprofessionals

- Share student-related information

- Explain the role of the paraprofessional

Planning and Scheduling

- Coordinate schedules

- Establish goals, set plans

- Establish time for planning

- Consider strengths and interests of paraprofessionals when aligning tasks

Instructional Support

- Provide regular feedback regarding each paraprofessional's work performance

- Support paraprofessionals in providing instruction to students

- Provide support and direction to paraprofessionals who work in independent capacities

Modeling for Paraprofessionals

- Model for paraprofessionals in a caring and respectful manner when interacting with students

Public Relations

- Inform administrators, teachers, and parents of the responsibilities and roles paraprofessionals have in the educational program

- Advocate for the paraprofessional regarding training and leave time, modifications in responsibility, involvement in group decisions, etc.

On-the-Job Training

- Provide opportunities for on-the-job training for paraprofessional skill development

Management of Paraprofessionals

- Maintain regular positive and supportive interaction with paraprofessionals

- Contribute to the evaluation of paraprofessional performance

- Support skill improvement

Let's take a closer look at some of these roles.

Communicating with Paraprofessionals

When working as a team, communication is critical. Many problems and challenges can be averted by establishing a relationship based on respect and professionalism. You might, for example, start by making a list of all the things you know about the paraprofessional in your classroom—her knowledge, experience, skills, cultural background, and other ways that she might contribute to the work in the classroom (Morgan & Ashbaker, 2001). This will help you to identify things you don't know and motivate you to find out more. When you are working with a paraprofessional who is very similar to you in age, background, culture or personality, it can be very comforting and supportive. On the other hand, when you and your paraprofessional are very different from one another, it is an excellent opportunity for the classroom as a whole, since you will grow and learn more from your different perspectives and understandings.

At the beginning of the school year (or whenever you take on your position), start by having a planning meeting without the children present. Discuss your ideas about the roles and responsibilities for each person in the classroom. Listen to your paraprofessional's ideas, too, since you can draw from other's experience that you might not have. Be sure to take a firm approach in making the final decisions, though, since you are the instructional leader. Some teachers, especially those who are younger than the paraprofessional, may find it difficult to take a stand and feel like they are being "mean" or overly aggressive. Try to make sure the paraprofessional feels heard—which means using the same active listening skills you use with children. Be sure to stay positive, kind, and accepting, while stating your decisions clearly.

Once the school year is underway, ensure good communication by scheduling regular meetings. Ideally, this should be done daily at the start or end of the day to discuss curriculum planning, tasks, and behavioral issues that come up. This time should be a priority that is not pre-empted by other meetings or tasks. When leading this meeting, be sure to ask the paraprofessional what observations she has made during the day, and seek input in curriculum planning. You can create a simple agenda that includes discussing what went well, what needs improvement, concerns about individual children, plans for the next day (or week), and specific steps to take. Although you are in charge, it should feel like a collaborative, shared process. Too often paraprofessionals have been treated with a lack of respect and it can be easy for them to disengage from this process, feeling that no one will value their ideas.

You can use symbolic gestures to communicate respect for the paraprofessional you are working with. Be sure his or her name is on the classroom door, along with your own. If you use a title such as Mrs. or Ms. for yourself, be sure you use a title for your assistant, both in writing and in speaking. Provide her a mailbox for communication. Her authority needs to be respected and valued in the classroom as well as yours.

As well as formal communication times, you will also be communicating throughout the day in more subtle ways. If you see that something needs to be done, be sure to ask for it. Don't assume that another teacher sees what you do, or can intuit what you want. Be clear and up front. If you're reading a story and you notice Matthew needs more support today to stay focused, ask the paraprofessional to sit with him. Don't assume she should figure that out on her own. Be sure to provide positive feedback when the paraprofessional is helpful. Adults need this in the same way children do in order to improve our practice.

In some situations, the paraprofessional might speak the home language of the families better than you. This can be a wonderful resource, but might lead to awkward situations if you are not open about communicating. If this is the situation you are in, be sure to communicate to your assistant what things you'd like to share with the parents, and always check in with her about what the family has communicated. Acknowledge the paraprofessional's helpfulness and be careful you don't get into a power struggle.

Consider having a communication journal or place to put short notes to each other as reminders. Often by the end of the day, you've forgotten some of the things you wanted to communicate so having a place to write down notes immediately can help. This is especially useful if you do not work the same hours as your paraprofessional. You might leave a quick note which she can check when she comes in. Similarly, she can leave you notes at the end of the day after you have left. This might include a list of things that need to be done, such as getting science materials ready for a group activity later in the day, or a note that a parent wanted to speak with you. You could also share information about particular children who need special attention or focus that day. Be sure to keep your notes in a location which can ensure confidentiality. You can also include a place to jot down items that can be discussed at your formal planning meetings and invite the paraprofessional to also add items to the agenda.

Conflicts

Like any relationship, conflicts will naturally occur when adults work together in the classroom. It's impossible to avoid conflict completely, or expect it should never occur. Instead, the goal is to resolve conflicts professionally and effectively. The first principle is always to talk directly to the paraprofessional about any concerns — and ask that she do the same. Going to a third party to complain (another teacher, a girlfriend, the director) is very appealing because it reduces our anxiety level, however, it is counterproductive, making the problem grow bigger. Instead, recognize that as the instructional leader, it is your role (no matter how uncomfortable) to bring up conflicts so they can be discussed. Here are some opening phrases that might help you get started:

- I noticed that things didn't go well at circle time today....what did you think?

- It seems like you might be feeling like things are not going well during reading groups. Can you tell me about it?

- I'm sorry I was so angry earlier today. I didn't mean to blow up, but I'm worried about...

- How do you think things are going in the classroom? Anything bothering you or that you feel needs to be changed?

- I'm sorry you were so upset earlier today. Let's talk about what we could do differently.

As in any interpersonal situation, it is helpful to also share positive feelings and observations, and to stay as calm as possible. Do not engage in defensive, back and forth arguments. The biggest mistake in resolving conflicts is not listening thoroughly to the other person. We all need to be heard and feel understood. You can acknowledge the other person's viewpoint even if you disagree and make the decision to do things differently. And you can apologize for your part in any conflict. For example, you might say, "I see what you mean. In the past the children were sent to time-out when they were hitting or taking the toys. I know a lot of teachers use that approach, however, I'd like to try something different." Or "I can understand why you were so angry that I left you to get all the children ready to go home. I saw that Mrs. Knight really needed my attention, so that's why I left. I appreciate so much all the work you did and I'm really sorry you got stuck with it." Think of resolving conflict as repairing relationships. Focus on what you can do to help each person feel validated and avoid the problem happening again.

Planning for Instructional Support

As you begin your planning and scheduling process, you'll want to keep in mind how you will use your "human resources" in the classroom. First find out if there is a job description for the paraprofessional. Often there is not, so it will be up to you to create a plan for job responsibilities. Too often classrooms become chaotic because you have expected the paraprofessional to do a job or take over something but you never made your expectations clear. You can start with the daily schedule. Throughout each activity of the day, think through where you and the paraprofessional (or other volunteers or aides) will be and what each person will be doing.

One technique for organizing staff, recommended by the Head Start Center for Inclusion, is called "zoning"(Ainslie, n.d.). Each area of the classroom is designated a particular zone and staff members are assigned each week to a particular zone, with particular responsibilities. For example, one person can be responsible for cleaning up the tables, while another person helps the children in the bathroom. Zones can also be arranged to provide one-on-one support for children with special needs or challenging behavior.

Get started with zoning by creating a chart that lists each person's area of responsibility and role. The advantages include limiting the amount of time that children are off-task or waiting for the next transition since the adults are spread out and more available for support. You can also rotate staff members through some of the tasks to build confidence and expertise. This rotation helps all the staff members understand the different roles in the classroom and how they fit together.

Responsibility and Role Chart

Activity	Teacher	Assistant Teacher	One-on-One Aide
Arrival/Greeting	At door to greet parents	Helps children get breakfast items	
Breakfast	Sits with children Zone A	Sits with children Zone B	
Table Toys/ Games	Helps children who are done early to choose materials	Help children at tables finish up eating and cleaning hands	Aide arrives
Whole Group Morning Message/ Movement	Prepares for and leads group	Assists children in getting to circle area, sits in back of children to support behavior	Sits next to Sammy during circle time; helps with other children as needed
Choice Time	Assists children in making choices & supports learning Zone A	Assists children in making choices & supports learning Zone B	Provides support to Sammy as needed; encourages peer interactions

Activity	Teacher	Assistant Teacher	One-on-One Aide
Clean Up	Begins clean up song; Assists in Zone A clean up	Assists in Zone B clean up	Helps Sammy clean up art area or other quiet section of classroom
Outside	Begins to help children get on coats; Playground Zone A	Begins to help children get on coats; Playground Zone B	Helps Sammy get coat and put it on; assists him outside
Handwashing/ Lunch	Assists children in bathroom with handwashing then sits with children at tables	Gets lunches on table, then begins to get cots out	Sits at Sammy's table and models conversation and helps with food
Nap	Puts on quiet music; reads story, then helps settle children down	Helps children settle onto cots and rubs backs	Helps Sammy and other children settle onto cots and rubs backs
Choice Time	Assists children in making choices & supports learning Zone B	Assists children in making choices & supports learning Zone A	Provides Sammy support as needed; encourages peer interactions
Clean Up	Gets materials ready for small groups	Helps with Clean Up in Zone A	Helps with Clean Up in Zone B; supports Sammy if he needs to move to quiet area
Small Groups	Leads small group activity Orange Group	Leads small group activity Yellow Group	Assists with adaptations for Sammy during small group as needed; Puts out snack materials
Snack	Prepares story materials then sits with children for snack	Sits with children during snack	Works on Sammy's independent practice during snack
Whole Group/ Story	Prepares for and leads group	Assists children in getting to circle area, sits in back of children to support behavior	Sits next to Sammy during circle time; helps with other children as needed

Activity	Teacher	Assistant Teacher	One-on-One Aide
Outside/ Parents pick up children	Is available to talk briefly with parents and take children inside if needed	Takes primary responsibility for playground activities	Assists Sammy as needed with coat and playing outside
Final Clean Up	Puts away instructional materials	Cleans tables/ art area	Cleans discovery area and water table; straightens other areas as needed
Team Meeting	Review day's activities; plan for tomorrow; review any concerns; share assessment notes		

In addition to scheduling with your classroom staff, review the types of instructional support you'd like. Take into consideration the type of qualifications, training, and experience the paraprofessional has (and doesn't have), and how those might be best used to help the children's learning. First check with your supervisor about any legal limits for paraprofessionals set by the school or the state. Remember that your overall goal is to increase student learning. This can happen by having the paraprofessional relieve you of jobs that allow you to do more instructional work, or by having the paraprofessional assist directly with the instructional activities. Be specific about the responsibilities you assign. If you've said you'd like her to "help the children with math" what exactly does that entail? Should she correct work? Go over a procedure you've already demonstrated to the children? Suggest new work for the children who are done?

Perhaps you've told your assistant to help monitor the children's behavior during choice time. Does that mean she can decide on the type of guidance strategies to use? How will you stay consistent in your approach with the children? Does she have the skills to notice agitation, redirect children, or use positive feedback? You'll need to be specific about the role she will play. If you would like your paraprofessional to lead a small group, you'll need to be specific about that role. Will you do the planning? Who will gather the materials? Who will assess the children on their progress?

Create consistent contingency plans for specific occasions. For example, if you are called out of the room, or need to speak with a parent, supervisor, or visitor, plan ahead that your paraprofessional will take over the activity. If there are fire drills, lock-down drills or just walks around the neighborhood, set plans for who leads the children out of the room, who turns off lights, locks up, etc. The more specific and detailed you can be in your planning and instructional guidance, the more smoothly things will go.

As you work through these responsibilities, also highlight what the paraprofessional is not assigned to do, or things you'd rather take responsibility for. Having written responsibilities will help to clarify your roles.

Make sure the paraprofessional understands the line of command if she has concerns (Morgan & Ashbaker, 2001). Most educational settings have well-designated hierarchies of administration and in some public schools these can be quite rigid. For example, if the paraprofessional has a concern about a particular child or family member, it would not be appropriate to go to the center director without bringing the concern to you first. The paraprofessional should know who your direct supervisor is if she ever has a concern about things you do as a teacher.

Monitoring and On-the-Job Training

Many teachers and paraprofessionals say that they do not watch each other in the classroom (Morgan & Ashbaker, 2001). These statements probably stem from the discomfort we get in thinking about being judged. Teachers might believe that monitoring the work of the paraprofessional is implying that they don't trust her work, and many teachers mistakenly believe that monitoring means finding things to criticize. It seems unlikely that teachers and paraprofessionals don't really watch each other, so it makes sense to be open and honest about working as a team and helping each other to improve.

It is likely that the predominant training your paraprofessional will get is ongoing modeling and support from you in the classroom. You will be constantly modeling interactions with children, instructional strategies, behavioral guidance techniques, and other professional behaviors. As you do this, there may be times you can communicate on the fly about your goals or strategies. You can also discuss the choices you make at daily or weekly planning meetings. Keep in mind that paraprofessionals often have considerable experience, and may be older than you. This can put you in a tricky position in which you will need to communicate respect and acknowledge the skills and experience the paraprofessional has, while carefully finding teachable moments in which you can suggest or model practices. Monitor the work of the paraprofessional carefully to learn her skill sets, and try to give her tasks that are within her abilities. You can try team teaching as a way of increasing skills in a supportive way.

Throughout the day you should communicate and acknowledge the strategies that you see the paraprofessionals using that are working well. Adults, like children, learn from detailed, specific, positive feedback. Too often we might assume that the other person knows when things are going well, but as the team leader, you can help by pointing out the positives. Let the paraprofessional know what skills and strategies you yourself are working on also, and ask for feedback.

Observational Modeling

Ask the paraprofessional to observe you as a way of improving both of your skills. Choose a particular skill you'd like to model and ask the paraprofessional to write observational notes that she will later share with you.

For example, you might say, "I've been trying to notice more quickly when Alexis becomes agitated, and working to regain her attention. What have you observed? Do you think it's working?" In this way, you are modeling an attitude toward professional improvement.

These planned observations can be more formal. For example, if you are working on creating a more positive climate in your classroom, you could ask the paraprofessional to observe for 15 minutes during center time and write down how many times you give positive feedback and how many times you use negative language. This can provide an opportunity for a discussion on why this is an important skill, and allow you to gather data on how well you are doing. Another example would be to ask your paraprofessional to observe a group activity and observe which children seem to have difficulty staying focused. As you share the data, you can discuss strategies for supporting these children in the future. With time and practice, these ideas for observation will come more naturally and the conversations about teaching strategies and specific children will become a regular part of your planning and communication.

Ideas for Observational Modeling

Focus of Observation	Information to Be Collected	How to Record the Information
Participation in Discussions	Which children are participating in discussions?	With a list of the children's names, check off who participates during the discussion.

Giving clear instructions	Do I give instructions clearly enough so that the children know what to do next?	Write down which children, if any, have trouble following directions or if they ask what to do.
Positive climate	How often do I give positive comments compared to negative ones?	During a 15 minute period, make tallies in two columns for positive and negative comments.
Adaptations for child with special needs	Are the adaptations to the lesson for Corrine working well? Is she able to participate fully?	Write brief notes during the lesson about how Corrine is participating.
Adhering to Positive Behavior Support Plan	Am I giving positive feedback to Frankie when he demonstrates the target skill of using his words to express frustration?	During choice time, observe Frankie and write down any instance when he uses words to express himself and whether or not he received positive feedback or encouragement.
Being prepared	Do I have all the materials I need to lead group activities?	For one week, use a blank calendar page to mark off each day whether or not I had all the materials ready or whether I had to go get things at the last minute.

Adapted from Morgan & Ashbaker, 2001, p. 62.

At a more formal meeting time, ask the paraprofessional what aspects of her job she feels comfortable with and what aspects she'd like to get more experience with. This opens the door for talking about personal goals and shows you value her work. Play the role of advocate for paraprofessional training. Be sure to communicate to your supervisor or others with decision-making power about the training needs you think are most important. Get together with other teachers and paraprofessionals at your center or school to come up with ideas, or research training opportunities in your area that paraprofessionals could be given paid time off to attend.

Sharing Professional Resources

Gather professional resources such as pamphlets from the National Association for the Education of Young Children, the Council for Exceptional Children, or the International Reading Association to share with your paraprofessional and aides.

Professional journals which are written for practitioners such as *Young Children*, or *Teaching Young Children,* published by NAEYC, are a good choice because they provide practical articles that are relevant to the classroom. You can also suggest membership and provide information on how to join NAEYC or other professional organizations. Many paraprofessionals will be pleased to be treated as an important member of the instructional team and will be very interested in furthering their professional development. Some would benefit from information on how to achieve paraprofessional credentials like the Child Development Associate (CDA) offered by the Council for Professional Recognition (http://www.cdacouncil.org/cda.htm). As part of your advocacy, inform parents, administrators and others in the school community about the responsibilities and roles that the paraprofessionals play in your classroom and any professional development they participate in.

Collaborative Teaching in an Inclusion Setting

It is becoming increasingly common for young children who have been identified as needing special services to be placed in inclusion classrooms. Inclusion has been defined in many different ways, leading the National Association for the Education of Young Children and the Division for Early Childhood to issue a position statement that clarifies the definition:

> Early childhood inclusion embodies the values, policies, and practices that support the right of every infant and young child and his or her family, regardless of ability, to participate in a broad range of activities and contexts as full members of families, communities, and society. The desired results of inclusive experiences for children with and without disabilities and their families include a sense of belonging and membership, positive social relationships and friendships, and development and learning to reach their full potential. The defining features of inclusion that can be used to identify high quality early childhood programs and services are access, participation, and supports (Division of Early Childhood & National Association for the Education of Young Children, 2009, p. 2).

It is likely that you could be co-teaching with a special education teacher. Researchers have found that certain attributes and attitudes of the general education teacher are important for inclusion to be successful. For example, Olson, Chalmers and Hoover (1997) asked supervisors to choose the teachers who were most successful at inclusion. They found that these teachers shared the following characteristics:

- They had tolerant, reflective, and flexible personalities. They were described as easy going, patient, and calm.

- They assumed responsibility for all children, including those with disabilities. One early childhood teacher said, "I was hired to teach children. I ... believe that all kids have the right to learn and that the best way for children to reach their potential literacy level is to interact with kids at all different levels."

- They worked as a team with the special education teacher, although they felt that they would like more time to collaborate.

- They changed their expectations enough to make appropriate accommodations while still maintaining a high level of challenge for the children. One first grade teacher said, "Obviously, special needs students don't learn the same as the other children in the room; not one of the 25 learn the same, so I do adjust my expectations and that is really important for me to do. If that means shortening the assignment or folding the paper four different times so they only have to see a few of the problems at a time, I will do that."

- They showed positive attitudes, acceptance, and warm interactions with their students, developing strong relationships with them.

When two teachers are working together in a room, it's important that you both work as equals. This means working together to decide on teaching strategies, curriculum modifications, behavior guidance strategies, and assessment strategies (The IRIS Center for Training Enhancements, n.d.-c). You can also provide valuable moral support to each other. This requires extra planning time, perhaps designated as "team" planning time, professional development related to inclusion topics, and your participation in IEP meetings for your students with disabilities.

The advantage of working in collaboration with another teacher is that you can draw on each other's strengths, learning techniques from each other. You may begin to consider your students as one group (rather than separate groups of regular and special education students) who have a variety of differing abilities and needs, whether they are classified or not. Both teachers can develop competency in working with all the students in the classroom, which will also help children who are at-risk for learning problems, but not classified.

Determining the Need and Role of the Paraprofessional in Inclusion

You may find yourself in a position to advocate for having a paraprofessional in your classroom in order to better support children with special needs. To determine the best use of a paraprofessional for an inclusion setting, start by identifying what the child can do independently, when adaptations are needed, and how much assistance is needed throughout the day. What activities will be targeted? How will the paraprofessional help increase socialization for the child, and encourage independence? The following chart can help you think through what the child needs assistance with (Adapted from Mueller & Murphy, 2001, p. 25).

Plan for Professional Support

Class Activity	Need for Paraprofessional	Areas to increase socialization (natural support, peers)	How indpendence will be encouraged	Total time needed for paraprofessional

Carrying out this evaluation process can help you communicate with other supervisors, administrators, or family members to determine the best support for children with special needs.

Working with other Special Education Professionals

Early childhood teachers are often the professionals who first notice children's disabilities or learning problems. It is helpful to know how to make referrals or get support for children who need more than you can provide alone. Many public schools, especially larger districts, have some type of pre-referral team who works with classroom teachers to help them provide support for children who seem to be

at risk. This can include providing reasonable accommodations and modifications in classroom procedures to see if this will improve the situation before a referral is made. Based on the results of these interventions, the team will also help make the decision to refer a child for formal evaluation by the Child Study Team.

Once a child has been referred to the Child Study Team, a group of specialists including a social worker, school psychologist, learning disabilities specialist, and often a speech/language specialist, work together for a formal evaluation. You can play an important role by providing information about the child's academic achievement and functional performance in the classroom. The most helpful data are observational records and assessments that you have which document the child's achievement and behavior in different settings and with different interventions you have tried. Be careful not to use diagnostic language like, "I think he has ADHD" since teachers are not qualified to diagnose, only to provide information about the child. Be as specific as possible and use behavioral descriptions. For example, instead of saying that a child is hyperactive and doesn't pay attention, it is more helpful to share data: "During whole-group activities, Carla can sit still for no more than three minutes. In a 15-minute activity she will get up from her spot on the carpet an average of 7 times. She has trouble answering any questions related to the activity when asked."

If a child in your class is eligible for special education services, you will be part of the Individualized Education Program (IEP) Team who will also include:

- At least one special education teacher or provider

- A representative of the school who is knowledgeable about specially designed instruction for students with disabilities, the general curriculum, and the availability of school resources

- The parents or guardians

- The student, as appropriate

- Someone who can interpret the instructional implications of evaluation results, who may be another team member

- Other people whom the parents or the school have chosen to invite

You will be asked to participate in discussions related to the child's involvement and progress in the general curriculum and participation in the regular education environment (as well as discussions about the supplementary aids and supports for teachers and other school staff that are necessary to ensure the child's progress in that environment). You must also have access to the IEP of any child with a disability in your classroom if you are responsible for implementing any of the goals of the IEP. You will also be informed of your specific responsibilities related to implementing the IEP and the specific accommodations, modifications, or supports that must be provided to the child.

Working successfully in early childhood classrooms requires the ability to work collaboratively with a variety of other professionals and paraprofessionals. This can be challenging, but also a rewarding way to enhance the lives of young children. Working as a team provides you with social and emotional support, extra help, and a wider perspective on teaching. With care and dedication, you can create working relationships that help you create a positive classroom.

ↁ   ↁ   ↁ

Chapter 12: Finding Joy in Teaching

Carrie had been teaching three-year olds for five years in a large child care center. The end of the year was approaching and she was thinking about how much she would miss the children in her class who were moving to the four-year old group. She still loves teaching even more now than in the beginning. She finally felt like she knew what she was doing. The first few years were hard. She found herself spending a great amount of time on preparing so many activities and keeping up with the assessment system and doing all the required paperwork. Sometimes she'd look at her friends who were working in the business world who made more money and got compensated for anything they did outside of working hours, and she would feel under-appreciated. But she continued to enjoy the satisfaction she got from watching children learn and grow. Carrie found that now she could focus on improving her teaching rather than just surviving.

Carrie realized that what helped her most was her friendship with Briana who was in the classroom down the hall from her. It was so wonderful to have someone to share ideas with, and who was there to listen to her when things were frustrating. In the beginning, she was often unsure about what methods to use, or how to handle some of the challenging behavior issues, but Briana would share her wisdom or spend time brainstorming ideas. Now they had become good friends and sometimes got together for social occasions, too. Having the support of Briana also helped Carrie to avoid some of the negativity in the school. She rarely went into the teachers' lounge because she found that the complaints and discussions of students were dragging down her spirit.

As she ended her fifth year, Carrie was also thinking about graduate school. Her district would reimburse her for the cost of one course each semester and she wanted to take advantage of this wonderful opportunity. The challenge was to decide what direction she wanted to pursue. She was considering getting a Masters degree in special education since it would help her greatly with the children in her class who were struggling. But she was also considering getting certified as a Reading Specialist since she realized how important an early start in language arts is for children. And then there was the possibility of getting certified as a principal, although Carrie thought she still had so much to learn she couldn't yet imagine being in charge of a school. Well, she would continue to talk to other teachers to get more ideas and help in making up her mind.

Most of all, Carrie wanted to make sure that she kept her motivation up for teaching. She had experienced too many teachers in her own schooling that seemed burned out and tired of the job. And there were a couple of teachers in her school now who seemed to have lost their passion. Carrie was determined to find ways to keep up her joy in teaching!

Teaching is a difficult job. Perhaps because all of us have been through years of schooling, we are very familiar with what we think teaching is all about. However, a gap between teacher's expectations of what teaching will be like and the reality of the classroom experience can lead to stress and burnout (Friedman, 2006) Burnout is considered a loss of idealism and enthusiasm for work, which comes from experiencing stress over long periods of time (Matheny, 200). It's helpful to understand what this stress is all about. We experience stress when the demands placed on us by the school are greater than our resources to meet those demands. Researchers have identified three types of problems that result from this stress (Maslach & Schaufeli, 1993):

- Depersonalization, in which teachers distance themselves emotionally from other people and lose their personal connection to others at work, including poor attitudes towards students

- Reduced personal accomplishment, in which teachers lose their sense of accomplishment and find it hard to see the value in their work

- Emotional exhaustion, in which teachers feel that they don't have the emotional resources to deal with their job and they become highly vulnerable to other stress

Maintaining Your Motivation

Burnout occurs for many reasons, including the difficult nature of the job, especially (but not only) in high-stress schools in urban areas. Teachers typically work in isolation from other adults so they can begin to feel lonely and cut-off from social support (Bennett & LeCompte, 1990). Teachers in child care centers often work long hours with poor pay and few benefits. Because of the schedule teachers have and the way school buildings are arranged, it can be very difficult to find regular time to meet with other teachers in meaningful ways throughout the day. Instead, teachers' meetings are typically brief, and focused on administrative issues rather than providing time for discussions about teaching issues. The demands of the classroom can also be overwhelming—ranging from the constant need to address challenging behaviors, to finding time for mountains of paperwork—with little support provided. Emotional stress from being unable to meet these demands consistently ranks as the major reason why teachers leave the field (Darling-Hammond, 2001; Montgomery, 2005). The following are symptoms that researchers have identified which are warning signs of teacher burnout (Brown & Ralph, 1998)

- Dreading going to work or actually missing days

- Having difficulty in concentrating on tasks

- Feeling overwhelmed by the workload and having a related sense of inadequacy to the tasks given to them

- Withdrawing from colleagues or engaging in conflictual relationships with co-workers

- Feeling fatigue and low energy levels

- Experiencing insomnia, digestive disorders, headaches, and heart palpitations

Classroom management skills matter in preventing burnout. For example, when teachers feel they are able to handle student misbehavior, this reduces their emotional exhaustion (Tsouloupas & Barber, 2010). When teachers are not able to effectively manage the behavioral challenges in their classroom, the climate becomes negative and it can lead to "burnout cascade" (Jennings & Greenberg, 2009; Osher, 2008). As the climate becomes more negative, challenging behaviors increase, and the teacher often resorts to punishment instead of teaching self-regulation and prosocial behaviors. This becomes a vicious, self-sustaining cycle that becomes more and more destructive over time, leading to emotional exhaustion. As a teacher becomes more exhausted, it is harder for her to draw on her knowledge and skills for handling the classroom climate. Many teachers leave the profession, and others unhappily continue to teach, establishing rigid classrooms dominated by harsh interactions, coercion, and bitter resentment.

The good news is that the reverse is also possible: teachers who have strong social-emotional competency and effective classroom management skills gain a sense of self-efficacy and personal accomplishment. A positive cycle is set up that propels the future success of the teacher and children. Teachers who have developed their own social-emotional competence enjoy teaching more and feel more able to make a positive difference. So what constitutes social emotional competency in teachers? The following are some of the characteristics (Goddard, 2004):

- High self-awareness—being able to recognize your own emotions

- Being able to manage your actions even when you are emotionally upset

- High social awareness—being able to recognize the emotional state of others and forming positive social relationships

- High cultural sensitivity—recognizing that others may have a different perspective and realizing there is not one right way to have relationships or understand issues

- Strong boundaries—recognizing that you can't be everything to everyone and respectfully setting limits on what you will do in order to protect your own emotional health

- Being comfortable with ambiguity and uncertainty, including having trust and patience to let children figure things out

Stress Prevention

Stress is an inevitable part of teaching, however there are many coping techniques that teachers have found to be helpful in keeping themselves emotionally healthy and satisfied with their job. The following section outlines some strategies and techniques you can use to maintain your motivation and success. In order to work as prevention, these strategies need to be done *before* you are overwhelmed by stress. Make them a regular part of your life now and you will build up more resiliency to the inherent stress of the job.

Social Support

In order to combat the isolation that often happens in teaching, seek out other people who can offer you moral support, an ear to listen to you, and a way to feel that you are not alone. This might be another teacher (or teachers) at your center or school, 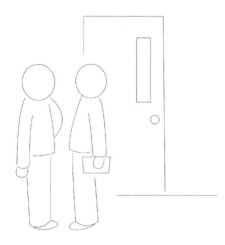 educators that you get together with at professional meetings, a mentor or educational leader who has supported you, or family members who understand your job well. It doesn't matter who your support people are, but rather that you feel like you have a safety net of people who will be there for you. Set aside time on a regular basis—perhaps each week, or monthly—to get together.

Also consider asking for help when things seem to be too much to handle. You can turn to parents, volunteers, assistants, even students to help out with some of the routine tasks to free yourself up a bit. It is often hard for us to let go of responsibilities because we might believe that someone else will not do them as well as we would. Focus instead on the benefits of letting go of some responsibilities.

Physical Health Support

Never underestimate how much your physical health can affect your emotional health. When we are tired, for example, our tolerance for any type of misbehavior is extremely low. We are more likely to be reactive, negative, and irrational. In our society, sleep deprivation has become almost the norm so we don't always realize we are not getting enough sleep. Therefore, our anxiety, sadness, anger, or frustration is greatly increased because we are simply tired. Over time, sleep deprivation affects brain functioning and can lead to exhaustion, poor decision-making, lack of impulse control, and lowered immune functioning (Ackermann, et al., 2012; Harrison & Horne, 2000). Changing your sleep habits is very challenging because there is so much to compete with going to sleep—spending time alone reading, talking to your significant other, socializing with friends, taking care of children, and so on. However, to prevent burnout, it's critical to put getting enough sleep higher on your priority list. Perhaps at first you can commit to going to bed earlier for a week or two so you can see the effects for yourself. This might convince you that it is worth getting more sleep and rearranging other activities to do so.

Similarly, good nutrition and exercise make a difference in your stress level. Some teachers find that an intense workout at the gym a few times a week helps them keep their sanity and find the energy they need in the classroom. Others find that an evening walk around the neighborhood or a yoga class helps them get exercise while also quieting their mind. Some teachers go hiking on the weekends or go running to prepare for marathons. Exercise is so important in affecting our moods that research shows that for people who are depressed, it is as effective as anti-depressant medication and the effects last longer (Miller, 2011). Exercise may be one of the best, overlooked strategies for coping with stress and preventing burnout.

Social Emotional Competence

We know that social emotional competence leads to better quality of life for the teacher in the classroom (and consequently the students), so we can take steps to improve that competence as a way of stress prevention. Let's face it: it's not always easy to stay calm, or be warm and supportive in the classroom. Children do things that often provoke strong emotional reactions in us such as disgust, sadness, anger, frustration, embarrassment, and helplessness. Yet teachers who maintain their composure when they are under pressure from behavioral issues and respond to them in a matter of fact way without taking it personally are more effective at classroom management (Jennings & Greenberg, 2009).

Regulating your emotions. Just as it is important to help children begin to regulate their emotions by labeling them, adults can improve at this, too. When you are stressed or feeling upset, try to label your emotion, being as specific as you can. The better you can identify what you are really feeling, the better you will be able to cope with that emotion. Here's a list of emotions that Goleman (2006) provides in his book on Emotional Intelligence:

- ***Fear.*** Anxiety, apprehension, nervousness, concern, consternation, misgiving, wariness, qualm, edginess, dread, fright, terror, and, in the extreme cases, phobia and panic.

- ***Anger.*** Fury, outrage, resentment, wrath, exasperation, indignation, vexation, acrimony, animosity, annoyance, irritability, hostility, and perhaps these are manifested in the extreme as hatred and violence.

- *Sadness.* Grief, sorrow, cheerlessness, gloom, melancholy, self-pity, loneliness, dejection, despair, and depression in the extreme case.

- *Enjoyment.* Happiness, joy, relief, contentment, bliss, delight, amusement, pride, sensual pleasure, thrill, rapture, gratification, satisfaction, euphoria, whimsy, ecstasy, and at the far edge, mania.

- *Love.* Acceptance, friendliness, trust, kindness, affinity, devotion, adoration, infatuation, and agape.

- *Disgust.* Contempt, disdain, scorn, abhorrence, aversion, distaste, and revulsion

- *Surprise.* Shock, astonishment, amazement, and wonder

- *Shame.* Guilt, embarrassment, chagrin, remorse, humiliation, regret, mortification, and contrition.

When emotions are uncomfortable, most of us try to do something to get rid of the feeling. Sometimes this can help us since emotions can signal to us that something needs to change in our lives. On the other hand, sometimes we can get more relief by tolerating or letting go of the emotion. We suffer more by focusing on how awful the emotion is and trying to push our uncomfortable emotions away. This can lead to anger, helplessness, and bitterness. When you are feeling upset, try to answer the following:

What would I call this feeling?

What situation triggered this feeling?

What does it feel like in my body (pressure in my chest, head hurts, etc.)?

What does this feeling make me want to do?

How do I want to respond to this feeling? Tolerate it or just observe it?

Let it go? Act on it to change the situation, if possible?

Social awareness. Practice labeling the emotions of the children (or adults) whom you find most challenging. The more you are able to empathize and understand how that child is feeling, the better you will be at choosing the right course of action. This should also help you to avoid taking things personally. Also work on your cultural understanding of children and their families so that you can realize when different perspectives and cultural traditions and values can help explain behaviors.

Setting limits. I have found that the people who are most attracted to teaching are often the people that give of themselves freely—caring for others, helping out, going the extra mile. This is a wonderful attribute to have; however, it can also lead to overwhelming stress.

It might help to think of your caring as a balance scale. Whenever you give to others, you need to balance this out with giving back to yourself. It is when this scale is out of balance that stress can run us down. You can handle this in two ways. First is to develop the ability to say "no" to requests when you need to. Has your boss asked you to take on another late shift at the day care center? Have the other teachers asked you to plan the parents' evening coming up? Have you started making new math games for center time while you are at home in the evening? Perhaps it's time to reconsider all these requests.

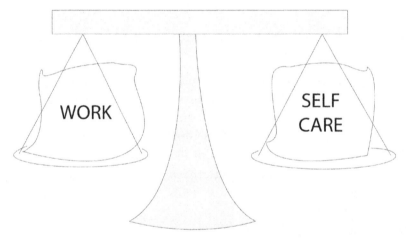

Work on getting past the feeling that others won't approve of you or will be disappointed if you say no. That may or may not be true. Often other people are fine with us saying no and will turn to someone else, or figure out a different solution. And if people are disappointed in us for saying no, then perhaps their expectations are out of line and we need to be okay with it. Setting boundaries in this way is critical for all professionals in the caring fields. If we let ourselves take on too much we lose our ability to be a caring professional.

Self-care strategies. The other part of this equation is to do more for yourself. Often the most caring people are those who forget to take care of themselves. And when teachers also have additional caring responsibilities at home, such as young children, a parent who is ill, or a husband who needs your attention, it is even more important to find time for self-care. Perhaps you can take some time to read that novel you love, get a manicure, sleep late once in a while, get some exercise, buy some favorite self-soother like scented candles, or make yourself your favorite food. It might be necessary to schedule these things into your life rather than relying on "finding time" for them, because you might never find the time. Don't let your schoolwork and job be the only activities in your life.

Relaxation. The same techniques that work for children also work for us. It's helpful to think about relaxation in two ways: the strategies you use to calm down on the spot when you are feeling strong emotions and those you use to keep your life calmer in general. The easiest and perhaps most effective tool for calming yourself on the spot is to focus on your breathing. This is aligned with the old adage to count to ten before taking action.

Improving Working Conditions

Sometimes a particular school, center, school administrator, or other aspect of your working conditions will be too stressful to be tolerated even with the suggestions given here. There are times that some working environments are too toxic and you will need to decide whether to move on to a different job. The truth is that child care centers, schools, and Head Start center environments vary greatly and you may find where you are is just not a good match for you. Rather than giving up on teaching, or finding yourself doubting your own abilities, it is worth trying a job in a different location, grade level, or type of setting.

Another possibility is to try to change some of the working conditions that you are finding stressful. You may be reluctant to "rock the boat" or complain, but nothing will change unless someone takes the first steps. For example, you can send a letter to the appropriate committee outlining your suggestions and including the names of other teachers who support you. You could also volunteer your time to serve on decision-making committees at your school. You might be surprised at how much of a difference you can make if you channel your complaints into thoughtful problem-solving steps.

The way you approach changing work conditions is as important as what you want to change. The first step is to identify the problem and to come up with a proposed solution. It is unlikely anything will change if you just complain about your situation; instead you need to be prepared with a possible solution (or more than one). Next you need to figure out who has the power, responsibility, or motivation to make the change happen. It is probably a waste of time to complain to your director about state regulations that are impacting your work. Instead, you'd want to target the state department who reviews the regulations and find out who is responsible for changes. There are many opportunities if you are willing to take the first steps. Here's an example: you and the other teachers are unhappy with the report cards you need to use. First, consider what alternatives you'd recommend (what's your solution to the problem?). Next figure out who makes the decision about report cards. Ask around, starting with your director or supervisor. Once you find out who has the ability to make the change, then you can begin your communication campaign.

Steps in Creating Organizational Change

1. *Identify the problem clearly and precisely.* "We don't have adequate time to complete child observation reports, therefore parents are not getting a complete picture of their child's academic progress" rather than "We are overworked."

2. *Identify possible solutions.* "We'd like to have another teacher's aide for an hour each morning" or "We'd like to have an extra planning period once a week."

3. *Identify who has the authority, responsibility or motivation to make the change happen.* Seek information from your supervisor or other leaders. Ask directly, "Who is in charge of making decisions about hiring teacher aids?" "Who makes the decisions about planning time for the teachers?"

4. *Present your case.* Communicate in a positive, professional way including a clear statement of the problem, how your solution would work, and what the benefits would be if things were changed. Give the impression that you are concerned about the quality of your work and the outcomes for students and families. Do not whine, complain, or criticize.

5. *Be persistent.* You might not be successful right away. Change can happen slowly, but the more you keep trying the more likely you are to be successful. If you are told that your solution is not possible you can respond, "Thank you so much for considering this. Could I check in with you next spring to see if other solutions are possible?" Make it clear you are serious, committed, and willing to follow through. Consider volunteering for any committee or role that puts you in a decision-making position.

Learning to Learn

When you graduate from a teacher certification program, you are prepared to be a novice teacher. Teaching effectively is a complicated skill that requires continual professional development and you will not know all you need to know when you first start working as an educator. You may be lucky enough to be working for a center or school that provides professional development. However, you will also want to think through your own personal needs for professional growth as these may be different from those of other people you are working with. For example, you may find that your math skills are not as strong as you'd like and you'd want to take advantage of opportunities to continue to learn both pedagogical techniques as well as more content knowledge in mathematics. You might have a special interest in early literacy and would like to improve your skills in working with struggling students. Or you may find that you want to learn more about promoting social and emotional skills in young children. Here are some steps to use in thinking through your professional development needs:

Developing a Professional Improvement Plan

1. *Review your strengths.* What do you do particularly well that you could continue to build on?

2. *Review your weaknesses.* What areas do you feel unsure about? What aspects of teaching are most challenging for you?

3. *Review your needs.* What are the most pressing issues you are facing right now in your setting? You might have a variety of strengths and weakness, but which ones relate most to your current situation? For example, you may have a child in your classroom with Asperger's Syndrome and you'd like to learn more about how to support him. You might have recently changed age groups or grade levels and would learn more about the content you need to teach. Perhaps you have many multicultural students and would like to gain knowledge about cultural values and practices.

4. *Develop goals.* Come up with one or two goals that you have for your own professional growth. For each of the goals, write up action steps to help you make the plan concrete.

Here's an example of one teacher's Professional Improvement Plan. She is a preschool teacher who has been working in a community-based child care center for two years, as the head teacher in the four-year-old class. This year she has a group of children who are learning English as their second language. She wants to learn more about how to support children with limited-English proficiency (LEP) in her classroom.

Professional Improvement Plan

Goal 1. Learn more about the issues in working with LEP children.

- Action step 1. Gather information from center's professional development library.

- Action step 2. Attend LEP workshops at the state NAEYC conference.

- Action step 3. Research what graduate courses are available in teaching ESL

- Action step 4. Introduce new activities in the classroom based on the information gathered.

Goal 2. Connect to families of the LEP children

- Action step 1. Reach out to families and offer individual conferences to get information on how to help their children.

- Action step 2. Read articles on working with families with LEP from on-line databases available through the library.

Keeping up with a continuous improvement plan will not only help you become a more effective teacher, it can also help prevent burnout and keep you interested and motivated in teaching as your career. Some important sources for professional development opportunities include the National Association for the Education of Young Children and their state affiliate groups. They sponsor an annual conference, offer professional journals, and many books, pamphlets, and videos as professional resources. For information visit www.naeyc.org. Other professional associations also provide journals, materials and information about teaching young children:

- The International Reading Association: www.reading.org

- The Division for Early Childhood of The Council for Exceptional Children: http://www.dec-sped.org/

- Association for Childhood Education International: www.acei.org

- National Council of Teachers of Mathematics: www.nctm.org

- National Child Care Association: www.nccanet.org

- National Association of Child Care Professionals: www.naccp.org

Finding Joy

Hopefully the suggestions in this chapter will help you maintain your enthusiasm for teaching, find support when you need it, and be prepared for the challenges, stress, and satisfaction of teaching. Teaching should be joyful and meaningful, and if it is not, that doesn't mean you have to just accept being miserable. Think through the changes you can make, and give them time to work. If you are still unhappy, it might be time to change where you work, what age group you work with, or even consider a different way to work with children than in the classroom.

As you move on in your career, never lose sight of the fact that you are an important person in the lives of the children you teach, and their families. You make an important contribution to your community, and you help create a better world. May you always find joy in these accomplishments!

References

Abdullah, M. H. (2002). Bibliotherapy. *ERIC Clearinghouse on Reading, English and Communication, Digest 177.*

Ackermann, K. Revell, V., Lao, O., Rombouts, E., Skene, D., Kayser, M. (2012). Diurnal rhythms in blood cell populations and the effect of acute sleep deprivation in healthy young men. *Sleep, 35*(7), 933-40.

Ainslie, K. (n.d.). Tips for teachers: Zoning in the preschool classroom. Retrieved May 24, 2010, from http://depts.washington.edu/hscenter/sites/default/files/01_15m_inclusion_inservice/06_zoning/documents/zoning_tips_for_teachers.pdf

Ainsworth-Darnell, J. W., & Downey, D. B. (1998). Assessing the oppositional culture explanation for racial/ethnic differences in school performance. *American Sociological Review, 63*, 536-553.

Alber, S. R. , & Heward, W. L. (1997). Recruit it or lose it! Training students to recruit positive teacher attention. *Intervention in School and Clinic, 32*, 275-282.

Alexander, K. L., Entwisle, D. R., & Herman, R. (1999). In the eye of the beholder: Parents' and teachers' ratings of children's behavioral style. In C. L. Shehan (Ed.), *Contemporary perspectives on family research: Vol. 1. Revisioning children as active agents of family life.* Greenwich, CT: JAI Press.

Ashford, J., LeCroy, C. W., & Lortie, K. L. (2006). *Human behavior in the social environment* (3rd ed.). Belmont, CA: Thompson.

Bailey, B. (2001). *Conscious discipline: 7 basic skills for brain smart classroom management.* Oviedo, FL: Loving Guidance, Inc.

Beauboeuf-Lafontant, T. (2002). A womanist experience of caring: Understanding the pedagogy of exemplary Black women teachers. *The Urban Review, 34*(1), 71-86.

Beaulieu, C. (2004). Intercultural study of personal space: A case study. *Journal of Applied Social Psychology, 34*(4), 794-805.

Belfiore, P. J., Basile, Pulley, S. & Lee, D. L. (2008). Using a high probability command sequence to increase classroom compliance: The role of behavioral momentum. *Journal of Behavioral Education, 17*(2), 160-171.

Bennett, K. P. , & LeCompte, M. D. (1990). *The Way Schools Work: A Sociological Analysis of Education.* New York: Longman.

Bermúdez, A. B., & Márquez, J. A. (1996). An examination of a four-way collaborative to increase parental involvement in the school. *The Journal of Educational Issues of Language Minority Students, 16*, 1-10.

Berry, J. W. (1996). *Let's talk about feeling sad.* New York: Scholastic.

Bodrova, E., & Leong, D. J. (2007). *Tools of the mind: The Vygotskian approach to early childhood education* (2nd ed.). Upper Saddle River, NJ: Pearson.

Bodrova, E., & Leong, D. J. (2008). Developing self-regulation in kindergarten: Can we keep the crickets in the basket? *Young Children, 63*(2), 56-58.

Bondy, E., & Ross, D. D. (2008). The teacher as warm demander. *Educational Leadership, 66*(1), 54-58.

Boykin, A. W. (1978). Psychological/behavioral verve in academic/task performance: Pre-theoretical considerations. *Journal of Negro Education, 47*, 343-354.

Bronson, P., & Merriman, A. (2009). *Nurture shock: New thinking about children.* New York: Hatchett Book Group.

Brophy, J. (2006). History of research on classroom management. In C. M. Evertson & C. S. Weinstein (Eds.), *Handbook of classroom management: Research, practice and contemporary issues* (pp. 17-43). New York: Routledge.

Brown, M. , & Ralph, S. (1998). The identification of stress in teachers. In J. D. V. Varma (Ed.), *Stress in teachers: Past, present and future* (pp. 37-56). London: Whurr Publishers Ltd.

Buck, G. H. (1999). Smoothing the rough edges of classroom transitions. *Intervention in School and Clinic, 34*(4), 224-235.

California Services for Technical Assistance and Training (CalSTAT). (2012). Classroom management. Module 4: Teaching students how to behave: Social skills.

Carter, K., & Doyle, W. (2006). Classroom management in early childhood and elementary classrooms. In C. M. Evertson & C. S. Weinstein (Eds.), *Handbook of classroom management: Research, practice and contemporary issues.* New York: Lawrence Erlbaum Associates.

Cazden, C. B. (2001). *Classroom discourse: The language of teaching and learning* (2nd ed.). Portsmouth, NH: Heinemann.

Center on the Social and Emotional Foundations of Learning. (n.d.). *Tucker Turtle Takes Time to Tuck and Think* Retrieved January 6, 2009, from http://www.vanderbilt.edu/csefel/scriptedstories/tuckerturtle.ppt

Chapman, A. (1995-2012). Gender bias in education. *Critical Multicultural Pavilion Research Room.* Retrieved August 20, 2012, from http://www.edchange.org/multicultural/papers/genderbias.html

Chen, X., Rubin, K. H., Cen, G., Hastings, P.D., Chen, H., & Stewart, S.L. (1998). Child-rearing attitudes and behavioral inhibition in Chinese and Canadian toddlers: A cross-cultural study. *Developmental Psychology, 34*(4), 677-686.

Child Welfare Information Gateway. (2007). Recognizing child abuse and neglect: Signs and symptoms. Retrieved July 6, 2010, from http://www.childwelfare.gov/pubs/factsheets/signs.cfm

Child Welfare Information Gateway. (2008). Mandatory reporters of child abuse and neglect. Retrieved July 6, 2010, from http://www.childwelfare.gov/systemwide/laws_policies/statutes/manda.cfm

Chinese for Affirmative Action. (2006). Lost without translation: Language barriers faced by limited-English proficient parents with children in the San Francisco Unified School District. Retrieved January 12, 2011, from http://www.caasf.org/PDFs/Lost%20Without%20Translation%20[CAA].pdf

Conroy, M. A. (2005). A descriptive analysis of positive behavioral intervention research with young children with challenging behavior. *Topics in Early Child-*

hood Special Education, 25(3), 157-166.

Cooper, H. (2007). *The battle over homework: Common ground for administrators, teachers, and parents* (3rd ed.). Thousand Oaks, CA: Corwin.

Cooper, H., Robinson, J. C. & Patall, E. A. (2006). Does homework improve academic achievement? A synthesis of research, 1987–2003. *Review of Educational Research, 76*(1), 1-62.

Cross, T., Bazron, B., Dennis, K., & Isaacs, M. (1989). *Towards a culturally competent system of care, volume I.* Washington, D.C.: Georgetown University Child Development Center, CASSP Technical Assistance Center.

Curtis, J. L.. (1998). *Today I feel silly: And other moods that make my day.* New York HarperCollins.

Darling-Hammond, L. (2001). The challenge of staffing our schools. *Educational Leadership, 58,* 12-17.

Darragh, J. (2007). Universal design for early childhood education: ensuring access and equity for all. *Early Childhood Education Journal, 35*(2), 167-171.

Denham, S.A., Blair, K.A., DeMulder, E., Levitas, J., Sawyer, K., Auerbach-Major, S., & Queenan, P. (2003). Preschool emotional competence: Pathway to social competence. *Child Development, 74*(1), 238-256.

Derman-Sparks, L., & Edwards, J. O. (2010). *Anti-bias education for young children and ourselves.* Washington, DC: National Association for the Education of Young Children.

Devereux Early Childhood Initiative. (2004). *Building protective factors through gross motor game play.* Villanova, PA: Devereux Foundation.

DeVries, R., & Kohlberg, L. (1990). *Constructivist early education: overview and comparison with other programs.* Washington, D.C.: National Association for the Education of Young Children.

DeVries, R., & Zan, B. (1994). *Moral classrooms, moral children: Creating a constructivist atmosphere in early education.* New York: Teachers College Press.

Doctoroff, S. (2001). Adapting the physical environment to meet the needs of all young children for play. *Early Childhood Education Journal, 29*(2), 105-109.

Division of Early Childhood, & National Association for the Education of Young Children. (2009). *Early Childhood Inclusion.* Retrieved May 17, 2010, from http://www.dec-sped.org/uploads/docs/about_dec/position_concept_papers/ PositionStatement_Inclusion_Joint_updated_May2009.pdf

Downey, D. B., & Pribesh, S. (2004). When race matters: Teacher's evaluations of students' classroom behavior. *Sociology of Education, 77*(4), 267-282.

Duckworth, A. L., & Seligman, M. E. P. (2005). Self-discipline outdoes IQ in predicting academic performance of adolescents. *Psychological Science, 16*(12), 939-944.

Dunlap, G., Strain, P. S., Fox, L., Carta, J. J., Conroy, M., Smith, B. J., . . . Sowell, C. (2006). Prevention and intervention with young children's challenging behavior: Perspectives regarding current knowledge. *Behavioral Disorders, 32*(1), 29-45.

Dweck, C. S. (2007). The perils and promise of praise. *Educational Leadership, 65*(2), 34-39.

Early Childhood Equity Initiative. (n.d.). *Equity/anti-bias classroom assessment.* Washington, D.C.: Teaching for Change.

Eigsti, I., Zayas, V., Mischel, W., Shoda, Y., Ayduk, O., Dadlani, M. B., Davidson, M. C., . . . Casey, B. J. (2006). Predictive cognitive control from preschool to late adolescence and young adulthood. *Psychological Science, 17*, 478-484.

Emberley, E., & Miranda, A. (1997). *Glad Monster Sad Monster.* Boston: Little Brown and Company.

Emmer, E. T., Evertson, C. M., & Anderson, I. (1980). Effective classroom management at the beginning of the school year. *Elementary School Journal, 80*(5), 219-231.

Epstein, A. (2009). *Me, you, us: Social-emotional learning in preschool.* Ypsilanti, MI: High Scope Press.

Epstein, J. L., & Sanders, M. G. (2002). Family, school, and community partnerships. In M. H. Bornstein (Ed.), *Handbook of parenting, Volume 5: Practice issues in parenting.* Mahwah, NJ: Lawrence Erlbaum.

Evertson, C. M., Anderson, C., Anderson, L., & Brophy, J. (1980). Relationships between classroom behaviors and student outcomes in junior high mathematics and English classes. *American Educational Research Journal, 17*, 43-60.

Evertson, C. M., & Anderson, I. (1979). Beginning school. *Educational Horizons, 57*(4), 164-168.

Evertson, C. M., Emmer, E. T., Clements, B. S., & Worsham, M E. (2008). *Classroom management for elementary teachers* (8th ed.). Boston: Allyn & Bacon.

Faber, A., & Mazlish, E. (1995). *How to talk so kids can learn at home and at school.* NY: Scribner.

Ferguson, C., Ramos, M., Rudo, Z., & Wood, L. (2008). *The school-family connection: Looking at the larger picture: A review of current literature.* Austin, TX: National Center for Family and Community Connections with Schools.

Finders, M., & Lewis, C. (1994). Why some parents don't come to school. *Educational Leadership, 51*(8), 50-54.

Friedman, I. (2006). Classroom management and teacher stress and burn out. In C. M. Evertson & C. S. Weinstein (Eds.), *Handbook of classroom management: research, practice, and contemporary issues* (pp. 925-944). Mahwah, NJ: Lawrence Erlbaum.

Gandini, L. (1998). Educational and caring spaces. In C. Edwards, L. Gandini, & G. Forman, (Eds.) *The hundred languages of children: The Reggio Emilia approach to early childhood education - Advanced Reflections.* (pp. 161-178). Norwood, NJ: Ablex

Gartrell, D. (2006). The beauty of class meetings. *Young Children, 61*(6), 54-55.

Gartrell, D. (2010). *A guidance approach for the encouraging classroom* (5th ed.). Belmont, Ca: Wadsworth.

Gayle-Evans, G. (2004). It is never too soon: A study of kindergarten teachers' implementation of multicultural education in Florida's classrooms. *The Professional Educator, 26*(2), 1-15.

Gerber, S. B., Finn, J. D., Achilles, C. M., & Boyd-Zaharias, J. (2001). Teacher aides and students' academic achievement. *Education Evaluation and Policy Analysis, 23*(2), 123-143.

Gilliam, W. S. (2005). *Prekindergarteners left behind: Expulsion rates in state prekindergarten systems.* New Haven, CT: Yale University Child Study Center.

Goddard, R. D., Hoy, W. K., Woolfolk Hoy, A. (2004). Collective efficacy beliefs: Theoretical developments, empirical evidence, and future directions. *Educational Researcher, 33*, 3-13.

Goleman, D. (2006). *Emotional intelligence: Why it can matter more than IQ* (10th Anniversary ed.). New York: Bantam.

Gray, C., & Garand, J. (1993). Social stories: Improving responses of students with autism with accurate social information. *Focus on Autistic Behavior, 8*(1), 1-10.

Gray, C. (2000). *The new social story book.* Arlington, TX: Future Horizons.

Greenfield, P. (1994). Independence and interdependence as cultural scripts. In P. Greenfield & R. Cocking (Eds.), *Cross-cultural roots of minority child development* (pp. 1-40). Mahwah, NJ: Erlbaum.

Greenfield, P., Keller, H., Fuligni, A., & Maynard, A. (2003). Cultural pathways through universal development. *Annual Review of Psychology, 54*, 461-490.

Gurian, M., & Stevens, K. (2010). *Boys and girls learn differently: A guide for teachers and parents* (10th ed.). San Francisco: Jossey-Bass.

Hall, E. T. (1977). *Beyond culture.* Garden City, NY: Anchor Press/Doubleday.

Han, H. S. & Thomas, M. S. (2010). No child misunderstood: Enhancing early childhood teachers' multicultural responsiveness to the social competence of diverse children. *Early Childhood Education Journal, 37*, 469-476.

Hanley, G. P., Iwata, B. A., & McCord, B. E. (2003). Functional analysis of problem behavior: A review. *Journal of Applied Behavior Analysis, 36*(2), 147-185.

Harriott, W. A., & Martin, S. S. (2004). Using culturally responsive activities to promote social competence and classroom community. *Teaching Exceptional Children, 37*(1), 48-54.

Harrison, Y, & Horne, J. (2000). The impact of sleep deprivation on decision-making: A review. *Journal of Experimental Psychology: Applied, 6*(3), 236-249.

Hastings, R. P. (2003). The relationship between student behaviour patterns and teacher burnout *School Psychology International, 24*(1), 115-127.

Hawken, L. S., Vincent, C. G., & Schumann, J. (2008). Response to Intervention for social behavior: Challenges and opportunities. *Journal of Emotional and Behavioral Disorders, 16*(4), 213-225.

Hayes, R. (2005). Conversation, negotiation, and the word as deed: Linguistic interaction in a dual language program. *Linguistics and Education, 16*, 93-112.

Hemmeter, M. L., Ostrosky, M., & Fox, L. (2006). Social and emotional foundations for early learning: A conceptual model for intervention. *School Psychology Review, 35*(4), 583-601.

Hemmeter, M. L., Ostrosky, M., Santos, R. M., & Joseph, G. (2006). Promoting children's success: Building relationships and creating supportive environments: Center on the Social and Emotional Foundations for Early Learning.

Henderson, A. T., & Mapp, K. L. (2002). A new wave of evidence: The impact of school, family and community connections on student achievement. Annual Synthesis 2002. National Center for Family & Community Connections with Schools (Ed.). Austin, TX: Southeast Educational Development Laboratory.

Holmes, R. M., Pellegrini, A. D., & Schmidt, S. L. (2006). The effects of different recess timing regimens on preschoolers' classroom attention. *Early Child Development and Care, 176,* 735-743.

Hughes, J. N., & Kwok, O. (2006). Classroom engagement mediates the effect of teacher-student support on elementary students' peer acceptance: A prospective analysis. *Journal of School Psychology, 43*(6), 465-480.

Irvine, J. J. (2002). African American teachers' culturally specific pedagogy: The collective stories. In J. J. Irvine (Ed.), *In search of wholeness: African American teachers and their culturally specific teacher practices* (pp. 139-146). New York: Palgrave McMillan.

Isaacs, M. , & Benjamin, M. (1991). *Towards a culturally competent system of care, volume II: Programs which utilize culturally competent principles.* Washington, D.C: Georgetown University Child Development Center, CASSP Technical Assistance Center.

Ivey, M. L., Heflin, L. J., & Alberto, P. (2004). The use of Social Stories to promote independent behaviors in novel events for children with PDD-NOS. *Focus on Autism and Other Developmental Disabilities, 19*(3), 149-160.

Jennings, P. A., & Greenberg, M. T. (2009). The prosocial classroom: Teacher social and emotional competence in relation to student and classroom outcomes. *Review of Educational Research, 79*(1), 491-525.

Jones, K., Evans, C., Byrd, R., Campbell, K. . (2000). Gender equity training and teaching behavior. *Journal of Instructional Psychology, 27*(3), 173-178.

Joseph, G. E., & Strain, P. S. (2006). Building positive relationships with young children. *The Center on the Emotional and Social Foundations of Early Learning.* University of Illinois at Urbana-Champaign.

Judge, S., Floyd, K., & Jeffs, T. (2008). Using an assistive technology toolkit to promote inclusion. *Early Childhood Education Journal, 36,* 121-126.

Jung, S., Sainato, D. M., & Davis, C. A. (2008). Using high-probability request sequences to increase social interactions in young children with autism. *Journal of Early Intervention, 30*(3), 163-187.

Kaiser, B., & Rasminsky, J. S. (2007). *Challenging behavior in young children: Understanding, preventing and responding effectively* (2nd ed.). Boston: Pearson.

Katz, K. (2007). *The color of us.* New York: Holt.

Katz, P. A. (2003). Racists or tolerant multiculturalists? How do they begin? *American Psychologist, 58*(11), 897-909.

Kaufman, C. (2010). *Executive function in the classroom: practical strategies for improv-*

ing performance and enhancing skills for all students. Baltimore: Paul H. Brookes.

Kirmani, M. H. & Laster, B. P. (1999). Responding to religious diversity in classrooms. *Educational Leadership, 55*(7), 61-63.

Knopf, H. T., & Swick, K. J. (2007). How parents feel about their child's teacher/school: Implications for early childhood professionals. *Early Childhood Education Journal, 34*(4), 291-296.

Kohn, A. (1993). *Punished by rewards.* Boston: Houghton Mifflin.

Kohn, A. (2006). *The homework myth: Why our kids get too much of a bad thing.* New York: De Capo Press.

Kounin, J. (1970). *Discipline and group management in classrooms.* New York: Holt, Rinehart & Winston.

Kritchevsky, S., Prescott, E., & Walling, L. (1969). *Planning environments for young children: Physical space.* Washington, D.C.: National Association for the Education of Young Children.

Kume, T., Tokui, A., Hasegawa, N. & Kodama, K.. (2000). *A comparative study of communication styles among Japanese, Americans, and Chinese: Toward an understanding of cultural friction.* Retrieved February 8, 2010, from http://coe-sun.kuis.ac.jp/public/paper/kuis/kume3.pdf

Landrum, T. J., & Kauffman, J. M. (2006). Behavioral approaches to classroom management. In C. M. Evertson & C. S. Weinstein (Eds.), *Handbook of classroom management: Research, practice, and contemporary issues* (pp. 47-71). New York: Routledge.

Lemov, D. (2010). *Teach like a champion: 49 techniques that put students on the path to college.* San Francisco: Jossey-Bass.

Lortie, D. (2002). *Schoolteacher: A sociological study with a new preface.* Chicago: University of Chicago Press.

Lyman, F. (1981). The responsive classroom discussion. In A. S. Anderson (Ed.), *Mainstreaming Digest.* College Park, MD: University of Maryland College of Education.

Marshall, C.S., Reihartz, J. (1997). Gender issues in the classroom. *Clearinghouse, 70*(6), 333-338.

Marzano, R. J., Marzano, J. S., , & Pickering, D. J. . (2003). *Classroom management that works.* Alexandra, VA: ASCD.

Maslach, C., & Schaufeli, W. B. (1993). Historical and conceptual development of burnout. In C. Maslach, W. B. Schaufeli & T. Marek (Eds.), *Professional burnout: Recent developments in theory and research* (pp. 1-16). Washington, DC: Taylor & Francis.

Maslow, A. H. (1943). A theory of human motivation. *Psychological Review, 50,* 370-396.

Maslow, A. H. (1971). *The farther reaches of human nature.* New York: Viking Press.

Maslow, A. H. (1968). *Toward a psychology of being.* Princeton, NJ: Van Nostrand.

Maslow, A. H. (1999). *Toward a psychology of being, 3rd Edition.* New York: Wiley.

Matheny, K. B., Gfroerer, C. A., & Harris, K. (200). Work stress, burnout, and coping at the turn of the century: An Adlerian perspective. *Journal of Individual Psychology, 56*(1), 74-87.

Matson, J. L., & Minshawi, N. F. (2007). Functional assessment of challenging behavior: Toward a strategy for applied settings. *Research in Developmental Disabilities, 28*, 353-361.

Maxwell, L.E. (2007). Competency in child care settings: The role of the physical environment. *Environment and Behavior, 39*(2), 229-245.

McIntosh, K., Herman, K., Sanford, A., McGraw, K., & Florence, K. (2004). Teaching transitions: Techniques for promoting success *between* lessons. *Teaching Exceptional Children, 37*(1), 32-28.

Miller, M. (2011). Understanding depression. *A Harvard Medical School Special Health Report.* Cambridge, MA: Harvard Medical School.

Minami, M. (2002). *Culture-specific language styles: The development of oral narrative and literacy.* Clevedon, UK: Multilingual Matters.

Mischel, W., Shoda, Y., & Rodriguez, M.I. (1989). Delay of gratification in children. *Science, 244*(4907), 933-938.

Montgomery, C., & Rupp, A. A. (2005). A meta-analysis for exploring the diverse causes and effects of stress in teachers. *Canadian Journal of Education, 28*, 458-486.

Moore, G.T. (1996). A question of privacy: Places to pause and child caves. *Child Care Information Exchange, 112,* 91-95.

Morgan, J., & Ashbaker, B. Y. (2001). *A teacher's guide to working with paraeducators and other classroom aides.* Alexandria, VA: Association for Supervision and Curriculum Development.

Morrow, L. M. & Smith, J. K. (1990). The effects of group size on interactive storybook reading. *Reading Research Quarterly, 25*(3), 213-231

Mueller, P. H., & Murphy, F. V. (2001). Determining when a student needs paraeducator support. *Teaching Exceptional Children, 33*(6), 22-27.

Mulrine, A. (2001). Are boys the weaker sex? *U.S. News & World Report, 131*(4), 40-48.

Najavits, L. M. (2002). *Seeking safety.* New York: Guilford.

NAEYC. (2005). *Standard 9: Physical environment. A guide to the NAEYC Early Childhood Program Standard and Related Accreditation Criteria.* Washington, DC: NAEYC.

National Education Association. (2002-2010). *Research spotlight on homework.* Retrieved July 6, 2010, from http://www.nea.org/tools/16938.htm

Office of the United Nations High Commissioner for Human Rights. (November 1989). *Convention on the rights of the child: Article 31.*

Ogbu, J. (1991). Minority responses and school experiences. *Journal of Psychohistory, 18,* 433-456.

Ogbu, J. (Ed.). (2008). *Minority status, oppositional culture, & schooling (Sociocultural, Political, and Historical Studies in Education).* New York: Routledge.

Okagaki, L., & Diamond, K. E. (2003). Responding to cultural and linguistic differences in the beliefs and practices of families with young children. In C. Copple (Ed.), *A world of difference: Readings on teaching young children in a diverse society*. Washington, DC: National Association for the Education of Young Children.

Okagaki, L., & Sternberg, R. (1993). Parental beliefs and children's school performance. *Child Development, 52*, 413-429.

Olson, M. R., Chalmers, L., & Hoover, J. H. (1997). Attitudes and attributes of general education teachers identified as effective inclusionists. *Remedial and Special Education, 18*(1), 28-33.

Osher, D., Sprague, J., Weissberg, R. P., Axelrod, J., Keenan, S., Kendziora, K., et al. (2008). A comprehensive approach to promoting social, emotional, and academic growth in contemporary schools. In A. Thomas & J. Grimes (Eds.), *Best practices in school psychology* (5th ed., Vol. 5, pp. 1263–1278). Bethesda, MD: National Association of School Psychologists.

Paley, V. (1993). *You can't say you can't play*. Cambridge, MA: Harvard University Press.

Parette, H. P., Quesenberry, A. C., & Blum, C. (2010). Missing the boat with technology usage in early childhood settings: A 21st century view of developmentally appropriate practice. *Early Childhood Education Journal, 37*, 335-343.

Parker, W. C. (2001). Classroom discussion: Models for leading seminars and deliberations. *Social Education, 65*(2), 111-115.

Patall, E. A., Cooper, H., & Robinson, J. C. (2008). Parent involvement in homework: A research synthesis. *Review of Educational Research, 78*(4), 1039–1101.

Pecaski McLennan, D. M. (2009). "ready, set, grow!" Nurturing young children through gardening. *Early Childhood Education Journal, 37*, 329-333.

Pellegrini, A., & Smith, P. K. (1998). School recess: Implications for education and development. Review of Educational Research, 63(1), 51-67

Pfister, M. (1992). *The rainbow fish*. New York: North South Books.

Pomerantz, E. M., Moorman, E. A., & Litwack, Scott D. (2007). The how, whom, and why of parents' involvement in children's academic lives: More is not always better. *Review of Educational Research, 77*(3), 373-410.

Ponitz, C. C., McClelland, M. M., Matthews, J. S., & Morrison, F. J. (2009). A structured observation of behavioral self-regulation and its contribution to kindergarten outcomes. *Developmental Psychology, 45*(3), 605-619.

Public Agenda. (2000). *Questionnaire and full survey results: National poll of parents of public school students*. New York: Author.

Quilty, K. M. (2007). Teaching paraprofessionals how to write and implement social stories for students with autism spectrum disorders. *Remedial and Special Education, 28*(3), 182-189.

Read, M. A. (2007). Sense of place in child care environments. Early Childhood Education Journal, 34(6), 387-392.

Rothbart, M. K., & Bates, J. E. (2006). Temperament in children's development. In R. L. W. Damon, & N. Eisenberg (Ed.), *Handbook of child psychology. Volume 3, Social, emotional, and personality development* (6th ed., pp. 99-153). New York:

Wiley.

Ryan, A. L., Halsey, H. N., & Matthews, W. J. (2003). Using functional assessment to promote desirable student behavior in schools. *Teaching Exceptional Children, 35*(5).

Sadker, D., & Sadker, M. (1994) *Failing at fairness: How our schools cheat girls.* Toronto: Simon & Schuster, Inc.

Scheuermann, B., & Hall, J. (2012). *Positive behavioral supports for the classroom* (2nd ed.). Upper Saddle River, NJ: Pearson.

Schneider, N., & Goldstein, H. (2009). Social Stories improve the on-task behavior of children with language impairment. *Journal of Early Intervention, 31*(3), 250-264.

Shippen, M. E., Simpson, R. G., & Crites, S. A. (2003). A practical guide to functional behavioral assessment. *Teaching Exceptional Children, 35*(5), 36-44.

Skouge, J. R., Rao, K., & Boisvert, P. C. (2007). Promoting early literacy for diverse learners using audio and video technology. *Early Childhood Education Journal, 35*(1), 5-11.

Sridhar, D., & Vaughn, S. (2000). Bibliotherapy for all. *Teaching Exceptional Children, 33*(2), 74-83.

Starkey, P., & Klein, A. (2000). Fostering parental support for children's mathematical development: An intervention with Head Start families. *Early Education and Development, 11*(5), 659-680.

Starr, L. (2005). Meeting *with* the parents: Making the most of parent-teacher conferences. *Education World.* Retrieved January 8, 2010, from http://www.educationworld.com/a_curr/TM/WS_curr291_conf3.shtml

Sugai, G., Horner, R. H., Dunlap, G., Hieneman, M., Lewis, T. J., Nelson, C. M.,... Wilcox, B. (1999). Applying positive behavioral support and functional behavior assessment in schools. Washington, D.C.: OSEP Center on Positive Behavioral Interventions and Support.

Tabors, F. (2004). What early childhood educators need to know: Developing effective programs for linguistically and culturally diverse children and families. In C. Copple (Ed.), *A world of difference: Readings on teaching young children in a diverse society.* Washington, D.C.: National Association for the Education of Young Children.

Tangney, J. P., & Dearing, R. L. (2002). *Shame and guilt.* New York: Guilford Press.

Tannen, D. (2001). *You just don't understand: Men and women in conversation* (New paperback ed.). New York: Quill.

The IRIS Center for Training Enhancements. (n.d.-a). *Addressing disruptive and noncompliant behaviors (part 1): Understanding the acting-out cycle.* Retrieved April 21, 2010, from http://iris.peabody.vanderbilt.edu/bi1/cresource.htm

The IRIS Center for Training Enhancements. (n.d.-b). *Addressing disruptive and noncompliant behaviors (part 2): Behavioral interventions.* Retrieved January 4, 2010, from http://iris.peabody.vanderbilt.edu/bi2/chalcycle.htm

The IRIS Center for Training Enhancements. (n.d.-c). *Effective school practices: Promot-*

ing collaboration and monitoring student's academic achievement. Retrieved May 16, 2010, from http://iris.peabody.vanderbilt.edu/esp/chalcycle.htm

The IRIS Center for Training Enhancements. (n.d.-d). *Who's in charge? Developing a comprehensive behavior management system.* Retrieved December 1, 2009, from http://iris.peabody.vanderbilt.edu/parmod/chalcycle.htm

Thompson, R. A. (1994). Emotional regulation: A theme in search of a definition. In N. A. Fox (Ed.), *The development of emotional regulation: Biological and behavioral considerations* (Vol. 59, pp. 25-52): Monographs of the Society for Research in Child Development.

Torres-Guzman, M. (1998). Language culture, and literacy in Puerto Rican communities. In B. Perez (Ed.), *Sociocultural contexts of language and literacy.* Mahwah, NJ: Erlbaum.

Tsouloupas, C., Carson, R., Matthews, R., Grawitch, M., & Barber, L. (2010). Exploring the association between teachers' perceived student misbehaviour and emotional exhaustion: The importance of teacher efficacy beliefs and emotion regulation. *Educational Psychology, 30*(2), 173-189.

U.S. Department of Education National Center for Education Statistics. (2001). *The kindergarten year: Findings from the Early Childhood Longitudinal Study, Kindergarten Class or 1998-99 (NCES 2001-023).* Washington, D.C.: Author.

Vergeront, J. (1987). *Places and spaces for preschool and primary: Indoors.* Washington, D.C.: NAEYC.

Viorst, J. (2009). *Alexander and the terrible, horrible, no good, very bad day.* New York: Atheneum.

Voorhis, V. (2004). Reflecting on the homework ritual: Assignments and designs. *Theory into Practice, 43*(3), 205-212.

Vygotsky, L. (1978). *Mind in society: the development of higher psychological processes.* Cambridge, MA: Harvard University Press.

Wallace, T., Shin, J., Bartholomay, T., & Stahl, B. J. (2001). Knowledge and skills for teachers supervising the work of paraprofessionals. *Exceptional Children, 67*(4), 520-533.

Wardle, F. (2004). Supporting multiracial and multiethnic children and their families. In C. Copple (Ed.), *A world of difference: Readings on teaching young children in a diverse society.* Washington, D.C.: National Association for the Education of Young Children.

Ware, F. (2002). Black teachers' perceptions of their professional roles and practices. In J. J. Irvine (Ed.), *In search of wholeness: African American teachers and their culturally specific classroom practices* (pp. 33-46). New York: Palgrave.

Ware, F. (2006). Warm demander pedagogy: Culturally responsive teaching that supports a culture of achievement for African American students. *Urban Education, 41*(4), 427-456.

Webster-Stratton, C. (1991). *The teachers and children videotape series: Dina dinosaur school.* Seattle, WA: The Incredible Years.

Weinstein, C. S. (1991). The classroom as social context for learning. *Annual Review of Psychology, 42,* 492-525.

Wilson, M. B. (2012). *Interactive modeling.* Turner Falls, MA: Northeast Foundation for Children.

Wolfgang, C. H. (2004). Child guidance through play: Teaching positive social behaviors (Ages 2-7). Boston: Pearson.

Wolfgang, C. H., & Glickman, C. D. (1986). *Solving discipline problems: Strategies for classroom teachers* (2nd ed.). Boston: Allyn & Bacon.

Wong, H, & Wong, R. (2004). *The first days of school: How to be an effective teacher.* Mountain View: Harry K. Wong Publications.

Wood, B. K., Cho Blair, K., & Ferro, J. B. (2009). Young children with challenging behavior: function-based assessment and intervention. *Topics in Early Childhood Special Education, 29*(2), 68-78.

Young, C. (2010). *Narrate the positive.* Retrieved from http://teacherevolution. com/2010/09/13/narrate-the-positive/

Index

About the Author

Muriel K. Rand, is Professor of Early Childhood Education at New Jersey City University. She has spent 20 years working with preschool and elementary teachers in urban public schools. She began her career as a preschool teacher and has been preparing new teachers since 1995. She writes *The Positive Classroom* blog which focuses on classroom management strategies for teachers of young children: www.thepositiveclassroom.org/

Dr. Rand has published *The Positive Classroom* and two books of teaching cases: *Voices of Student Teachers: Cases from the Field* (Merrill, 2003) and *Giving it Some Thought: Cases for Early Childhood Practice* (NAEYC, 2000). She is also a prolific and successful grant writer. She holds an Ed.D. and an M.S.W. degree from Rutgers University. She can be contacted at murielrand@thepositiveclassroom.org.

About the Illustrator

Catherine L. Rand is a free-lance artist, award-winning sculptor, and writer. Her interests include a passion for traveling, learning languages, and film. She has studied in Paris with Rutgers University and in Ireland at University College, Dublin.

Ms. Rand is a member of Phi Beta Kappa and holds a B.A. in Art History and Sculpture from Rutgers University.

Made in the USA
Coppell, TX
03 January 2022

70773953R00155